LONGMAN PREPARATION ~~SERIES~~ FOR THE TOEIC® TEST

INTERMEDIATE COURSE   5TH EDITION

LISTENING AND READING

Lin Lougheed

The TOEIC® Test total package are reprinted by permission of Educational Testing Service, the copyright owner. However, any other testing information is provided in its entirety by Pearson ELT. No endorsement of this publication by Educational Testing Service should be inferred.

Longman Preparation Series for the TOEIC® Test: Listening and Reading, Intermediate Course, Fifth Edition

Copyright © 2012 by Pearson Education, Inc.
All rights reserved.

No part of this publication may be reproduced, stored in a retrieval system, or transmitted in any form or by any means, electronic, mechanical, photocopying, recording, or otherwise, without the prior permission of the publisher.

Pearson Education, 10 Bank Street, White Plains, NY 10606

Staff credits: The people who made up the *Longman Preparation Series for the TOEIC® Test: Listening and Reading* team—representing editorial, production, design, and manufacturing—are Aerin Csigay, Dave Dickey, Pam Fishman, Mike Kemper, Barbara Perez, Liza Pleva, Robert Ruvo, and Adina Zoltan.

Development: Helen B. Ambrosio Publishing Services, Inc.
Text composition: ElectraGraphics, Inc.
Text font: Palatino
Cover photographs: Shutterstock.com
Cover design: Barbara Perez

Photo Credits: All photos are used under license from Shutterstock.com except for the following: **Page 2** Copyright © Educational Testing Service. Reprinted with permission; **pp. 7, 10, 29** (bottom), **30** (top), **120** (top), **121** (both), **122** (bottom), **123** (bottom), **124** (top), **165** (top) **262** (top), Instructional Design International, Inc., Washington D.C.; **p. 119** Copyright © Educational Testing Service. Reprinted with permission; **p. 122** (top) iStockphoto.com; **p. 123** (top) Royalty-Free/Corbis; **p. 260** Copyright © Educational Testing Service. Reprinted with permission; **p. 262** (bottom) Pearson Education; **p. 264** (bottom) Pearson Education; **p. 300** Copyright © Educational Testing Service. Reprinted with permission; **p. 342** Copyright © Educational Testing Service. Reprinted with permission.

Library of Congress Cataloging-in-Publication Data

Lougheed, Lin
    Longman preparation series for the TOEIC test: listening and reading. Introductory course / Lin Lougheed.—5th ed.
        p. cm.
    ISBN 978-0-13-286148-9 (with answer key)—ISBN 0-13-286148-8 (with answer key)—
ISBN 978-0-13-286151-9 (without answer key)—ISBN 0-13-286151-8 (without answer key)—
ISBN 0-13-286142-9—ISBN 0-13-286146-1—ISBN 0-13-286152-6—ISBN 0-13-286143-7—
ISBN 0-13-286145-3 1. Test of English for International Communication—Study guides.
2. English language—Business English—Examinations—Study guides. 3. English language—Textbooks for foreign speakers. I. Lougheed, Lin, 1946– Longman preparation series for the TOEIC test. Introductory course. II. Title.

PE1128.L646 2012
428.0076—dc23

2011037693

Printed in the United States of America

ISBN 10: 0-13-138277-2 (with answer key)
ISBN 13: 978-0-13-138277-0 (with answer key)

 2 3 4 5 6 7 8 9 10—V001—17 16 15 14 13 12

ISBN 10: 0-13-286142-9 (without answer key)
ISBN 13: 978-0-13-286142-7 (without answer key)

 2 3 4 5 6 7 8 9 10—V001—17 16 15 14 13 12

CONTENTS

INTRODUCTION — vii

To the Student	viii
Goals	viii
TOEIC Study Contract	ix
On Your Own	x
To the Teacher	xiii
LIPP Service Examples	xiii
About the TOEIC Test	xvi
Tips for Taking the TOEIC Test	xvi
TOEIC Test Directions and Answer Sheets	xvii
General Directions	xvii
Specific Directions	xvii
TOEIC Test Answer Sheets	xvii
Proven Tips for Doing Well on the Test	xviii

LISTENING COMPREHENSION — 1

PART 1: PHOTOS	**2**
Strategy Overview	3
Language Strategies	3
Context / Vocabulary / What do you see? / Analyze This	
Test Strategies	3
Prepositions / Similar Sounds	
Photos of People	4
Photos of Things	16
Grammar Tip	28
Vocabulary Tip	28
Strategy Practice	29
PART 2: QUESTION-RESPONSE	**33**
Strategy Overview	
Language Strategies	33
Statements / Occupations / Activities / Time / Location / Reason / How / Auxiliaries	
Test Strategies	33
Similar Words / Repeated Words	
Statements	34
Occupations	38
Activities	41

Time	45
Location	49
Reason	53
How	57
Auxiliaries	61
Grammar Tip	65
Vocabulary Tip	65
Strategy Review	66

PART 3: CONVERSATIONS **67**

Strategy Overview	67
Language Strategies	67
Occupations / Activities / Time / Locations / Reasons	
Test Strategies	67
Read before listening / Listen for specifics	
Occupations	68
Activities	72
Time	76
Locations	80
Reasons	84
Grammar Tip	90
Vocabulary Tip	90
Strategy Practice	91

PART 4: TALKS **95**

Strategy Overview	95
Language Strategies	95
Advertisements / Weather / News / Recorded Announcements / Special Announcements / Business Announcements	
Test Strategies	95
Read before listening / Listen for specifics	
Advertisements	96
Weather	98
News	100
Recorded Announcements	103
Special Announcements	106
Business Announcements	109
Grammar Tip	114
Vocabulary Tip	114
Strategy Practice	115

LISTENING COMPREHENSION REVIEW **119**

READING 133

PART 5: INCOMPLETE SENTENCES — 134

Strategy Overview — 134
  Language Strategies — 134
    Word Form
  Test Strategies — 134
    Context
Word Form: Nouns — 135
Word Form: Verbs — 137
Word Form: Adjectives — 139
Word Form: Adverbs — 141
Word Form: Pronouns — 143
Context: Nouns — 145
Context: Verbs — 147
Context: Adjectives — 149
Context: Adverbs — 151
Context: Conjunctions — 153
Context: Prepositions — 155
Grammar Tip — 157
Vocabulary Tip — 157
Strategy Practice — 158

PART 6: TEXT COMPLETION — 162

Strategy Overview — 162
  Language Strategies — 162
    Verb Patterns / Modifier Choices
  Test Strategies — 162
    Context
Verbs — 163
  Verb Tenses — 163
  Modal Auxiliaries — 170
Modifiers — 172
  Adjectives: Comparative and Superlative Forms — 172
  Adverbs of Frequency — 175
  Verbal Adjectives: Present and Past Participles — 177
Context — 179
  Word Meaning — 179
  Part of Speech — 179
  Pronoun — 179
  Verb Tenses — 179
Grammar Tip — 182
Vocabulary Tip — 182
Strategy Practice — 183

CONTENTS   V

PART 7: READING COMPREHENSION	**188**
Strategy Overview	188
Language Strategies	188
Words in Context	
Test Strategies	188
Skimming / Scanning / Reading Fast	
Advertisements	189
Forms	197
Letters, E-mail, Faxes, and Memos	205
Tables, Indexes, and Charts	212
Instructions and Notices	219
Grammar Tip	226
Vocabulary Tip	226
Strategy Practice	227

READING REVIEW	**234**

PRACTICE TEST ONE	**259**

PRACTICE TEST TWO	**299**

PRACTICE TEST THREE	**341**

ANSWER SHEETS	**381**
Practice Test Score Conversion	386
Practice Test Estimated Score Conversion Table	387

CD-ROM CONTENTS	**398**

INTRODUCTION

TO THE STUDENT

The TOEIC® (Test of English for International Communication) test measures your ability to understand English. It also measures your ability to take a standardized, multiple-choice test in English. In order to score well on the TOEIC test, you must have two goals: improve your proficiency in English and improve your test-taking skills. The *Longman Preparation Series for the TOEIC® Test: Listening and Reading* will teach you *language strategies* and *test strategies* that will help you reach these goals and score well on the TOEIC test.

Goals

IMPROVING YOUR PROFICIENCY IN ENGLISH

The *Longman Preparation Series for the TOEIC® Test* will help you improve your English language skills. This book will help you build your vocabulary by exposing you to words that commonly appear on the TOEIC test. You will learn words used in a variety of business contexts such as negotiating contracts, marketing, planning conferences, using computers, writing correspondence, hiring personnel, and making investments. You will also learn words frequently used in more general contexts such as travel, entertainment, shopping, dining, and other everyday situations.

The *Longman Preparation Series for the TOEIC® Test* will also help you review English grammar. You will see grammar structures in TOEIC contexts and get practice with grammar items that are commonly tested on the TOEIC test.

IMPROVING YOUR TEST-TAKING SKILLS

The *Longman Preparation Series for the TOEIC® Test* will help you develop skills that will improve your ability to take the TOEIC test efficiently. You will become familiar with the types of questions asked on the test and you will learn to analyze test items for tricks and traps that are commonly hidden in the answer choices. In addition, these general guidelines will help you take the test more effectively:

- **Read the directions carefully.**
  Study the directions and the sample questions in this book carefully so that you will already be familiar with the test format when you take the actual test.

- **Work rapidly and carefully.**
  When you take the test, do not spend too much time on any one question. Work as fast as you can.

- **Guess.**
  There is no penalty for guessing. Try to answer every question, but when you really do not know the answer, make a guess.

- **Mark only one answer per question.**
  Questions with more than one answer marked will be counted wrong even if one of the answers marked is correct.

TOEIC Study Contract

A contract is a type of agreement. It is a document that describes work you agree to do. You can make a contract with yourself that describes how much time you will spend studying English each week. When you sign the contract, it means that you promise to do the work.

Complete the contract below with your name and the number of hours you plan to study English each week. Sign and date the contract. This is a promise to yourself to follow your study plan. Keep track of the hours that you study everyday to make sure that you fulfill the terms of your contract.

STUDY CONTRACT

I, _____, make a promise to study for the TOEIC test by following a regular study plan. I will use *Longman Preparation Series for the TOEIC® Test: Listening and Reading, Intermediate Course* and, in addition, I will study English on my own.

I will study English for _____ hours a week. I will divide my study time as follows.

Listening to English: _____ hours a week

Writing in English: _____ hours a week

Speaking English: _____ hours a week

Reading English: _____ hours a week

_____   _____

Signed   Date

INTRODUCTION   IX

On Your Own

There are a variety of ways you can study English on your own. Here are some suggestions. Add some of your own ideas to the list.

INTERNET-BASED ACTIVITIES

Listening

_____ YouTube
_____ Pod casts
_____ Movies (Trailers)
_____ TV shows
_____ News channels (BBC, CNN, NBC)
_____ _____

Speaking

_____ Talk to English speakers with Skype
_____ Chat with other users of social websites, like Facebook, Yahoo, etc.
_____ _____

Writing

_____ Write a blog
_____ Post comments on blogs
_____ Post comments on an online forum
_____ Start a Facebook page in English
_____ Use Twitter in English
_____ _____

Reading

_____ Read blogs
_____ Read online newspaper articles
_____ Look for information on topics that interest you
_____ _____

OTHER WAYS TO STUDY ON YOUR OWN

Listening

_____ Listen to English-language radio broadcasts
_____ Watch English-language movies and TV in English
_____ Watch English-language TV programs
_____ Listen to songs in English
_____ _____

Speaking

_____ Find a friend to practice conversations with
_____ Summarize your daily activities to yourself aloud
_____ _____

Writing

_____ Write to an English-speaking pen pal
_____ Keep a journal in English
_____ Write essays on topics of importance to you
_____ Write lists of things you see, do, and want to do
_____ _____

Reading

_____ Read books in English
_____ Read newspaper articles in English
_____ Read magazine articles in English
_____ _____

SAMPLE SELF-STUDY ACTIVITIES

You can use any kind study material to practice English in a variety of ways. Websites, books, magazine articles, and TV shows, for example, can all be used for listening, speaking, reading, and writing activities. Here are some ways you can use different resources to practice your English skills.

Shop for a product

Think of a product you would like to buy. Try www.amazon.com or another shopping site in English and look for the product you are interested in. Read the descriptions and the reviews. (*Read*) Based on what you read, decide whether or not you want to buy the product. Now write about the product. (*Write*) Pretend you are writing an article for a magazine. Write a description of the product. Tell why you want (or don't want) to buy it. Next, talk about the product. (*Speak*) Record yourself as you describe it. Listen to your recording, correct your mistakes, and record yourself again. Some websites have video reviews on a product (e.g., www.cnet.com). Watch these video reviews. (*Listen*) Then choose a different kind of product and repeat the activities.

Plan a vacation

Go to www.tripadvisor.com or another travel website in English. Choose a city you would like to visit and fill in the dates for your imaginary trip. Look at the suggested hotels and read the reviews, then choose which hotel you would like to stay at. Read about the different things to do and see in the city and choose some that you are interested in. (*Read*) Now write about the city. Pretend that you are writing an article for a travel magazine and describe your imaginary trip for tourists. (*Write*) Next, give a presentation about the city. Record yourself as you describe your imaginary trip to the city. (*Speak*) Listen to your recording, correct your mistakes, and record yourself again. (*Listen*) Then choose a different city and repeat the activities.

Find out about any subject

Think of a topic you would like to know more about and look for information about it online. One place to look is http://simple.wikipedia.org/wiki/Main_Page. This website is written in simple English. Read information about your topic on this or other websites. (*Read*) Now write a short essay about your topic. (*Write*) Next, talk about your topic. Record yourself as you speak. (*Speak*) Listen to your recording, correct your mistakes, and record yourself again. (*Listen*) Then choose a different topic and repeat the activities.

Report the news

Listen to an English language news report on the radio, watch a news program on TV, or read the news in English online. (*Listen and read*) Take notes as you listen or read and use them to write a short summary of the news. (*Write*) Next, record yourself as you give a spoken summary of the news. (*Speak*) Listen to your recording, correct your mistakes, and record yourself again. Then choose a different news story and repeat the activities.

Summarize a TV show or movie

Watch a TV show or movie in English. (*Listen*) Take notes as you watch and use them to write a summary of the show or movie. (*Write*) Include your opinion. Say whether or not you liked it and why. Next, record yourself as you give a spoken summary of the show or movie. (*Speak*) Listen to your recording, correct your mistakes, and record yourself again. (*Listen*) Then watch another TV show or movie and repeat the activities.

Review a book

Read a book in English. (*Read*) Then pretend that you are writing a book review for a magazine. Write a short summary of the book and explain your opinion of it. Explain what you liked and didn't like about the book and why. Compare it to other books you have read. (*Write*) Next, talk about the book. Record yourself as you give a spoken review of the book. (*Speak*) Listen to your recording, correct your mistakes, and record yourself again. (*Listen*) Then read another book and repeat the activities.

TO THE TEACHER

As a teacher, you want your students to become proficient in English, but you know your student's first goal is to score well on the TOEIC test. Fortunately, with the *Longman Preparation Series for the TOEIC® Test: Reading and Listening*, both your goals and the students' goals can be met. All activities in the Longman Preparation Series match those on the actual TOEIC test. Every practice exercise a student does prepares him or her for a similar question on the test. You do not, however, have to limit yourself to this structure. You can take the context of an item and adapt it to your own needs. I call this teaching technique "LIPP service:" Look at; Identify; Paraphrase; Personalize. LIPP service makes the students repeat the target words and ideas in a variety of ways. Repetition helps students learn English. Variety keeps them awake. Here are some examples on how LIPP service can "serve" you in your classroom for each of the seven parts of the TOEIC test.

LIPP Service Examples

PART 1: PHOTOS

L   Have the students look at the photo.

I   Have the students identify all the words in the photo. Have them determine who is in the photo, what they are doing, and where they are standing. If there are no people, have them determine what is in the photo and describe it.

P   Have the students paraphrase the sentences they used when identifying the people or objects in the photo. This can be very simple, but it teaches the versatility and adaptability of language. For example, the students identify in the picture a man getting on the bus. Paraphrase: *A passenger is boarding the bus.* The students can also enrich the sentence by adding modifiers: *A young man is about to get on the city bus.*

P   Have the students personalize their statements. Start with simple sentences such as *I am getting on the bus* and expand to short stories: *Every morning, I wait for the bus on the corner. The bus stop is between Fifth and Sixth Street on the west side of the street. There are often many people waiting for the bus, so we form a line.*

PART 2: QUESTION-RESPONSE

L   Have the students listen to the question and three responses.

I   Have the students identify all the words in the question and three responses. They can take dictation from the audio program or from you.

P   Have the students paraphrase the question or statement they hear. *You're coming, aren't you?* can be paraphrased as *I hope you plan to come.* Options such as, *Yes, of course,* can be paraphrased as *Sure.*

P   Have the students personalize their statements. The students can work in pairs and develop small dialogues: *You're coming to my house tonight, aren't you? No, I'm sorry. I have to study.*

INTRODUCTION   **XIII**

PART 3: CONVERSATIONS

L   Have the students listen to the conversations and look at the three questions and answer options in the book.

I   Have the students identify all the words in the short conversations, the three written questions, and possible answers.

P   Have the students paraphrase the sentences. The method is the same as for Parts 1 and 2. The students will demonstrate their understanding of the individual sentences by providing a paraphrase.

P   Have the students personalize their statements. If the conversation is about dining out, the students can make up their own short conversation about a dining experience that they had. They should work in pairs or small groups for this exercise.

PART 4: TALKS

L   Have the students listen to the talks and look at the question(s) and answer options in the book.

I   Have the students identify all the words in the talks, the written question(s), and possible answers.

P   Have the students paraphrase the sentences.

P   Have the students personalize their statements. Have them work in pairs or groups to create a similar talk. Have different individuals from the same group stand and give the talk. It will be interesting to see which vocabulary and grammar patterns they choose to share.

PART 5: INCOMPLETE SENTENCES

L   Have the students look at the statement and four responses.

I   Have the students identify all the words in the statement and four responses.

P   Have the students paraphrase the statement. They can also create sentences with the answer options that did not complete the blank in the original statement.

P   Have the students personalize their statements. The students may find it difficult to find something in common with the whole statement, but they might be able to isolate one word and create some personal attachment. For example, in *Our clients are satisfied with their computer system*, your students may not have clients, but they will probably have a computer: *I am satisfied with my personal computer*.

PART 6: TEXT COMPLETION

L   Have the students look at the statement and four answer options.

I   Have the students identify all the words in the statement and the four answer options.

P   Have the students paraphrase the statement. They can also create sentences with the answer options that did not complete the blank in the original statement.

P Have the students personalize their statements. For example, in *Our offices are modern and spacious*, your students may not work in offices, but they probably live in apartments: *My apartment is modern, but it's not very spacious.*

PART 7: READING COMPREHENSION

L Have the students look at the passage or passages.

I Have the students identify all the words in the passage(s).

P Have the students paraphrase the passage(s). If a passage is an advertisement, have them create a new advertisement for the same product. If a passage is a timetable, have them put the timetable in a different format.

P Have the students personalize the passage(s). An advertisement can be turned into a student's personal classified ad. A diary can be turned into a student's own schedule. A report can be turned into a student's essay on the same subject. With a little imagination, you can find a way to personalize almost any reading passage.

ABOUT THE TOEIC TEST

The Test of English for International Communication (TOEIC) is a multiple-choice test of English for adult, nonnative speakers of the language. The test uses the language of international business. It has two sections: Listening Comprehension and Reading.

Listening Comprehension	Part 1 Photos	10	45 minutes
	Part 2 Question-Response	30	
	Part 3 Conversations	30	
	Part 4 Talks	30	
	TOTAL	100	
Reading	Part 5 Incomplete Sentences	40	75 minutes
	Part 6 Text Completion	12	
	Part 7 Reading Comprehension		
	• Single Passages	28	
	• Double Passages	20	
	TOTAL	100	

The TOEIC test is scored on a scale of 10 to 990. Only correct responses count toward your score. These correct responses are added and converted to a TOEIC score.

Tips for Taking the TOEIC Test

- **Be familiar with the directions before you take the exam.**
  The directions are the same on every exam. If you study the directions in this book, which are identical to those on the actual TOEIC test, you don't need to read them on the day of the exam. Instead you can study the photos, read the answer options, and take more time to answer the questions themselves.

- **Work rapidly, but carefully.**
  Train yourself to work quickly. Train yourself to be thorough.

- **Guess.**
  If you do not know the answer, guess. You are not penalized for wrong answers, and you may get it right.

- **Mark only one answer per question.**
  Any question with more than one answer blackened will be counted as wrong.

- **Use the strategies and tips that you learned in this book.**
  This book was written so you can score higher on the TOEIC test. Use these strategies and tips for success.

TOEIC TEST DIRECTIONS AND ANSWER SHEETS

General Directions

These directions are provided by the Educational Testing Service (ETS) and are reprinted here with their permission. Read them and make sure you understand them. These directions are the same on every test.

Test of English for International Communication

General Directions

This test is designed to measure your English language ability. The test is divided into two sections: Listening and Reading.

You must mark all of your answers on the separate answer sheet. For each question, you should select the best answer from the answer choices given. Then, on your answer sheet, you should find the number of the question and fill in the space that corresponds to the letter of the answer that you have selected. If you decide to change an answer, completely erase your old answer and then mark your new answer.

Specific Directions

Each part of the TOEIC test begins with specific directions for that part. In this book, you will find these directions at the beginning of each study section and in the Practice Tests. Read them and be sure you understand them.

TOEIC Test Answer Sheets

The Answer Sheets used in this book are similar to those used in the TOEIC test. The precise format of the Answer Sheets varies from test site to test site.

To record a response to a test question, find the number on the answer sheet that corresponds to the test question and make a solid mark with a pencil, filling in the space that corresponds to the letter of the answer they have chosen.

INTRODUCTION XVII

PROVEN TIPS FOR DOING WELL ON THE TEST

Scientists from many U.S. universities, such as Purdue University, University of North Texas, St. Lawrence University, University of Chicago, and Trinity College, Hartford, have conducted research on the best ways to prepare for standardized tests like the TOEIC test. Here is a summary of some of the results of their research:

1. **Take a lot of practice tests.**
   Taking a lot of practice tests will train your brain to retrieve the information it needs from your memory. It will also improve your test-taking skills.

2. **Study in a quiet place.**
   You might think that listening to music or talking to your friends will help you relax, but distractions make it more difficult to retain the information that you are studying.

3. **Review the night before the test.**
   On the night before the test, review and practice the most difficult material. This will keep it fresh in your mind.

4. **Keep your regular hours the week before the test.**
   Go to sleep and wake up at your normal time. Staying up too late or waking up too early to study can interfere with your memory.

5. **Eat right.**
   During the week leading up to the test, make sure to eat well-balanced meals with plenty of fruit and vegetables. On the morning of the test, eat a high fiber, low sugar breakfast, such as whole grain cereal. Good food will provide your brain with the energy it needs to function well.

6. **Relax.**
   Try to remove stress from your life. Before the day of the test, make sure you are very familiar with the test procedures. Know what you can bring with you and what you have to leave at home. Make sure you know how to go to the test center. If you can, go to the test center, find the room, locate the restroom, water fountains, or coffee bar. Know how to get there and how long it takes to get there.

7. **Be confident.**
   If you have studied and practiced regularly, slept well, and eaten right, then you know that you will do your best on the day of the test.

Source: Shellenbarger, Sue. "Toughest Exam Question: What Is the Best Way to Study?" *Wall Street Journal* 26 October 2011. Online.

LISTENING COMPREHENSION

In the first section of the TOEIC® test, you will have the chance to show how well you understand spoken English. There are four parts to this section:

Part 1	Photos
Part 2	Question-Response
Part 3	Conversations
Part 4	Talks

In this part of the *Intermediate Course* for the TOEIC Test, you will learn strategies to help you on the Listening Comprehension section. Each part begins with activities to help you develop these strategies. Each part ends with listening comprehension questions similar to those on the TOEIC test.

NOTE: The TOEIC test directions for each part of the TOEIC test will be given at the beginning of the section. Read the directions carefully to be sure you understand them.

Part 1: Photos

These are the directions for Part 1 of the TOEIC® test. Study them now. If you understand these directions now, you will not have to read them during the test.

LISTENING TEST

In the Listening test, you will be asked to demonstrate how well you understand spoken English. The entire Listening test will last approximately 45 minutes. There are four parts, and directions are given for each part. You must mark your answers on the separate answer sheet. Do not write your answers in the test book.

PART 1

Directions: For each question in this part, you will hear four statements about a picture in your test book. When you hear the statements, you must select the one statement that best describes what you see in the picture. Then find the number of the question on your answer sheet and mark your answer. The statements will not be printed in your test book and will be spoken only one time.

Example

Sample Answer

Statement (C), "They're standing near the table," is the best description of the picture, so you should select answer (C) and mark it on your answer sheet.

STRATEGY OVERVIEW

LANGUAGE STRATEGIES

The following strategies will help you examine the photos in Part 1 of the TOEIC.

- Determine the Context – Give the photo a title and tell yourself a story about it.

- Vocabulary – Name the people and things you see in the photo.

- What do you see? – Ask yourself questions about the photo: What are the people doing? What has been done to the things? Where are they?

- Analyze – Interpret the photo: What is the situation? Why are the people doing this? Why are the things here?

TEST STRATEGIES

Some answer choices are made to confuse you. They are written to seem correct, but they really are not. Here are some common types of confusion you may see in the Part 1 answer choices.

- Similar Sounds – answer choices may use words that sound similar to words for people, things, or activities in the photo.

- Incorrect Prepositions – answer choices may incorrectly identify the position of people or things in the photo by using an incorrect preposition.

PHOTOS OF PEOPLE

PHOTO 1

CONTEXT
Title: At the Desk

The young man is working at his desk. He has his laptop computer next to him, and it is open. He is using a calculator and writing on a piece of paper at the same time. There is a stack of papers next to him and a cup in front of him. There is a pen in a penholder next to the cup. The man looks like he is concentrating hard on his work.

LANGUAGE STRATEGIES

Vocabulary

DIRECTIONS: Find these items in the photo.

desk	chair	paper	calculator
cup	tie	shirt	computer

What Do You See?

A. DIRECTIONS: Read these statements about what you see in the photo. The statements may or may not be true. Put (Y) for *yes* beside the statements that match the photo. Put (N) for *no* beside the statements that do not match the photo. Correct the statements that are not true.

4   LISTENING COMPREHENSION

1. _____ The man is looking at the computer.

2. _____ The computer is closed.

3. _____ The man is holding the cup in his hand.

4. _____ He is sitting in a chair at the desk.

5. _____ He is wearing a tie.

B. DIRECTIONS: You will be tested on what *is* in the photograph, not what ***could be*** in the photograph. Put (Y) beside the statements that are correct. Put (?) beside the statements that could be true, but you cannot be sure from the photo.

1. _____ The computer is turned on.

2. _____ He is working on his budget.

3. _____ He has a pen in his hand.

4. _____ The cup is empty.

5. _____ The computer is next to the man.

Analyze This

DIRECTIONS: What do you think about the photo? Read each statement. Put (Y) for *yes*, (N) for *no*, or (?) for *maybe* next to each statement. Give reasons for your answers.

1. _____ It's a large office.

Reason: _____

2. _____ The man works with computers a lot.

Reason: _____

3. _____ He prefers tea to coffee.

Reason: _____

4. _____ He's using a desktop computer.

Reason: _____

5. _____ He's writing in a notebook.

Reason: _____

TEST STRATEGIES

Prepositions

🎧 **DIRECTIONS:** Listen and complete the sentences with the prepositions you hear.

1. His hand is _____ the calculator.

2. The calculator is _____ the piece of paper.

3. The computer is _____ the desk.

4. He's sitting _____ the desk.

5. The man is looking at the numbers _____ the calculator.

Similar Sounds

🎧 **A. DIRECTIONS:** Listen. Which word or phrase do you hear first? Mark (A) or (B).

1. (A) coffee   (B) coughing   (A) (B)

2. (A) good-bye   (B) shirt and tie   (A) (B)

3. (A) sheet of paper   (B) neat paper   (A) (B)

4. (A) drinking from the cup   (B) thinking something up   (A) (B)

5. (A) colder   (B) holder   (A) (B)

🎧 **B. DIRECTIONS:** Listen. Which statement do you hear first? Mark (A) or (B).

1. (A) The man drinks coffee in his office.   (A) (B)
   (B) The man is coughing in his office.

2. (A) He's saying good-bye.   (A) (B)
   (B) He's wearing a shirt and tie.

3. (A) The man is using a sheet of paper.   (A) (B)
   (B) The man is choosing some neat paper.

4. (A) He's drinking from the cup.   (A) (B)
   (B) He's thinking something up.

5. (A) The tea is next to the holder.   (A) (B)
   (B) The tea is getting colder.

Extra Practice

DIRECTIONS: On a separate piece of paper, write about what is happening in the photo. Use the vocabulary in this section.

PHOTO 2

CONTEXT
Title: _____

There are many tables in this restaurant. The restaurant is outside in a garden. There are some trees and plants in the garden. Some of the tables are covered with umbrellas. Some of the tables are under a tree. There are many empty tables.

At one of the tables, a waitress is taking an order. She is holding a pen and a small notebook or pad of paper. She writes the customers' orders on this pad. There are two customers, a man and a woman, at this table.

There is a tablecloth on the table. The table is set with glasses and plates. One knife is visible. There is a menu on the table by the man and an ashtray in the middle of the table.

LANGUAGE STRATEGIES

Vocabulary

DIRECTIONS: Find these items in the photo.

table	umbrella	tablecloth	chair
customer	waitress	pad of paper	plate

What Do You See?

A. DIRECTIONS: Read these statements about what you see in the photo. The statements may or may not be true. Put (Y) for *yes* beside the statements that match the photo. Put (N) for *no* beside the statements that do not match the photo. Correct the statements that are not true.

1. _____ There are customers at every table.

2. _____ The restaurant is inside.

3. _____ The customers are giving their orders to the waitress.

4. _____ There are tablecloths on all the tables.

5. _____ There are umbrellas at every table.

B. DIRECTIONS: You will be tested on what *is* in the photograph, not what ***could be*** in the photograph. Put (Y) for yes beside the statements that describe what you see in the photo. Put (?) beside the statements that could be true, but you cannot be sure from the photo.

1. _____ The couple is ordering dessert.

2. _____ The restaurant is very popular.

3. _____ The waitress is taking an order from the couple.

4. _____ The waitress is standing.

5. _____ The restaurant is not full.

Analyze This

DIRECTIONS: What do you think about the photo? Put (Y) for *yes*, (N) for *no*, or (?) for *maybe* beside each statement. Give a reason for your answer.

1. _____ The restaurant is expensive.

Reason: _____

2. _____ It is lunchtime.

Reason: _____

3. _____ It is a hot day.

Reason: _____

4. _____ The tablecloth is clean.

Reason: _____

5. _____ The waitress is giving the customers menus.

Reason: _____

TEST STRATEGIES

Prepositions

🎧 **DIRECTIONS:** Listen and complete the sentences with the prepositions you hear.

1. The couple is sitting _____ the table.

2. The restaurant is _____ the garden.

3. A tablecloth is _____ the table.

4. The waitress is standing _____ front _____ the customers.

5. The man and woman are _____ each other.

Similar Sounds

🎧 **A. DIRECTIONS:** Listen. Which word or phrase do you hear first? Mark (A) or (B).

1.	(A) cup of	(B) couple		Ⓐ	Ⓑ
2.	(A) talking together	(B) taking their order		Ⓐ	Ⓑ
3.	(A) waiter is setting	(B) waitress is sitting		Ⓐ	Ⓑ
4.	(A) a dress	(B) address		Ⓐ	Ⓑ
5.	(A) on the right	(B) wearing white		Ⓐ	Ⓑ

🎧 **B. DIRECTIONS:** Listen. Which statement do you hear first? Mark (A) or (B).

1. (A) The waitress is serving a cup of coffee. Ⓐ Ⓑ
   (B) The waitress is serving the couple coffee.

2. (A) The waitress is taking their order. Ⓐ Ⓑ
   (B) The waitresses are talking together.

3. (A) The waiter is setting the table. Ⓐ Ⓑ
   (B) The waitress is sitting at the table.

4. (A) The woman is wearing a dress. Ⓐ Ⓑ
   (B) The man is writing his address.

5. (A) The waiter is wearing white. Ⓐ Ⓑ
   (B) The waitress is on the right.

Extra Practice

DIRECTIONS: On a separate piece of paper, write about what is happening in the photo. Use the vocabulary in this section.

PHOTO 3

CONTEXT
Title: _____

There are two men sitting at a table. The table is very long. There are papers and books on the table. There are also two bottles. One bottle is not open. The other bottle is open. Its cap is on the table. There is a glass on a napkin.

Both men are wearing jackets. Both men are wearing ties. One man is wearing glasses. They are looking at each other. Both men have their hands on the table.

LANGUAGE STRATEGIES

Vocabulary

DIRECTIONS: Find these items in the photo.

bottle	cap	glass	napkin
tie	glasses	shirt	hand

10   LISTENING COMPREHENSION

What Do You See?

A. DIRECTIONS: Read these statements about what you see in the photo. The statements may or may not be true. Put (Y) beside the statements that match the photo. Put (N) beside the statements that do not match the photo. Correct the statements that are not true.

1. _____ There are three bottles on the table.

2. _____ Only one man is wearing a tie.

3. _____ Both men are wearing glasses.

4. _____ There is a napkin under the glass.

5. _____ A bottle cap is on the table.

B. DIRECTIONS: You will be tested on what *is* in the photograph, not what *could be* in the photograph. Put (Y) beside the statements that describe what you see in the photo. Put (?) beside the statements that could be true, but you cannot be sure from the photo.

1. _____ The men are wearing jackets.

2. _____ The men are wearing suits.

3. _____ There is water in the bottle.

4. _____ Each man has a bottle beside him.

5. _____ Both men drink a lot of water.

Analyze This

DIRECTIONS: What do you think about the photo? Put (Y) for *yes*, (N) for *no*, or (?) for *maybe* beside each statement. Give reasons for your answers.

1. _____ It's night time.

Reason: _____

2. _____ The men are reading the newspaper.

Reason: _____

3. _____ It is an important meeting.

Reason: _____

4. _____ The men know each other very well.

Reason: _____

5. _____ They're discussing business.

Reason: _____

TEST STRATEGIES

Prepositions

🎧 **DIRECTIONS:** Listen and complete the sentences with the prepositions you hear.

1. The glass is _____ top _____ the napkin.

2. The books are _____ front _____ the men.

3. The men are sitting _____ each other.

4. The cap is _____ the table.

5. A window is _____ them.

Similar Sounds

🎧 **A. DIRECTIONS:** Listen. Which word or phrase do you hear first? Mark (A) or (B).

1. (A) waiter	(B) water		Ⓐ	Ⓑ
2. (A) hurt	(B) shirt		Ⓐ	Ⓑ
3. (A) took a cap	(B) took a nap		Ⓐ	Ⓑ
4. (A) disc is in	(B) discussing		Ⓐ	Ⓑ
5. (A) Jack ate at	(B) jacket at		Ⓐ	Ⓑ

🎧 **B. DIRECTIONS:** Listen. Which statement do you hear first? Mark (A) or (B).

1. (A) The water is in the bottle. Ⓐ Ⓑ
   (B) The waiter has a bottle.

2. (A) He brought it himself. Ⓐ Ⓑ
   (B) He bought it himself.

3. (A) I took a cap from the table. Ⓐ Ⓑ
   (B) I took a nap at the table.

4. (A) They're discussing computers. Ⓐ Ⓑ
   (B) Their disc is in the computer.

5. (A) You know you need a jacket at the restaurant. Ⓐ Ⓑ
   (B) You know what Jack ate at the restaurant.

Extra Practice

DIRECTIONS: On a separate piece of paper, write about what is happening in the photo. Use the vocabulary in this section.

12 LISTENING COMPREHENSION

PHOTO 4

CONTEXT
Title: _____

The man is a carpenter. He is inside an unfinished building. He is holding three boards over his shoulder. He is wearing a hard hat and work gloves. He is also wearing a tool belt, and it is filled with tools. There is a measuring tape attached to his belt. Behind him is an unfinished wall. There is a window on the other side of the wall.

LANGUAGE STRATEGIES

Vocabulary

DIRECTIONS: Find these items in the photo.

carpenter	hard hat	tool belt	boards
lumber	gloves	beams	ceiling

PHOTOS   13

What Do You See?

A. DIRECTIONS: Read these statements about what you see in the photo. The statements may or may not be true. Put (Y) for *yes* beside the statements that match the photo. Put (N) for *no* beside the statements that do not match the photo. Correct the statements that are not true.

1. _____ He's carrying some lumber.

2. _____ The carpenter has a tool in his hand.

3. _____ The pockets of his belt are empty.

4. _____ His hat is on his head.

5. _____ The ceiling is finished.

B. DIRECTIONS: You will be tested on what *is* in the photograph, not what ***could be*** in the photograph. Put (Y) beside the statements that describe what you see in the photo. Put (?) beside the statements that could be true, but you cannot be sure from the photo.

1. _____ He's going to use the boards to finish the wall.

2. _____ He's been working hard all day.

3. _____ The window is open.

4. _____ The boards aren't very heavy.

5. _____ His hands are protected by gloves.

Analyze This

DIRECTIONS: What do you think about the photo? Put (Y) for *yes*, (N) for *no*, or (?) for *maybe* beside each statement. Give reasons for your answers.

1. _____ The carpenter is skilled at his job.

Reason: _____

2. _____ The room is too dark to work in.

Reason: _____

3. _____ The carpenter has a lot of tools.

Reason: _____

4. _____ The room is clean and orderly.

Reason: _____

5. _____ He enjoys working as a carpenter.

Reason: _____

TEST STRATEGIES

Prepositions

DIRECTIONS: Listen and complete the sentences with the prepositions you hear.

1. He has a tool belt _____ his waist.

2. He's wearing protective gloves _____ his hands.

3. There is a window _____ the wall.

4. There are tools _____ his pockets.

5. He's standing _____ the wall.

Similar Sounds

A. DIRECTIONS: Listen. Which word or phrase do you hear first? Mark (A) or (B).

1.	(A) hat	(B) mat		Ⓐ	Ⓑ
2.	(A) wall	(B) ball		Ⓐ	Ⓑ
3.	(A) fools	(B) tools		Ⓐ	Ⓑ
4.	(A) cold and bored	(B) holding boards		Ⓐ	Ⓑ
5.	(A) window	(B) windy		Ⓐ	Ⓑ

B. DIRECTIONS: Listen. Which statement do you hear first? Mark (A) or (B).

1. (A) The man's wearing a hard hat.   Ⓐ   Ⓑ
   (B) The man's standing on a mat.

2. (A) There's a wall behind him.   Ⓐ   Ⓑ
   (B) There's a ball behind him.

3. (A) He's carrying a lot of tools.   Ⓐ   Ⓑ
   (B) He's worrying about all the fools.

4. (A) The carpenter is holding boards.   Ⓐ   Ⓑ
   (B) The carpenter is cold and bored.

5. (A) The light comes through the window.   Ⓐ   Ⓑ
   (B) The night is cold and windy.

Extra Practice

DIRECTIONS: On a separate piece of paper, write about what is happening in the photo. Use the vocabulary in this section.

PHOTOS OF THINGS

PHOTO 5

CONTEXT
Title: _____

Cars are parked along a city street. There are parking meters along the curb. There is also a "no parking" sign on a tall signpost. Beyond that sign there are some other signs, but they are impossible to read. Farther down the sidewalk there are some people walking. In the background there are skyscrapers. There are some trees that don't have any leaves on their branches. There is a grassy area to the left of the sidewalk.

LANGUAGE STRATEGIES

Vocabulary

DIRECTIONS: Find these items in the photo.

curb	sidewalk	branches	skyscraper
grass	signpost	cars	parking meter

16 LISTENING COMPREHENSION

What Do You See?

A. DIRECTIONS: Read these statements about what you see in the photo. The statements may or may not be true. Put (Y) for *yes* beside the statements that match the photo. Put (N) for *no* beside the statements that do not match the photo. Correct the statements that are not true.

1. _____ There is a sign next to each parking meter.

2. _____ The cars are parked in a parking lot.

3. _____ The parking meters are next to the curb.

4. _____ The people are getting into a car.

5. _____ The leaves are falling from the tree branches.

B. DIRECTIONS: You will be tested on what *is* in the photograph, not what **could be** in the photograph. Put (Y) beside the statements that describe what you see in the photo. Put (?) beside the statements that could be true, but you cannot be sure from the photo.

1. _____ It costs one dollar an hour to park here.

2. _____ The street is in a city.

3. _____ Overnight parking is not allowed here.

4. _____ The people on the sidewalk just parked their car.

5. _____ You have to pay to park on this street.

Analyze This

DIRECTIONS: What do you think about the photo? Put (Y) for *yes,* (N) for *no,* or (?) for *maybe* beside each statement. Give reasons for your answers.

1. _____ The sidewalk runs along a park.

Reason: _____

2. _____ The drivers of the cars are at work now.

Reason: _____

3. _____ It's a winter day.

Reason: _____

4. _____ There are some stores nearby.

Reason: _____

5. _____ There is a lot of traffic on the street.

Reason: _____

PHOTOS **17**

TEST STRATEGIES

Prepositions

🎧 **DIRECTIONS:** Listen and complete the sentences with the prepositions you hear.

1. The signpost is _____ two parking meters.

2. The sign is _____ the top of the signpost.

3. The meters are _____ the cars.

4. The skyscrapers are _____ the trees.

5. The cars are _____ the curb.

Similar Sounds

🎧 **A. DIRECTIONS:** Listen. Which word or phrase do you hear first? Mark (A) or (B).

1. (A) tall   (B) wall   Ⓐ Ⓑ
2. (A) row   (B) go   Ⓐ Ⓑ
3. (A) meet her   (B) meters   Ⓐ Ⓑ
4. (A) curb   (B) curve   Ⓐ Ⓑ
5. (A) skyscrapers   (B) landscape   Ⓐ Ⓑ

🎧 **B. DIRECTIONS:** Listen. Which statement do you hear first? Mark (A) or (B).

1. (A) The signpost is very tall.   Ⓐ Ⓑ
   (B) The signpost is by the wall.

2. (A) The cars are parked in a row.   Ⓐ Ⓑ
   (B) The cars are ready to go.

3. (A) He's going to meet her on the street.   Ⓐ Ⓑ
   (B) The parking meters are on the street.

4. (A) The cars are parked by the curb.   Ⓐ Ⓑ
   (B) The park is around the curve.

5. (A) The skyscrapers are in the background.   Ⓐ Ⓑ
   (B) The landscape has a nice background.

Extra Practice

DIRECTIONS: On a separate piece of paper, write about what is happening in the photo. Use the vocabulary in this section.

PHOTO 6

CONTEXT
Title: _____

The restaurant is ready for customers. There is a row of tables along one side of the room by the windows. The tables are set with silverware, glasses, and placemats. Most of the tables are set for two people. The tables each have a chair on one side and a bench on the other. The chairs and benches all have cushions. In the background are some tables that are set for more than two people. The room is decorated with potted plants and is filled with natural light.

LANGUAGE STRATEGIES

Vocabulary

DIRECTIONS: Find these items in the photo.

silverware	plants	bench	cushions
placemats	fork	knife	spoon

PHOTOS   19

What Do You See?

A. DIRECTIONS: Read these statements about what you see in the photo. The statements may or may not be true. Put (Y) for *yes* beside the statements that match the photo. Put (N) for *no* beside the statements that do not match the photo. Correct the statements that are not true.

1. _____ The restaurant is filled with customers.

2. _____ There are plates on the tables.

3. _____ There are three cushions on each chair.

4. _____ There are glasses on the tables.

5. _____ Each place is set with a fork, knife, and spoon.

B. DIRECTIONS: You will be tested on what *is* in the photograph, not what *could be* in the photograph. Put (Y) beside the statements that describe what you see in the photo. Put (?) beside the statements that could be true, but you cannot be sure from the photo.

1. _____ The glasses on the tables are empty.

2. _____ The benches are comfortable to sit on.

3. _____ There aren't any napkins on the tables.

4. _____ The plants need to be watered soon.

5. _____ The chairs face the windows.

Analyze This

DIRECTIONS: What do you think about the photo? Put (Y) for *yes*, (N) for *no*, or (?) for *maybe* beside each statement. Give reasons for your answers.

1. _____ The food at this restaurant is delicious.

Reason: _____

2. _____ This is a popular place to eat.

Reason: _____

3. _____ There are two chairs at each table.

Reason: _____

4. _____ People are seated at some of the tables.

Reason: _____

5. _____ The window curtains are closed.

Reason: _____

TEST STRATEGIES

Prepositions

🎧 **DIRECTIONS:** Listen and complete the sentences with the prepositions you hear.

1. The knife is _____ the spoon.

2. The glasses are _____ the placemats.

3. The bench is _____ the window.

4. The chair is _____ the bench.

5. The plant is _____ two benches.

Similar Sounds

🎧 **A. DIRECTIONS:** Listen. Which word or phrase do you hear first? Mark (A) or (B).

1.	(A) chairs	(B) stairs		Ⓐ	Ⓑ
2.	(A) mats	(B) cats		Ⓐ	Ⓑ
3.	(A) ready	(B) reading		Ⓐ	Ⓑ
4.	(A) each	(B) peach		Ⓐ	Ⓑ
5.	(A) dinner	(B) thinner		Ⓐ	Ⓑ

🎧 **B. DIRECTIONS:** Listen. Which statement do you hear first? Mark (A) or (B).

1. (A) The chairs are by the table.   Ⓐ Ⓑ
   (B) The stairs are next to the table.

2. (A) There are two mats on each table.   Ⓐ Ⓑ
   (B) The cats are under the table.

3. (A) They're ready to serve dinner.   Ⓐ Ⓑ
   (B) They're reading the dinner menu.

4. (A) Each table has two placemats.   Ⓐ Ⓑ
   (B) A peach was placed on the table.

5. (A) They set the table for dinner.   Ⓐ Ⓑ
   (B) They won't get any thinner.

Extra Practice

DIRECTIONS: On a separate piece of paper, write about what is happening in the photo. Use the vocabulary in this section.

PHOTOS

PHOTO 7

CONTEXT
Title: _____

There is a row of houses down one side of the street. It is a narrow street. A sidewalk runs along the street in front of the houses. Some of the houses have a stone wall in front. Some have bushes in front. Most of the houses seem to be three stories high. They have peaked roofs, and there are chimneys on many of the roofs. The street is empty. There are no cars or people.

LANGUAGE STRATEGIES

Vocabulary

DIRECTIONS: Find these items in the photo.

chimney	bushes	sidewalk	posts
stone wall	roof	story	windows

LISTENING COMPREHENSION

What Do You See?

A. DIRECTIONS: Read these statements about what you see in the photo. The statements may or may not be true. Put (Y) for *yes* beside the statements that match the photo. Put (N) for *no* beside the statements that do not match the photo. Correct the statements that are not true.

1. _____ There are cars parked in front of the houses.

2. _____ There is a line painted down the left-hand side of the street.

3. _____ All the houses have bushes in front of them.

4. _____ One of the houses is one story high.

5. _____ It is nighttime.

B. DIRECTIONS: You will be tested on what *is* in the photograph, not what ***could be*** in the photograph. Put (Y) beside the statements that describe what you see in the photo. Put (?) beside the statements that could be true, but you cannot be sure from the photo.

1. _____ The houses all look similar to each other.

2. _____ Some of the houses have chimneys.

3. _____ There are gardens behind the houses.

4. _____ It is early in the morning.

5. _____ Large families live in these houses.

Analyze This

DIRECTIONS: What do you think about the photo? Put (Y) for *yes*, (N) for *no*, or (?) for *maybe* beside each statement. Give reasons for your answers.

1. _____ There is a park across the street.

Reason: _____

2. _____ The houses are expensive to buy.

Reason: _____

3. _____ There are stores in some of the houses.

Reason: _____

4. _____ There is more than one family living in some of the houses.

Reason: _____

5. _____ Some of the houses are for sale.

Reason: _____

PHOTOS 23

TEST STRATEGIES

Prepositions

🎧 **DIRECTIONS:** Listen and complete the sentences with the prepositions you hear.

1. There is a wall _____ the sidewalk and the houses.

2. The chimney is _____ the roof.

3. There are bushes _____ the houses.

4. The bushes are _____ the wall.

5. There are two small posts _____ the sidewalk.

Similar Sounds

🎧 **A. DIRECTIONS:** Listen. Which word or phrase do you hear first? Mark (A) or (B).

1. (A) stories	(B) stores	Ⓐ	Ⓑ
2. (A) wall	(B) tall	Ⓐ	Ⓑ
3. (A) street	(B) feet	Ⓐ	Ⓑ
4. (A) around a corner	(B) rounded corners	Ⓐ	Ⓑ
5. (A) row	(B) snow	Ⓐ	Ⓑ

🎧 **B. DIRECTIONS:** Listen. Which statement do you hear first? Mark (A) or (B).

1. (A) The houses are three stories high. Ⓐ Ⓑ
   (B) There are stores in the houses.

2. (A) The house has an old stone wall. Ⓐ Ⓑ
   (B) The old stone house is tall.

3. (A) The street is very narrow. Ⓐ Ⓑ
   (B) His feet are very narrow.

4. (A) The street goes around a corner. Ⓐ Ⓑ
   (B) The window has rounded corners.

5. (A) The houses are all in a row. Ⓐ Ⓑ
   (B) The houses are covered with snow.

Extra Practice

DIRECTIONS: On a separate piece of paper, write about what is happening in the photo. Use the vocabulary in this section.

24   LISTENING COMPREHENSION

PHOTO 8

CONTEXT
Title: _____

This is an office with a few pieces of furniture. There is a desk, but there is nothing on top of the desk. There is a chair behind the desk, and behind the chair there is a floor lamp. On the other side of the room there is a cabinet with drawers and shelves. Three round mirrors hang on the wall over the cabinet. There is striped wallpaper on the wall. There are both blinds and curtains hanging on the window. The sun is shining through the window, making a shadow of the desk on the floor.

LANGUAGE STRATEGIES

Vocabulary

DIRECTIONS: Find these items in the photo.

curtains	blinds	shadow	wallpaper
mirror	cabinet	drawers	shelves

PHOTOS 25

What Do You See?

A. DIRECTIONS: Read these statements about what you see in the photo. The statements may or may not be true. Put (Y) for *yes* beside the statements that match the photo. Put (N) for *no* beside the statements that do not match the photo. Correct the statements that are not true.

1. _____ The mirrors are square.

2. _____ The curtains are open.

3. _____ There is a box on one of the shelves.

4. _____ There is a computer on the desk.

5. _____ It's a rainy day.

B. DIRECTIONS: You will be tested on what *is* in the photograph, not what **could be** in the photograph. Put (Y) beside the statements that describe what you see in the photo. Put (?) beside the statements that could be true, but you cannot be sure from the photo.

1. _____ This office is in someone's home.

2. _____ The furniture is all brand new.

3. _____ The desk faces away from the window.

4. _____ The drawers are empty.

5. _____ The chair isn't very comfortable.

Analyze This

DIRECTIONS: What do you think about the photo? Put (Y) for *yes,* (N) for *no,* or (?) for *maybe* beside each statement. Give reasons for your answers.

1. _____ It is a woman's office.

Reason: _____

2. _____ The room is dirty.

Reason: _____

3. _____ The chair is too heavy to move around.

Reason: _____

4. _____ This office is rarely used.

Reason: _____

5. _____ The mirrors are all the same size.

Reason: _____

TEST STRATEGIES

Prepositions

🎧 **DIRECTIONS:** Listen and complete the sentences with the prepositions you hear.

1. The mirrors are _____ the cabinets.

2. The lamp is _____ the chair.

3. There is a box _____ the shelf.

4. The wallpaper is covered _____ stripes.

5. The cabinet is _____ the wall.

Similar Sounds

🎧 **A. DIRECTIONS:** Listen. Which word or phrase do you hear first? Mark (A) or (B).

1. (A) floor lamp   (B) four lamps   (A) (B)
2. (A) shelves   (B) shells   (A) (B)
3. (A) on the wall are round (B) fall on the ground (A) (B)
4. (A) box   (B) socks   (A) (B)
5. (A) floor   (B) door   (A) (B)

🎧 **B. DIRECTIONS:** Listen. Which statement do you hear first? Mark (A) or (B).

1. (A) There is a floor lamp by the window.   (A) (B)
   (B) There are four lamps by the window.

2. (A) There is a box on one of the shelves.   (A) (B)
   (B) There is a box filled with some shells.

3. (A) The mirrors on the wall are round.   (A) (B)
   (B) The mirrors fall on the ground.

4. (A) The box is in the cabinet.   (A) (B)
   (B) The socks are in the cabinet.

5. (A) The curtains touch the floor.   (A) (B)
   (B) The curtains touch the door.

Extra Practice

DIRECTIONS: On a separate piece of paper, write about what is happening in the photo. Use the vocabulary in this section.

PHOTOS 27

GRAMMAR TIP

Possessive Adjectives

Possessive adjectives can help you know what the topic of the sentence is.

his	refers to a man or boy
her	refers to a woman or girl
its	refers to a thing or animal
their	refers to two or more people, things, or animals

The man is going to pay the bill. His wallet is in his hand.
The woman is reading. Her book is on the table.
The umbrella doesn't work. Its handle is broken.
The friends are going on a trip. Their taxi is waiting by the door.

VOCABULARY TIP

More Than One Meaning

Some words have two or more meanings. Here are a few examples:

Word	Meaning 1	Meaning 2
glasses	objects used for holding drinks	objects used for seeing better
sign	to write your name	a board with information
park	to leave your car in a certain place	a public outdoor area
leaves	goes away	parts of a tree or plant

The glasses are filled with water.
The man is putting on his glasses.

The woman is signing the letter.
There is a sign on the wall.

They parked the car on the street.
The park has many flowers.

He leaves through the back door.
The leaves fell off the tree.

STRATEGY PRACTICE

DIRECTIONS: Look at the photos and listen to the four statements. Choose the statement that most closely matches the photo.

1. Ⓐ Ⓑ Ⓒ Ⓓ

2. Ⓐ Ⓑ Ⓒ Ⓓ

PHOTOS 29

3. Ⓐ Ⓑ Ⓒ Ⓓ

4. Ⓐ Ⓑ Ⓒ Ⓓ

30   LISTENING COMPREHENSION

5. Ⓐ Ⓑ Ⓒ Ⓓ

6. Ⓐ Ⓑ Ⓒ Ⓓ

PHOTOS 31

7. Ⓐ Ⓑ Ⓒ Ⓓ

8. Ⓐ Ⓑ Ⓒ Ⓓ

PART 2: QUESTION-RESPONSE

PART 2

Directions: You will hear a question or statement and three responses spoken in English. They will not be printed in your test book and will be spoken only one time. Select the best response to the question or statement and mark the letter (A), (B), or (C) on your answer sheet.

Example

Sample Answer

You will hear: Where is the meeting room?

You will also hear: (A) To meet the new director.
(B) It's the first room on the right.
(C) Yes, at two o'clock.

Your best response to the question "Where is the meeting room?" is choice (B), "It's the first room on the right," so (B) is the correct answer. You should mark answer (B) on your answer sheet.

STRATEGY OVERVIEW

The exercises on the following pages will help you develop strategies for listening to the questions and choosing the best response. They will help you use context clues to guess what the question and response are about, and will help you improve your vocabulary.

LANGUAGE STRATEGIES

Listen for words that tell you whether it is a statement or a question and that are associated with these topics:

- Statements – Listen for statements that begin with a person's name, a pronoun, or an object.
- Occupations – Listen for *Who?* questions.
- Activities – Listen for *What?* questions.
- Time – Listen for *When?*, *How often?*, and *How long?* questions.
- Location – Listen for *Where?* questions.
- Reason – Listen for *Why?* questions.

TEST STRATEGIES

Some answer choices are made to confuse you. They are written to seem correct, but they really are not. Here are some common types of confusion in answer choices.

- Similar Words – Listen for similar words. Some words sound similar (*read, need*) or have similar meanings (*came, arrived*). Answer choices that contain words similar to words in the statement/question are not necessarily the correct answer.
- Repeated Words – Listen for repeated words. Answer choices that repeat words used in the statement/question are not necessarily the correct answer.

STATEMENTS

LANGUAGE STRATEGY PRACTICE

Practice A

DIRECTIONS: Match these statements with the correct responses.

1. _____ I came before noon.

2. _____ The meeting is either tomorrow or Friday.

3. _____ I bought two tickets to the concert.

4. _____ Our lease expires next month.

5. _____ I put the mail on your desk.

6. _____ The early morning flight is delayed.

7. _____ The product designer wants a blue box.

8. _____ My favorite restaurant is closed today.

9. _____ I'll rent a car if you want.

10. _____ The applicants aren't qualified for the job.

a. The plane must have a mechanical problem.

b. You'll enjoy the music, I'm sure.

c. Let's take taxis. It's easier than parking a car.

d. I'm sorry, but I had to leave at 11:30.

e. I'll open it later.

f. In that case, we'll have dinner in the cafeteria.

g. Actually, we met yesterday without you.

h. There must be someone with the qualifications.

i. We should renew it or find a new space.

j. I think red is a better choice.

Practice B

DIRECTIONS: Write possible responses to these statements.

1. My toothache is becoming really painful.

_____

2. We need someone to write a business plan.

_____

3. A computer virus shut down our network.

_____

4. In the summer, we don't wear coats or ties in the office.

_____

5. This letter should be sent overnight.

_____

6. The training program lasts all week.

_____

7. I think we're out of printer paper.

_____

8. Our expenses are greater than our revenues.

_____

9. The northbound train is on Track 1.

_____

10. The product warranty is only valid for a year.

_____

Practice C

DIRECTIONS: Read the questions and the possible responses below. Mark the correct answer.

1. It's raining very hard.   (A) (B) (C)
   - (A) They're in the yard.
   - (B) Then I'll take an umbrella.
   - (C) This training course isn't easy.

2. I got new shoes.   (A) (B) (C)
   - (A) They look very nice.
   - (B) The news I got was old.
   - (C) Please help me choose.

3. This pen doesn't work.   (A) (B) (C)
   - (A) She doesn't work without a pencil.
   - (B) Here, use mine.
   - (C) He does it at work.

4. I haven't seen John all week.   Ⓐ Ⓑ Ⓒ
    (A) He's away on a trip.
    (B) You've seen John every day this week.
    (C) Yes, he seems weak.

5. Mary seems like a nice person.   Ⓐ Ⓑ Ⓒ
    (A) I like ice cream, too.
    (B) He personally doesn't like mice.
    (C) Yes, she's very friendly.

6. I can't find my keys.   Ⓐ Ⓑ Ⓒ
    (A) I can find the peas.
    (B) Yes, that's the right kind.
    (C) I saw them on your desk.

7. I love the food in this restaurant.   Ⓐ Ⓑ Ⓒ
    (A) I'm ready for a rest.
    (B) Really? I've never eaten here before.
    (C) You don't like a good meal.

8. I don't know how to swim.   Ⓐ Ⓑ Ⓒ
    (A) It's easy. I'll show you how.
    (B) He doesn't know how to win.
    (C) What a nice swimsuit.

9. Susan's plane doesn't get in until midnight.   Ⓐ Ⓑ Ⓒ
    (A) Please don't fight on the train.
    (B) Susan does look plain at night.
    (C) That's OK. I can pick her up.

10. That store is closed on Sunday.   Ⓐ Ⓑ Ⓒ
    (A) This is a really fun day at the shore.
    (B) But it's open on Monday.
    (C) Someday we'll store our clothes away.

36 LISTENING COMPREHENSION

Practice D

DIRECTIONS: Look at each of the statements and answer choices in Practice C. In each one, circle all the words that are the same or are similar in meaning, if any. Underline all the words that are opposite in meaning, if any. Cross out the words that might sound similar, if any.

Not every conversation will have words that are the same, similar, opposite, or sound similar.

Example:

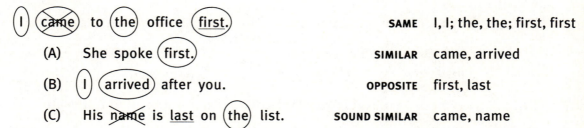

TEST STRATEGY PRACTICE

Practice E

DIRECTIONS: Listen to the statements, which are followed by three responses. They are not written out for you. Listen carefully to understand what the speakers say. You are to choose the best response to each question.

1. Ⓐ Ⓑ Ⓒ
2. Ⓐ Ⓑ Ⓒ
3. Ⓐ Ⓑ Ⓒ
4. Ⓐ Ⓑ Ⓒ
5. Ⓐ Ⓑ Ⓒ
6. Ⓐ Ⓑ Ⓒ
7. Ⓐ Ⓑ Ⓒ
8. Ⓐ Ⓑ Ⓒ
9. Ⓐ Ⓑ Ⓒ
10. Ⓐ Ⓑ Ⓒ

OCCUPATIONS

LANGUAGE STRATEGY PRACTICE

Practice A

DIRECTIONS: Match these questions with the correct answers.

1. _____ Who left the copy machine on?
2. _____ Who was the winner of the lottery?
3. _____ Who did not receive a paycheck?
4. _____ Who came to work during the snowstorm?
5. _____ Who recommended the new lawyer?
6. _____ Who answered your e-mail message?
7. _____ Who rode the subway this morning?
8. _____ Who fixes your car?
9. _____ Who hired you?
10. _____ Who helped you write this report?

a. Ms. Marsden gave me this job.

b. Our legal office suggested her name.

c. I wrote all of it myself.

d. The boss never misses a day even in bad weather.

e. The shipping clerk won $14 million.

f. I did not get one.

g. I think everybody drove today.

h. Mr. King sent me a very nice answer.

i. I did, but I'm still making copies.

j. I go to a very good mechanic on State Street.

Practice B

DIRECTIONS: Write possible answers to these questions.

1. Who designed this building?

_____

2. Who is working in the mailroom?

_____

3. Who is making coffee?

_____

38 LISTENING COMPREHENSION

4. Who typed this letter?

_____

5. Who is the new secretary?

_____

6. Who is going to the conference next week?

_____

7. Who took this telephone message?

_____

8. Who uses this desk?

_____

9. Who can fix the coffee machine?

_____

10. Who will be at the dinner tonight?

_____

Practice C

DIRECTIONS: Read the questions and the possible responses below. Mark the correct answer.

1. Who turned on the lights?   Ⓐ   Ⓑ   Ⓒ
   (A) They are on all the time.
   (B) It isn't dark outside.
   (C) I'll turn them off.

2. Who makes the decisions in this office?   Ⓐ   Ⓑ   Ⓒ
   (A) We get new office supplies every week.
   (B) She decided on a desk for her office.
   (C) The office manager usually does.

3. Who ordered two boxes of copy paper?   Ⓐ   Ⓑ   Ⓒ
   (A) Mary read two newspapers every morning.
   (B) I asked for twenty-two cartons of wrapping paper.
   (C) John put in the order yesterday.

4. Who is in charge of advertising?   Ⓐ   Ⓑ   Ⓒ
   (A) There was a charge for the ad.
   (B) The vice president of marketing.
   (C) He is very large.

5. Who is going to get this memo?   Ⓐ Ⓑ Ⓒ
   (A) Everyone in the department.
   (B) I typed the memo myself.
   (C) They are going together.

6. Who sent you that package?   Ⓐ Ⓑ Ⓒ
   (A) I'll mail it this afternoon.
   (B) The stamps cost fifty cents.
   (C) It came from the London office.

7. Who left these folders on my desk?   Ⓐ Ⓑ Ⓒ
   (A) Martha's assistant put them there.
   (B) They're on your desk.
   (C) You can get more folders in the supply room.

8. Who will be at the meeting tomorrow?   Ⓐ Ⓑ Ⓒ
   (A) The meeting's in the big conference room.
   (B) All the department heads will be there.
   (C) I'll be finished eating soon.

9. Who has read this article?   Ⓐ Ⓑ Ⓒ
   (A) It was written by a marketing expert.
   (B) It's a very interesting article.
   (C) I have, and I thought it was interesting.

10. Who was the last person to leave the office?   Ⓐ Ⓑ Ⓒ
    (A) It lasted a long time.
    (B) I think Bob was here until 10:00.
    (C) It's the last office on the left.

Practice D

DIRECTIONS: Look at each of the questions and answer choices in Practice C. In each one, circle all the words that are the same or are similar in meaning, if any. Underline all the words that are opposite in meaning, if any. Cross out the words that might sound similar, if any.

Not every conversation will have words that are the same, similar, opposite, or sound similar.

Example:

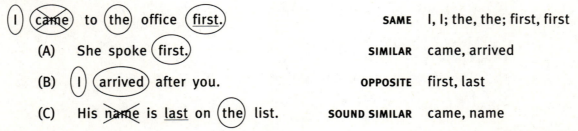

	SAME	I, I; the, the; first, first
(A) She spoke first.	SIMILAR	came, arrived
(B) I arrived after you.	OPPOSITE	first, last
(C) His name is last on the list.	SOUND SIMILAR	came, name

40   LISTENING COMPREHENSION

TEST STRATEGY PRACTICE

Practice E

DIRECTIONS: Listen to the questions, which are followed by three responses. They are not written out for you. Listen carefully to understand what the speakers say, and choose the best response to each question.

1. (A) (B) (C)   6. (A) (B) (C)
2. (A) (B) (C)   7. (A) (B) (C)
3. (A) (B) (C)   8. (A) (B) (C)
4. (A) (B) (C)   9. (A) (B) (C)
5. (A) (B) (C)   10. (A) (B) (C)

ACTIVITIES

LANGUAGE STRATEGY PRACTICE

Practice A

DIRECTIONS: Match these questions with the correct answers.

1. _____ What is this machine used for?

2. _____ What is your profession?

3. _____ What did your doctor tell you?

4. _____ What's for lunch?

5. _____ What is the best way to get there?

6. _____ What did they do last Saturday?

7. _____ What's on TV tonight?

8. _____ What's on that shelf?

9. _____ What do you like to read?

10. _____ What do you want a pen for?

a. Tuna fish sandwiches.

b. I'm an accountant.

c. The train is the cheapest and most comfortable.

d. To record my telephone calls.

e. To exercise more and eat less.

f. There's an interesting program about science.

g. I want to write down a phone number.

h. They went to the movies.

i. Paper and envelopes.

j. I enjoy novels.

QUESTION-RESPONSE   **41**

Practice B

DIRECTIONS: Write possible answers to these questions.

1. What did you put on my desk?

2. What is your favorite food?

3. What did you do last night?

4. What are you looking for?

5. What is the book about?

6. What do you do on your birthday?

7. What did she wear to the party?

8. What did you get in the mail?

9. What happened to your phone?

10. What did they do in New York?

Practice C

DIRECTIONS: Read the questions and the possible responses below. Mark the correct answer.

1. What do you see on his desk?　　Ⓐ　Ⓑ　Ⓒ
   (A) There are papers and books on it.
   (B) His desk is in the corner.
   (C) It's on his desk.

42　LISTENING COMPREHENSION

2. What street do they live on?
   (A) They live on New York Avenue.
   (B) That's where we live.
   (C) This is a busy street.

3. What did the printer do with our order?
   (A) We ordered more envelopes.
   (B) The print has an odor.
   (C) He misplaced it.

4. What does this briefcase cost?
   (A) He spoke briefly.
   (B) It's on sale for $150.
   (C) I lost my briefcase.

5. What are you doing after work?
   (A) I'm going home.
   (B) I like my work very much.
   (C) We are late for work.

6. What did you buy at the store?
   (A) It's not a big store.
   (B) It's right by my house.
   (C) I got some batteries.

7. What do you want for lunch?
   (A) Just a sandwich.
   (B) Let's eat at 12:30.
   (C) It doesn't cost much.

8. What did your boss tell you?
   (A) I don't want to sell it.
   (B) She asked me to help with the project.
   (C) Don't tell me about it.

9. What will we discuss at the meeting?
   (A) The meeting is at 10:00.
   (B) We'll talk about next year's budget.
   (C) Let's go by bus.

10. What is in that bag?
    (A) It's a new book I bought.
    (B) I'll take it back.
    (C) This bag is too heavy.

QUESTION-RESPONSE 43

Practice D

DIRECTIONS: Look at each of the questions and answer choices in Practice C. In each one, circle all the words that are the same or are similar in meaning, if any. Underline all the words that are opposite in meaning, if any. Cross out the words that might sound similar, if any.

Not every conversation will have words that are the same, similar, opposite, or sound similar.

Example:

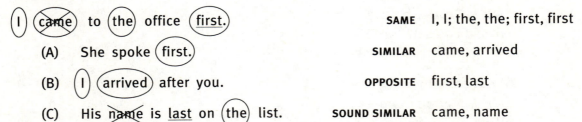

TEST STRATEGY PRACTICE

Practice E

DIRECTIONS: Listen to the questions, which are followed by three responses. They are not written out for you. Listen carefully to understand what the speakers say, and choose the best response to each question.

1. Ⓐ Ⓑ Ⓒ
2. Ⓐ Ⓑ Ⓒ
3. Ⓐ Ⓑ Ⓒ
4. Ⓐ Ⓑ Ⓒ
5. Ⓐ Ⓑ Ⓒ
6. Ⓐ Ⓑ Ⓒ
7. Ⓐ Ⓑ Ⓒ
8. Ⓐ Ⓑ Ⓒ
9. Ⓐ Ⓑ Ⓒ
10. Ⓐ Ⓑ Ⓒ

TIME

LANGUAGE STRATEGY PRACTICE

Practice A

DIRECTIONS: Match these questions with the correct answers.

1. _____ When are you leaving?
2. _____ When did you notice the problem?
3. _____ When do you think he will arrive?
4. _____ When are you taking the exam?
5. _____ When will you call your lawyer?
6. _____ When did you get the package?
7. _____ When did Mrs. Schmidt return from vacation?
8. _____ When can I see you?
9. _____ When did John send that e-mail message?
10. _____ When will you buy a new car?

a. She got back last week.
b. I'm leaving at noon.
c. I'll call him tomorrow.
d. After I study more, I'll take it.
e. I received it this morning.
f. He sent it yesterday.
g. He's expected on the 10:30 plane.
h. Let's get together tomorrow morning.
i. As soon as I have enough money.
j. I became aware of it last month.

Practice B

DIRECTIONS: Write possible answers to these questions.

1. When can you revise the report?

   _____

2. When will the store be painted?

   _____

3. When did they develop this new product?

   _____

4. When did she join the firm?

   _____

QUESTION-RESPONSE **45**

5. When are you going to go on vacation?

6. When did you see Sally?

7. When will the new computers arrive?

8. When is the office party?

9. When will your membership expire?

10. When was this office last cleaned?

Practice C

DIRECTIONS: Read the questions and the possible responses below. Mark the correct answer.

1. When are you leaving for France?   (A) (B) (C)
   (A) I like living in France.
   (B) Not since 1945.
   (C) My plane leaves at 7:45.

2. When will the meeting be over?   (A) (B) (C)
   (A) In about two hours.
   (B) I'll meet you later.
   (C) We talked it over.

3. When can we expect our check?   (A) (B) (C)
   (A) We did a thorough check already.
   (B) We didn't expect him so soon.
   (C) We will send your check out tomorrow.

4. When does the weather turn cold?   (A) (B) (C)
   (A) Usually not until December.
   (B) We'll go whether you are there or not.
   (C) The rain turned to snow yesterday.

5. When will the project be finished?   (A) (B) (C)
   (A) We finished the project on time.
   (B) Next month, we hope.
   (C) Yes, we predict it will be finished.

46   LISTENING COMPREHENSION

6. When will the plane arrive? Ⓐ Ⓑ Ⓒ
   (A) It'll be here in about 25 minutes.
   (B) They plan to arrive.
   (C) I never drive.

7. When did you call him? Ⓐ Ⓑ Ⓒ
   (A) You can call me tomorrow.
   (B) Everyone calls him Bob.
   (C) I spoke to him last night.

8. When do you have lunch? Ⓐ Ⓑ Ⓒ
   (A) I usually eat around noon.
   (B) I always go to the cafeteria downstairs.
   (C) I had a really big lunch.

9. When did Jane start her new job? Ⓐ Ⓑ Ⓒ
   (A) That job took a long time.
   (B) She began it last month.
   (C) She really likes her work.

10. When will the copy machine be fixed? Ⓐ Ⓑ Ⓒ
    (A) The machine is broken.
    (B) I made some copies this morning.
    (C) Someone will come to repair it tomorrow.

Practice D

DIRECTIONS: Look at each of the questions and answer choices in Practice C. In each one, circle all the words that are the same or are similar in meaning, if any. Underline all the words that are opposite in meaning, if any. Cross out the words that might sound similar, if any.

Not every conversation will have words that are the same, similar, opposite, or sound similar.

Example:

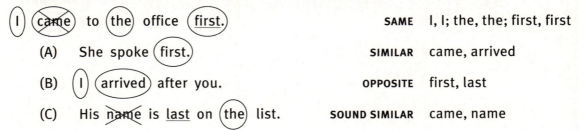

QUESTION-RESPONSE 47

TEST STRATEGY PRACTICE

Practice E

DIRECTIONS: Listen to the questions, which are followed by three responses. They are not written out for you. Listen carefully to understand what the speakers say, and choose the best response to each question.

1. (A) (B) (C)
2. (A) (B) (C)
3. (A) (B) (C)
4. (A) (B) (C)
5. (A) (B) (C)
6. (A) (B) (C)
7. (A) (B) (C)
8. (A) (B) (C)
9. (A) (B) (C)
10. (A) (B) (C)

LOCATION

LANGUAGE STRATEGY PRACTICE

Practice A

DIRECTIONS: Match these questions with the correct answers.

1. _____ Where will the bus stop?
2. _____ Where are you meeting your clients?
3. _____ Where did she study English?
4. _____ Where were you last night?
5. _____ Where can I buy a newspaper?
6. _____ Where did you grow up?
7. _____ Where is the magazine I lent you?
8. _____ Where is Ms. Salerian's office?
9. _____ Where can we park the car?
10. _____ Where is the bank?

a. There's a newsstand in the lobby.

b. It stops at the next corner.

c. She started in high school and then continued on her own.

d. They will meet me here.

e. I stayed at the office until midnight.

f. There's a garage in the building next door.

g. It's on my desk.

h. In a small town.

i. It's right across the street.

j. Down the hall to the left.

Practice B

DIRECTIONS: Write possible answers to these questions.

1. Where are you going to play golf?

_____

2. Where are the supplies kept?

_____

3. Where will the new employee sit?

_____

4. Where can I buy a used car?

_____

5. Where did you file the insurance policies?

_____

6. Where is the sugar?

_____

7. Where did you buy your new suit?

_____

8. Where will the party be?

_____

9. Where will you be tonight?

_____

10. Where can I put these books?

_____

Practice C

DIRECTIONS: Read the questions and the possible responses below. Mark the correct answer.

1. Where is the cafeteria?   Ⓐ   Ⓑ   Ⓒ
   (A) Coffee usually keeps me awake.
   (B) In the basement of the next building.
   (C) It's open until midnight.

2. Where will you be waiting?   Ⓐ   Ⓑ   Ⓒ
   (A) By the front door.
   (B) I weigh about 185 pounds.
   (C) This is the waiting room.

3. Where did you find your glasses?   Ⓐ   Ⓑ   Ⓒ
   (A) On the floor of my car.
   (B) The glasses were dirty.
   (C) Yes, I would like a glass of water.

4. Where is the nearest phone?   Ⓐ   Ⓑ   Ⓒ
   (A) I don't know her phone number.
   (B) My home is miles from here.
   (C) There is one in my office.

50   LISTENING COMPREHENSION

5. Where is the conference room?   Ⓐ Ⓑ Ⓒ
   (A) The conference starts in ten minutes.
   (B) Turn left at the end of the hall.
   (C) We do not have individual rooms.

6. Where's the hotel?   Ⓐ Ⓑ Ⓒ
   (A) It's near the airport.
   (B) I didn't tell anyone.
   (C) It's not an expensive hotel.

7. Where did you leave your cell phone?   Ⓐ Ⓑ Ⓒ
   (A) Your phone is ringing.
   (B) He sells phones.
   (C) I think I left it on the bus.

8. Where does Lucy work?   Ⓐ Ⓑ Ⓒ
   (A) Her office is downtown.
   (B) She works very hard.
   (C) Let's walk in the park.

9. Where did you go on your vacation?   Ⓐ Ⓑ Ⓒ
   (A) The room is vacant.
   (B) We flew to Miami.
   (C) It was a great vacation.

10. Where's a good place to get dinner?   Ⓐ Ⓑ Ⓒ
    (A) I think you're getting thinner.
    (B) I prefer a late dinner.
    (C) There's a nice restaurant on the corner.

Practice D

DIRECTIONS: Look at each of the questions and answer choices in Practice C. In each one, circle all the words that are the same or are similar in meaning, if any. Underline all the words that are opposite in meaning, if any. Cross out the words that might sound similar, if any.

Not every conversation will have words that are the same, similar, opposite, or sound similar.

Example:

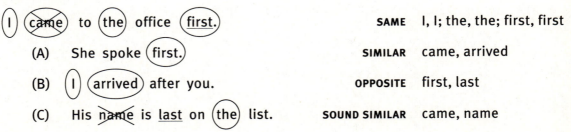

QUESTION-RESPONSE 51

TEST STRATEGY PRACTICE

Practice E

DIRECTIONS: Listen to the questions, which are followed by three responses. They are not written out for you. Listen carefully to understand what the speakers say, and choose the best response to each question.

1. (A) (B) (C)
2. (A) (B) (C)
3. (A) (B) (C)
4. (A) (B) (C)
5. (A) (B) (C)
6. (A) (B) (C)
7. (A) (B) (C)
8. (A) (B) (C)
9. (A) (B) (C)
10. (A) (B) (C)

REASON

LANGUAGE STRATEGY PRACTICE

Practice A

DIRECTIONS: Match these questions with the correct answers.

1. _____ Why are you wearing a suit?

2. _____ Why isn't the water hot?

3. _____ Why has the meeting been delayed?

4. _____ Why did she move to Japan?

5. _____ Why is the window open?

6. _____ Why aren't there any envelopes?

7. _____ Why do you look so tired?

8. _____ Why did George leave after lunch?

9. _____ Why don't you take a vacation this month?

10. _____ Why did he send you those flowers?

a. No one was available to meet until this afternoon.

b. The air conditioner is broken.

c. It's my birthday today.

d. He had an appointment this afternoon.

e. There's no hot water heater.

f. I forgot to order the office supplies.

g. She wanted to study Japanese.

h. I'm too busy at work this month.

i. I always wear one to work.

j. I didn't sleep well last night.

Practice B

DIRECTIONS: Write possible answers to these questions.

1. Why are you smiling?

_____

2. Why does she sit next to the window?

_____

3. Why isn't this project finished yet?

_____

QUESTION-RESPONSE 53

4. Why won't the car start?

_____

5. Why is the door closed?

_____

6. Why didn't you make coffee?

_____

7. Why did you bring an umbrella?

_____

8. Why can't John come to the party?

_____

9. Why do you always take the bus?

_____

10. Why aren't you hungry now?

_____

Practice C

DIRECTIONS: Read the questions and the possible responses below. Mark the correct answer.

1. Why were you late? (A) (B) (C)
   (A) I overslept this morning.
   (B) You ate very late last night.
   (C) I'll be there at eight o'clock.

2. Why can't she come with us? (A) (B) (C)
   (A) She has too much work to do.
   (B) We can't go with her.
   (C) She came by bus.

3. Why do first-year students study economics? (A) (B) (C)
   (A) They need the large, economy-size package.
   (B) It's a college requirement.
   (C) Yes, I caught the train at the station.

4. Why is the door closed? (A) (B) (C)
   (A) The wind blew it open.
   (B) Because I want some peace and quiet.
   (C) Her closet is full of clothes.

54 LISTENING COMPREHENSION

5. Why was the meeting postponed? Ⓐ Ⓑ Ⓒ
   (A) Yes, we met today.
   (B) Please post a notice about yesterday's meeting.
   (C) The lawyers had not finished writing their reports.

6. Why did you stay late at the office? Ⓐ Ⓑ Ⓒ
   (A) I had a lot of work to do.
   (B) Please wait in my office.
   (C) I'll spend the day at the office.

7. Why is Sam looking for a new job? Ⓐ Ⓑ Ⓒ
   (A) He knew about that job.
   (B) He booked a flight for Japan.
   (C) He wants to make more money.

8. Why hasn't that package arrived yet? Ⓐ Ⓑ Ⓒ
   (A) They'll arrive by jet.
   (B) They just mailed it yesterday.
   (C) I haven't learned how to drive yet.

9. Why isn't Mr. Lee here today? Ⓐ Ⓑ Ⓒ
   (A) He doesn't hear well.
   (B) He's at a conference in New York.
   (C) He usually sits here.

10. Why does it feel cold in here? Ⓐ Ⓑ Ⓒ
    (A) Yes, it's really old.
    (B) It's not very near.
    (C) Someone left the window open.

Practice D

DIRECTIONS: Look at each of the questions and answer choices in Practice C. In each one, circle all the words that are the same or are similar in meaning, if any. Underline all the words that are opposite in meaning, if any. Cross out the words that might sound similar, if any.

Not every conversation will have words that are the same, similar, opposite, or sound similar.

Example:

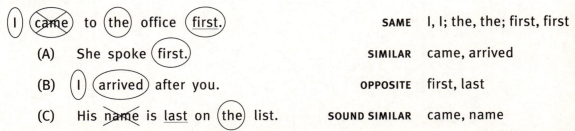

QUESTION-RESPONSE 55

TEST STRATEGY PRACTICE

Practice E

🎧 **DIRECTIONS:** Listen to the questions, which are followed by three responses. They are not written out for you. Listen carefully to understand what the speakers say, and choose the best response to each question.

1. Ⓐ Ⓑ Ⓒ
2. Ⓐ Ⓑ Ⓒ
3. Ⓐ Ⓑ Ⓒ
4. Ⓐ Ⓑ Ⓒ
5. Ⓐ Ⓑ Ⓒ
6. Ⓐ Ⓑ Ⓒ
7. Ⓐ Ⓑ Ⓒ
8. Ⓐ Ⓑ Ⓒ
9. Ⓐ Ⓑ Ⓒ
10. Ⓐ Ⓑ Ⓒ

HOW

LANGUAGE STRATEGY PRACTICE

Practice A

DIRECTIONS: Match these questions with the correct answers.

1. _____ How big is the conference room?
2. _____ How many people were at the meeting?
3. _____ How did you know my first name?
4. _____ How soon does the bank close?
5. _____ How far can you see without your glasses?
6. _____ How long does it take to get there?
7. _____ How often do you take a vacation?
8. _____ How much money do you need?
9. _____ How can I get in touch with you?
10. _____ How did you get here today?

a. It's bigger than the one we're in now.

b. Not very far—less than five meters.

c. About a dozen, if you count the officers.

d. In about an hour.

e. Your secretary told me.

f. Call me on my cell phone.

g. Just once a year.

h. About three hours by car.

i. Only a few dollars.

j. I drove my car.

Practice B

DIRECTIONS: Write possible answers to these questions.

1. How much is this table?

_____

2. How do you turn on the computer?

_____

3. How often do you play tennis?

_____

4. How old are his children now?

_____

QUESTION-RESPONSE **57**

5. How soon will you be leaving for your trip?

_____

6. How long is the movie?

_____

7. How far is the post office from here?

_____

8. How do you like your new job?

_____

9. How many envelopes do you need?

_____

10. How late did they arrive?

_____

Practice C

DIRECTIONS: Read the questions and the possible responses below. Mark the correct answer.

1. How much time do you have? Ⓐ Ⓑ Ⓒ
   (A) About ten o'clock.
   (B) I have another hour.
   (C) Just this watch.

2. How much does a new computer cost? Ⓐ Ⓑ Ⓒ
   (A) Without keyboard or monitor, it's about $500.
   (B) We have six new computers.
   (C) I bought it last month.

3. How will you get home? Ⓐ Ⓑ Ⓒ
   (A) I usually get home around 5 P.M.
   (B) As soon as it stops raining.
   (C) I'll probably walk.

4. How often does the bus come? Ⓐ Ⓑ Ⓒ
   (A) I always take the bus.
   (B) Every five minutes until six o'clock.
   (C) The bus stops in front of my house.

5. How many more file cabinets do you need? Ⓐ Ⓑ Ⓒ
   (A) We need five or six more.
   (B) I filed more than a hundred letters today.
   (C) Yes, I need to file my taxes soon.

58 LISTENING COMPREHENSION

6. How long did the meeting last?   Ⓐ Ⓑ Ⓒ
   (A) It was the last meeting of the week.
   (B) Only about thirty minutes.
   (C) About fifteen people were there.

7. How soon can you finish this report?   Ⓐ Ⓑ Ⓒ
   (A) I can have it for you by tomorrow morning.
   (B) I'm expecting an important call soon.
   (C) This is a very big room.

8. How can I make copies?   Ⓐ Ⓑ Ⓒ
   (A) Take all the copies you need.
   (B) I need ten copies.
   (C) Use the copy machine in my office.

9. How long is that article you wrote?   Ⓐ Ⓑ Ⓒ
   (A) It took about a week.
   (B) It's fifteen pages.
   (C) It's about the economic situation.

10. How was your trip?   Ⓐ Ⓑ Ⓒ
    (A) I went there last week.
    (B) It was very pleasant and relaxing.
    (C) I read a tour book.

Practice D

DIRECTIONS: Look at each of the questions and answer choices in Practice C. In each one, circle all the words that are the same or are similar in meaning, if any. Underline all the words that are opposite in meaning, if any. Cross out the words that might sound similar, if any.

Not every conversation will have words that are the same, similar, opposite, or sound similar.

Example:

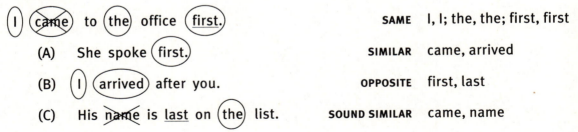

QUESTION-RESPONSE   59

TEST STRATEGY PRACTICE

Practice E

DIRECTIONS: Listen to the questions, which are followed by three responses. They are not written out for you. Listen carefully to understand what the speakers say, and choose the best response to each question.

1. (A) (B) (C)
2. (A) (B) (C)
3. (A) (B) (C)
4. (A) (B) (C)
5. (A) (B) (C)
6. (A) (B) (C)
7. (A) (B) (C)
8. (A) (B) (C)
9. (A) (B) (C)
10. (A) (B) (C)

AUXILIARIES

LANGUAGE STRATEGY PRACTICE

Practice A

DIRECTIONS: Match these questions with the correct answers.

1. _____ Can you work late this evening?
2. _____ Are they opening a branch office?
3. _____ Is there more paper in the supply room?
4. _____ Has the contract been signed?
5. _____ Will the chairperson resign?
6. _____ Did John get here on time today?
7. _____ Has the mail arrived yet?
8. _____ Were you calling about a package for me?
9. _____ Do you have my phone number?
10. _____ Do you know how to fix this fax machine?

a. She plans to resign tomorrow.

b. Yes, it's from Mr. Jones.

c. I'm sorry. I have another commitment.

d. Yes, I'm pretty sure it has been.

e. No, he was late again.

f. I think you should call a repair person.

g. Yes, I put your letters on your desk.

h. No, I'll order some more.

i. Yes, in Europe, I think.

j. No, please write it down for me.

Practice B

DIRECTIONS: Write possible answers to these questions.

1. Didn't you buy a new car?

_____

2. Have you given the new clerk something to do?

_____

3. Are you waiting for the express train?

_____

QUESTION-RESPONSE **61**

4. Will we be able to start production on schedule?

_____

5. Can they finish the chart by this afternoon?

_____

6. Is the manager going to be here today?

_____

7. Did you get the fax I sent you?

_____

8. Do you know how to speak French?

_____

9. Have you put the report on Martha's desk?

_____

10. Will everyone be at the meeting?

_____

Practice C

DIRECTIONS: Read the questions and the possible responses below. Mark the correct answer.

1. Have you used a word processing system before? Ⓐ Ⓑ Ⓒ
   (A) I processed it before I left yesterday.
   (B) Yes, we were trained on them at school.
   (C) It's a long process.

2. Did you send the report to the board members? Ⓐ Ⓑ Ⓒ
   (A) Yes, they reported to the board.
   (B) No, I'm waiting for your signature on the report.
   (C) They said the report was boring.

3. Can you take me to the train station? Ⓐ Ⓑ Ⓒ
   (A) Of course. I'll get my coat and we'll go.
   (B) Yes, I caught the train at the station.
   (C) We took a long time coming from the station.

4. Would you send this by overnight mail? Ⓐ Ⓑ Ⓒ
   (A) I'm sorry. It's too late for overnight service.
   (B) I mailed this to you last night.
   (C) No, overnight mail isn't too expensive.

5. Are the lawyers working on the new contracts?   Ⓐ Ⓑ Ⓒ
   (A) My lawyer's name is Ramon Carerra.
   (B) Yes, I contacted her by phone.
   (C) I asked them to get started this morning.

6. Will we discuss the budget at tomorrow's meeting?   Ⓐ Ⓑ Ⓒ
   (A) Yes, it's the first item on the agenda.
   (B) Yes, the meeting is tomorrow.
   (C) Yes, we'll take a bus to the meeting.

7. Do we need to order more office supplies?   Ⓐ Ⓑ Ⓒ
   (A) I just ordered some yesterday.
   (B) I wanted to give her a surprise.
   (C) Yes, that machine is out of order.

8. Are you going to the office party tonight?   Ⓐ Ⓑ Ⓒ
   (A) I'll be there three nights.
   (B) Yes, I'm looking forward to it.
   (C) It's the last office on the right.

9. Can you take this check to the bank for me?   Ⓐ Ⓑ Ⓒ
   (A) I'll check on it right away.
   (B) Certainly. I'll take it there after lunch.
   (C) It's the bank across the street.

10. Have you worked here very long?   Ⓐ Ⓑ Ⓒ
    (A) It won't take long to finish.
    (B) No, it's not a long way from here.
    (C) I started this job just last month.

Practice D

DIRECTIONS: Look at each of the questions and answer choices in Practice C. In each one, circle all the words that are the same or are similar in meaning, if any. Underline all the words that are opposite in meaning, if any. Cross out the words that might sound similar, if any.

Not every conversation will have words that are the same, similar, opposite, or sound similar.

Example:

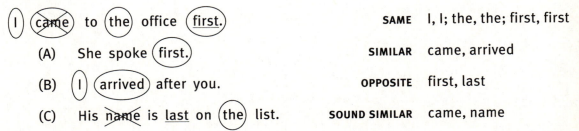

QUESTION-RESPONSE

TEST STRATEGY PRACTICE

Practice E

DIRECTIONS: Listen to the questions, which are followed by three responses. They are not written out for you. Listen carefully to understand what the speakers say, and choose the best response to each question.

1. (A) (B) (C)
2. (A) (B) (C)
3. (A) (B) (C)
4. (A) (B) (C)
5. (A) (B) (C)
6. (A) (B) (C)
7. (A) (B) (C)
8. (A) (B) (C)
9. (A) (B) (C)
10. (A) (B) (C)

GRAMMAR TIP

Polite Requests

The modals *can*, *could*, and *would* are often used to make polite requests. Even though these requests are in the form of yes/no questions, they are usually answered with polite responses rather than with a simple *yes* or *no*.

Polite Requests:
Can I borrow your pen?
Could you hand me that book?
Would you open the window, please?

Responses:
Of course.
Certainly.
I'd be glad to.
I'm sorry, I can't.

VOCABULARY TIP

Adjectives with *-ed*

Not all words that end with *-ed* are verbs. Sometimes they are adjectives.

Some common adjectives with *-ed*
interested
bored
scared
closed
tired
surprised

The woman is interested in her book.
The soccer fans looked bored.
The child is scared of the dog.
The restaurant is closed today.

QUESTION-RESPONSE **65**

STRATEGY REVIEW

DIRECTIONS: Listen and choose the appropriate response to the question or statement.

1. Ⓐ Ⓑ Ⓒ
2. Ⓐ Ⓑ Ⓒ
3. Ⓐ Ⓑ Ⓒ
4. Ⓐ Ⓑ Ⓒ
5. Ⓐ Ⓑ Ⓒ
6. Ⓐ Ⓑ Ⓒ
7. Ⓐ Ⓑ Ⓒ
8. Ⓐ Ⓑ Ⓒ
9. Ⓐ Ⓑ Ⓒ
10. Ⓐ Ⓑ Ⓒ
11. Ⓐ Ⓑ Ⓒ
12. Ⓐ Ⓑ Ⓒ
13. Ⓐ Ⓑ Ⓒ
14. Ⓐ Ⓑ Ⓒ
15. Ⓐ Ⓑ Ⓒ
16. Ⓐ Ⓑ Ⓒ
17. Ⓐ Ⓑ Ⓒ
18. Ⓐ Ⓑ Ⓒ
19. Ⓐ Ⓑ Ⓒ
20. Ⓐ Ⓑ Ⓒ

PART 3: CONVERSATIONS

PART 3

Directions: You will hear some conversations between two people. You will be asked to answer three questions about what the speakers say in each conversation. Select the best response to each question and mark the letter (A), (B), (C), or (D) on your answer sheet. The conversations will not be printed in your test book and will be spoken only one time.

STRATEGY OVERVIEW

The following exercises will help you develop strategies for listening to conversations and choosing the best response. They will help you use context clues to guess what the conversation is about. The exercises will also improve your vocabulary in specific ways.

LANGUAGE STRATEGIES

Listen for words in the conversations that are associated with these topics:

- Occupations – Listen for words about occupations to answer *Who?* questions.
- Activities – Listen for words about activities to answer *What?* questions.
- Time – Listen for words about time to answer *When?*, *How often?*, and *How long?* questions.
- Location – Listen for words about location to answer *Where?* questions.
- Reason – Listen for words about reasons to answer *Why?* questions.

TEST STRATEGIES

Use these strategies to determine the correct answers.

- Read before listening – Read the question and answer choices before you hear the audio.
- Listen for specifics – Listen for specific answers to the questions.

CONVERSATIONS **67**

OCCUPATIONS

LANGUAGE STRATEGIES

Vocabulary: Who

DIRECTIONS: Certain words are associated with certain occupations. Look at the words below. Cross out the words that do not match the occupation. What occupation is associated with the crossed-out words? Look at the example, and then do the exercise.

OCCUPATION	ASSOCIATED WORDS
Example:	
secretary	files, ~~singing~~, word processor, telephone, ~~song~~
singer	*singing, song*
1. cook	pots, kitchen, computer, knife, files
2. police officer	parking tickets, dessert, law, illegal, menu
3. teachers	class, mail, packages, exams, students
4. phone technician	telephone, novel, receiver, cord, write
5. computer programmer	files, software, memo, keyboard, monitor
6. bank teller	money, plane, deposit, withdrawal, fly
7. waiter	order, law, tip, customers, parking tickets
8. accountant	taxes, nails, receivables, wood, total
9. athlete	runner, training, sick, game, hospital

68 LISTENING COMPREHENSION

10.	doctor	menu, medicine, nurse, tip, hospital
	_____	_____
11.	musician	instrument, orchestra, pills, notes, prescription
	_____	_____
12.	actor	engine, stage, drama, repair, theater
	_____	_____
13.	taxi driver	passenger, campaign, fare, election, tip
	_____	_____
14.	sales clerk	film, camera, cash register, change, receipt
	_____	_____
15.	journalist	write, newspaper, flowers, seeds, reports
	_____	_____

Strategy Practice: Who

DIRECTIONS: Listen to the conversations on the audio and try to identify the occupation of the speakers. The words in the previous vocabulary exercise will be helpful to you. Remember to use the language strategies described on page 67.

1. Who are the speakers talking about?   Ⓐ Ⓑ Ⓒ Ⓓ
   - (A)   A hairstylist.
   - (B)   A ticketseller.
   - (C)   A concert pianist.
   - (D)   A singer.

2. Who are the speakers waiting for?   Ⓐ Ⓑ Ⓒ Ⓓ
   - (A)   The delivery person with lunch.
   - (B)   The telephone technician.
   - (C)   The television salesman.
   - (D)   The computer programmer.

3. Who are the speakers waiting for?   Ⓐ Ⓑ Ⓒ Ⓓ
   - (A)   A cab driver.
   - (B)   A friend.
   - (C)   A waitress.
   - (D)   A client.

CONVERSATIONS **69**

4. Who are the speakers?   Ⓐ   Ⓑ   Ⓒ   Ⓓ
   (A) Teachers.
   (B) Police officers.
   (C) Accountants.
   (D) Travel agents.

5. Who is coming this afternoon?   Ⓐ   Ⓑ   Ⓒ   Ⓓ
   (A) An athlete.
   (B) An accountant.
   (C) A carpenter.
   (D) A math teacher.

6. Who is giving advice?   Ⓐ   Ⓑ   Ⓒ   Ⓓ
   (A) A doctor.
   (B) A waiter.
   (C) An exercise coach.
   (D) An athlete.

7. Who is waiting?   Ⓐ   Ⓑ   Ⓒ   Ⓓ
   (A) A gardener.
   (B) A taxi driver.
   (C) A mail carrier.
   (D) A musician.

8. Who left a phone message?   Ⓐ   Ⓑ   Ⓒ   Ⓓ
   (A) A taxi driver.
   (B) A tennis coach.
   (C) A telephone repairperson.
   (D) An auto mechanic.

9. Who is Mr. Gomez?   Ⓐ   Ⓑ   Ⓒ   Ⓓ
   (A) A bookseller.
   (B) A hotel manager.
   (C) A travel agent.
   (D) A banker.

10. Who is the woman talking to?   Ⓐ   Ⓑ   Ⓒ   Ⓓ
    (A) An athlete.
    (B) A musician.
    (C) A travel agent.
    (D) A police officer.

Context

🎧 **DIRECTIONS:** On the TOEIC test, you will need to remember specific details from the conversation. You will have to improve your memory as well as your listening skills. Read the questions quickly before you listen to the conversation, and then listen for the answers.

CONVERSATION 1 (Questions 1–3)

1. Who is the woman talking to? Ⓐ Ⓑ Ⓒ Ⓓ
   (A) A hotel clerk.
   (B) A waiter.
   (C) A travel agent.
   (D) An elevator operator.

2. What is her room number? Ⓐ Ⓑ Ⓒ Ⓓ
   (A) 15.
   (B) 50.
   (C) 215.
   (D) 250.

3. Who recommended the restaurant to the woman? Ⓐ Ⓑ Ⓒ Ⓓ
   (A) Her brother.
   (B) Her mother.
   (C) Her friend.
   (D) Her employer.

CONVERSATION 2 (Questions 4–6)

4. Who did the man have an appointment with? Ⓐ Ⓑ Ⓒ Ⓓ
   (A) His dentist.
   (B) His secretary.
   (C) His hairstylist.
   (D) His rental agent.

5. Who missed the meeting? Ⓐ Ⓑ Ⓒ Ⓓ
   (A) The manager.
   (B) The woman.
   (C) Everybody.
   (D) Bob.

6. When is the next meeting? Ⓐ Ⓑ Ⓒ Ⓓ
   (A) Sunday.
   (B) Monday.
   (C) Tuesday.
   (D) Wednesday.

CONVERSATIONS **71**

ACTIVITIES

LANGUAGE STRATEGIES

Vocabulary: What

DIRECTIONS: Complete the sentences below using the following verb phrases.

eating dinner	making a sandwich
waiting for a bus	parking the car
buying a newspaper	driving a car
copying a letter	washing the floor
leaving a friend's home ✓	riding a bus
moving furniture	paying the taxi fare
picking up the mail	riding an elevator
buying a plane ticket	paying the bus fare

1. I said good-bye to Mr. Ogato. I hope to visit him again soon.

   I'm leaving a friend's home.

2. I put paper in the photocopier.

   _____

3. The children are cold standing at the bus stop.

   _____

4. Mr. Imamura is putting his desk by the window and his table in the corner.

   _____

5. I usually drive around for ten minutes until I find a place to park.

   _____

6. When we get on a bus, the driver wants us to pay our fare.

   _____

7. This elevator stops at every floor. I want an express elevator to the sixtieth floor.

   _____

8. She always pays attention to the traffic and wears her seat belt.

   _____

9. The round-trip fare from Chicago to Tokyo is $950.

   _____

10. We are sitting at a table. We have a lot of food on our plates.

   _____

72   LISTENING COMPREHENSION

11. She put butter on the bread and now she's slicing a tomato.

_____

12. I take the letters out of the mailbox.

_____

13. I always give the driver a 15 percent tip.

_____

14. They have a mop and a bucket of water.

_____

15. She gives the man fifty cents and takes a paper from the counter.

_____

Strategy Practice: What

DIRECTIONS: Listen to the conversations on the audio and then answer the following questions. Remember to use the language strategies described on page 67.

1. What are the speakers doing?   Ⓐ Ⓑ Ⓒ Ⓓ
   - (A) Typing a report.
   - (B) Eating lunch.
   - (C) Telling the time.
   - (D) Cooking.

2. What are the speakers doing?   Ⓐ Ⓑ Ⓒ Ⓓ
   - (A) Getting on a bus.
   - (B) Waiting for a bus.
   - (C) Taking a taxi.
   - (D) Paying a fare.

3. What are the speakers doing?   Ⓐ Ⓑ Ⓒ Ⓓ
   - (A) Painting the office.
   - (B) Buying a chair.
   - (C) Opening the window.
   - (D) Moving furniture.

4. What are the speakers doing?   Ⓐ Ⓑ Ⓒ Ⓓ
   - (A) Drinking coffee.
   - (B) Buying food.
   - (C) Sitting at a counter.
   - (D) Eating ice cream.

CONVERSATIONS

5. What is the woman doing?   Ⓐ Ⓑ Ⓒ Ⓓ
   (A) Paying her fare.
   (B) Giving change.
   (C) Going to the fair.
   (D) Changing her hair.

6. What is the woman going to do?   Ⓐ Ⓑ Ⓒ Ⓓ
   (A) Drive a car.
   (B) Take an elevator.
   (C) Wait for a train.
   (D) Walk up the stairs.

7. What are the speakers doing?   Ⓐ Ⓑ Ⓒ Ⓓ
   (A) Running in the park.
   (B) Looking for parking.
   (C) Walking across the street.
   (D) Taking the car to the mechanic.

8. What is the woman doing?   Ⓐ Ⓑ Ⓒ Ⓓ
   (A) Buying a ticket.
   (B) Giving directions.
   (C) Going to the bank.
   (D) Paying her taxes.

9. What are the speakers doing?   Ⓐ Ⓑ Ⓒ Ⓓ
   (A) Buying food.
   (B) Getting married.
   (C) Going to a restaurant.
   (D) Eating dinner.

10. What is the second man doing?   Ⓐ Ⓑ Ⓒ Ⓓ
    (A) Having lunch.
    (B) Comparing watches.
    (C) Leaving for home.
    (D) Arriving for a visit.

Context

🎧 **DIRECTIONS:** On the TOEIC test, you will need to remember specific details from the conversation. You will have to improve your memory as well as your listening skills. Read the questions quickly before you listen to the conversation, and then listen for the answers.

CONVERSATION 1 (Questions 1–3)

1. Who are the speakers waiting for?   Ⓐ Ⓑ Ⓒ Ⓓ
   - (A) A taxicab driver.
   - (B) A pilot.
   - (C) A train conductor.
   - (D) A newspaper delivery person.

2. What did the man just do?   Ⓐ Ⓑ Ⓒ Ⓓ
   - (A) He played a ball game.
   - (B) He arrived at the airport.
   - (C) He made a phone call.
   - (D) He wrote an editorial.

3. What is the woman going to do?   Ⓐ Ⓑ Ⓒ Ⓓ
   - (A) Read a book.
   - (B) Eat something.
   - (C) Read the newspaper.
   - (D) Buy some paper.

CONVERSATION 2 (Questions 4–6)

4. Who is the woman?   Ⓐ Ⓑ Ⓒ Ⓓ
   - (A) A pilot.
   - (B) A flight attendant.
   - (C) A waitress.
   - (D) A journalist.

5. What is the woman about to do?   Ⓐ Ⓑ Ⓒ Ⓓ
   - (A) Read a magazine.
   - (B) Relax.
   - (C) Serve lunch.
   - (D) Show a movie.

6. What does the man want to do?   Ⓐ Ⓑ Ⓒ Ⓓ
   - (A) Eat lunch.
   - (B) Watch a movie.
   - (C) Read a magazine.
   - (D) Tell jokes.

CONVERSATIONS **75**

TIME

LANGUAGE STRATEGIES

Vocabulary: When / How long / How often

DIRECTIONS: Time questions begin with *How long? How often? How soon? When?*
Write a question from each statement, using the question word or words provided.

1. The copy machine takes ten minutes to print a hundred pages.

   How long *does the copy machine take to print a hundred pages?*

2. Ms. Miller joined our staff in July.

   When _____

3. Mr. DeLorenzo has been in the hospital for two months.

   How long _____

4. The floors are cleaned every three months.

   How often _____

5. We are going to the reception at five o'clock.

   When _____

6. The mail usually comes before noon.

   When _____

7. It took all afternoon to fix the copy machine.

   How long _____

8. They tried to call him every night.

   How often _____

9. Mr. Gutfreund will be gone for two weeks.

   How long _____

10. She mailed the package last night.

    When _____

76 LISTENING COMPREHENSION

11. They've been working on this report all week.

How long _____

12. He sent the e-mail message this morning.

When _____

13. We have a staff meeting every Monday morning.

How often _____

14. Robert started his new job last week.

When _____

15. It will take about a week to paint all these offices.

How long _____

Strategy Practice: When / How long / How often

DIRECTIONS: Listen to the conversations on the audio and then answer the following questions. Remember to use the language strategies described on page 67.

1. How often are the offices cleaned? Ⓐ Ⓑ Ⓒ Ⓓ
   (A) Two times a week.
   (B) Three times a week.
   (C) Once a day.
   (D) Twice a day.

2. How long did it take to fix the coffee machine? Ⓐ Ⓑ Ⓒ Ⓓ
   (A) All day.
   (B) Two hours.
   (C) All morning.
   (D) Four hours.

3. How long does it take to make eight copies? Ⓐ Ⓑ Ⓒ Ⓓ
   (A) One minute.
   (B) Five minutes.
   (C) Eight minutes.
   (D) One hour.

4. How often has the man tried to call? Ⓐ Ⓑ Ⓒ Ⓓ
   (A) Once.
   (B) One more time.
   (C) Every five minutes.
   (D) Every hour.

CONVERSATIONS **77**

5. When does the mail come?   Ⓐ Ⓑ Ⓒ Ⓓ
   (A) In the morning.
   (B) At noon.
   (C) In the afternoon.
   (D) In the evening.

6. When was the check sent?   Ⓐ Ⓑ Ⓒ Ⓓ
   (A) Last week.
   (B) Yesterday.
   (C) Today.
   (D) On Friday.

7. When did Ms. Wallace join the company?   Ⓐ Ⓑ Ⓒ Ⓓ
   (A) The same year as Mr. Chu.
   (B) A month before Mr. Chu.
   (C) A year after Mr. Chu.
   (D) A month after Mr. Chu.

8. When are the speakers going?   Ⓐ Ⓑ Ⓒ Ⓓ
   (A) Five o'clock.
   (B) Six o'clock.
   (C) Seven o'clock.
   (D) Eight o'clock.

9. When did the woman visit her aunt?   Ⓐ Ⓑ Ⓒ Ⓓ
   (A) A long time ago.
   (B) Last week.
   (C) Yesterday.
   (D) This morning.

10. How long will Ms. Ono be away?   Ⓐ Ⓑ Ⓒ Ⓓ
   (A) One week.
   (B) Two weeks.
   (C) Three weeks.
   (D) Four weeks.

Context

> **DIRECTIONS:** On the TOEIC test, you will need to remember specific details from the conversation. You will have to improve your memory as well as your listening skills. Read the questions quickly before you listen to the conversation, and then listen for the answers.

CONVERSATION 1 (Questions 1–3)

1. When did the woman return from her vacation? (A) (B) (C) (D)
   - (A) Today.
   - (B) Last night.
   - (C) Yesterday afternoon.
   - (D) Last week.

2. Where will the man spend his vacation? (A) (B) (C) (D)
   - (A) In the mountains.
   - (B) At the lake.
   - (C) In Hong Kong.
   - (D) At the beach.

3. When will the man take his vacation? (A) (B) (C) (D)
   - (A) July.
   - (B) August.
   - (C) September.
   - (D) December.

CONVERSATION 2 (Questions 4–6)

4. When will the meeting begin? (A) (B) (C) (D)
   - (A) 8:00.
   - (B) 8:30.
   - (C) 9:30.
   - (D) 10:00.

5. When will Sherry speak? (A) (B) (C) (D)
   - (A) After the financial report.
   - (B) After the coffee break.
   - (C) Right after Tom's presentation.
   - (D) Right before lunch.

6. What will happen after lunch? (A) (B) (C) (D)
   - (A) Tom will speak.
   - (B) Coffee will be served.
   - (C) A committee will be organized.
   - (D) The manager will give a presentation.

CONVERSATIONS **79**

LOCATIONS

LANGUAGE STRATEGIES

Vocabulary: Where

DIRECTIONS: Certain words are associated with certain locations. Look at the words below. Cross out the words that do not match the location. What location is associated with the crossed-out words? Look at the example and then do the exercise.

LOCATION	ASSOCIATED WORDS
Example:	
plane	flight, ~~bed~~, flight attendant, ~~double room~~, seat belt
hotel	_bed, double room_
1. restaurant	order, tip, teacher, waiter, lesson
2. airplane	seat belt, deposit, landing, bank officer, wings
3. hotel	single room, Thailand, lobby, reservation, Malaysia
4. gas station	car, gas, fill up, waitress, oil, menu
5. travel agency	package tours, library card, tickets, hotels, bookshelves
6. train station	track, double room, train, room service, platform
7. library	book, gas, card, fill up, overdue, shelves, periodicals
8. bank	waiter, checking account, teller, deposit, tip
9. car rental agency	patient, insurance, rent, cars, nurse, reservation

80   LISTENING COMPREHENSION

10. import office   products, trade, export, engine, windshield

_____

11. post office   stamps, art, package, mail, exhibit

_____

12. clothing store   sand, dressing room, hanger, water, blouse

_____

13. park   bench, path, can, box, garden, aisle

_____

14. health club   cars, steam room, swimming pool, traffic light, exercise equipment

_____

15. kitchen   stove, cabinets, screen, tickets, sink

_____

Strategy Practice: Where

DIRECTIONS: Listen to the conversations on the audio and then answer the following questions. Remember to use the language strategies described on page 67.

1. Where are the speakers?   Ⓐ   Ⓑ   Ⓒ   Ⓓ
   - (A) At a gas station.
   - (B) In an elevator.
   - (C) In a kitchen.
   - (D) In an office.

2. Where are the speakers?   Ⓐ   Ⓑ   Ⓒ   Ⓓ
   - (A) At a fish store.
   - (B) At a restaurant.
   - (C) At the beach.
   - (D) At a party.

3. Where are the speakers?   Ⓐ   Ⓑ   Ⓒ   Ⓓ
   - (A) In a theater.
   - (B) On a train.
   - (C) In a plane.
   - (D) In a grocery store.

CONVERSATIONS   **81**

4. Where will the woman return the book?   (A) (B) (C) (D)
   - (A) To the bookstore.
   - (B) To the library.
   - (C) To her friend.
   - (D) To the post office.

5. Where are the sweaters made?   (A) (B) (C) (D)
   - (A) In the Philippines.
   - (B) In Thailand.
   - (C) In Hong Kong.
   - (D) In Malaysia.

6. Where are the speakers?   (A) (B) (C) (D)
   - (A) At an import company.
   - (B) At a restaurant.
   - (C) At a hotel.
   - (D) At an airport.

7. Where is this conversation taking place?   (A) (B) (C) (D)
   - (A) At a bank.
   - (B) At a bookstore.
   - (C) At a lost and found.
   - (D) At a library.

8. Where are the speakers going?   (A) (B) (C) (D)
   - (A) To the train station.
   - (B) To the watch repair shop.
   - (C) To a grocery store.
   - (D) To a coffee shop.

9. Where is this conversation taking place?   (A) (B) (C) (D)
   - (A) In Hawaii.
   - (B) At a travel agency.
   - (C) On a plane.
   - (D) In a gift shop.

10. Where are the speakers?   (A) (B) (C) (D)
   - (A) At a driving school.
   - (B) At an insurance agency.
   - (C) At a car rental agency.
   - (D) At an automobile showroom.

82   LISTENING COMPREHENSION

Context

🎧 **DIRECTIONS:** On the TOEIC test, you will need to remember specific details from the conversation. You will have to improve your memory as well as your listening skills. Read the questions quickly before you listen to the conversation, and then listen for the answers.

CONVERSATION 1 (Questions 1–3)

1. When will John arrive?   Ⓐ Ⓑ Ⓒ Ⓓ
   (A) Noon.
   (B) 2:00.
   (C) 2:15.
   (D) 2:50.

2. How long has he been gone?   Ⓐ Ⓑ Ⓒ Ⓓ
   (A) Four days.
   (B) Two weeks.
   (C) Three weeks.
   (D) One month.

3. Where will the woman take him?   Ⓐ Ⓑ Ⓒ Ⓓ
   (A) The train station.
   (B) The airport.
   (C) The office.
   (D) Home.

CONVERSATION 2 (Questions 4–6)

4. Where are these speakers now?   Ⓐ Ⓑ Ⓒ Ⓓ
   (A) In a waiting room.
   (B) At a restaurant.
   (C) At the beach.
   (D) At home.

5. How long have they been waiting?   Ⓐ Ⓑ Ⓒ Ⓓ
   (A) Five minutes.
   (B) Eight minutes.
   (C) Fifteen minutes.
   (D) One hour.

6. Where will they go later?   Ⓐ Ⓑ Ⓒ Ⓓ
   (A) Downtown.
   (B) To a theater.
   (C) To the movies.
   (D) To a ball game.

CONVERSATIONS **83**

REASONS

LANGUAGE STRATEGIES

Vocabulary: Why

DIRECTIONS: To complete each sentence, give a reason as an answer for the question.

1. She walked home in the snow.
   Why did she walk home in the snow?
   Because *she didn't want to drive.*

2. We will finish the report tomorrow.
   Why won't they finish the report today?
   Because _____

3. We used a pencil to sign the memo.
   Why didn't they use a pen?
   Because _____

4. My feet hurt.
   Why do your feet hurt?
   Because _____

5. She was late for work again.
   Why wasn't she on time?
   Because _____

6. Bob's clothes are wet.
   Why are Bob's clothes wet?
   Because _____

7. I tried to call you, but the line was busy.
   Why was the line busy?
   Because _____

8. Rita got a promotion at work.
   Why did Rita get a promotion?
   Because _____

9. She didn't eat anything for lunch.
   Why didn't she eat anything?
   Because _____

10. Please read this letter to me.
    Why don't you read the letter yourself?
    Because _____

Strategy Practice: Why

🎧 **DIRECTIONS:** Listen to the conversations on the audio and then answer the following questions. Remember to use the language strategies described on page 67.

1. Why was Ms. Boggs late?   Ⓐ Ⓑ Ⓒ Ⓓ
   (A) She had car trouble.
   (B) The bus broke down.
   (C) The bus didn't stop.
   (D) The train wasn't on time.

2. Why won't anyone come to the picnic?   Ⓐ Ⓑ Ⓒ Ⓓ
   (A) People work on Monday.
   (B) It's raining.
   (C) It starts at ten o'clock.
   (D) It's not fun.

3. Why was the man pleased?   Ⓐ Ⓑ Ⓒ Ⓓ
   (A) The woman finished the memo.
   (B) The woman is never late.
   (C) He has a new desk.
   (D) He likes to wait.

4. Why won't the speakers finish the letter today?   Ⓐ Ⓑ Ⓒ Ⓓ
   (A) They need a new pen.
   (B) They can't make it better.
   (C) They need five stamps.
   (D) There's not enough time.

5. Why can't the woman sign the memo?   Ⓐ Ⓑ Ⓒ Ⓓ
   (A) She doesn't have time.
   (B) It isn't typed yet.
   (C) Her pen doesn't work.
   (D) She can't think.

6. Why does the man want to be read to?   Ⓐ Ⓑ Ⓒ Ⓓ
   (A) He broke his glasses.
   (B) He forgot his glasses.
   (C) He lost his glasses.
   (D) He lent his glasses.

7. Why are the speakers taking the train?   Ⓐ Ⓑ Ⓒ Ⓓ
   (A) The roads are covered with snow.
   (B) They don't know how to drive.
   (C) The roads are closed.
   (D) It might rain.

CONVERSATIONS **85**

8. Why will the speakers walk?   Ⓐ   Ⓑ   Ⓒ   Ⓓ
- (A) They prefer walking.
- (B) They want to get some exercise.
- (C) The bus was full.
- (D) The car was out of gas.

9. Why didn't the man talk to the woman earlier?   Ⓐ   Ⓑ   Ⓒ   Ⓓ
- (A) Her line was busy.
- (B) She went to the doctor's.
- (C) He wasn't feeling well.
- (D) Her phone was broken.

10. Why did the woman's shoes hurt her feet?   Ⓐ   Ⓑ   Ⓒ   Ⓓ
- (A) They were old.
- (B) They were too big.
- (C) They were new.
- (D) They were too narrow.

Context

🎧 **DIRECTIONS:** On the TOEIC test, you will need to remember specific details from the conversation. You will have to improve your memory as well as your listening skills. Read the questions quickly before you listen to the conversation and then listen for the answers.

CONVERSATION 1 (Questions 1–3)

1. Why did the woman miss the meeting?   Ⓐ   Ⓑ   Ⓒ   Ⓓ
- (A) She had a problem with her car.
- (B) She didn't leave home on time.
- (C) She was feeling tired.
- (D) She was sick.

2. What time did the meeting start?   Ⓐ   Ⓑ   Ⓒ   Ⓓ
- (A) 1:00.
- (B) 8:00.
- (C) 9:00.
- (D) 10:00.

3. Why did the man leave his notes for his secretary?   Ⓐ   Ⓑ   Ⓒ   Ⓓ
- (A) She has to file them.
- (B) She wants to read them.
- (C) She will make copies of them.
- (D) She will rewrite them.

86   LISTENING COMPREHENSION

CONVERSATION 2 (Questions 4–6)

4. Where are the speakers going?   Ⓐ Ⓑ Ⓒ Ⓓ
   - (A) To a soccer game.
   - (B) To the theater.
   - (C) Out of town.
   - (D) To a park.

5. Why doesn't the woman want to drive?   Ⓐ Ⓑ Ⓒ Ⓓ
   - (A) It's difficult to find parking.
   - (B) Her car broke down.
   - (C) The bus is faster.
   - (D) The bus is free.

6. What time do they have to arrive?   Ⓐ Ⓑ Ⓒ Ⓓ
   - (A) 5:15.
   - (B) 5:30.
   - (C) 6:00.
   - (D) 7:00.

TEST STRATEGIES

DIRECTIONS: Read the questions before you hear the conversation. Then listen for specific details that answer the questions.

CONVERSATION 1 (Questions 1–3)

1. Who is the man talking to?   Ⓐ Ⓑ Ⓒ Ⓓ
   - (A) A taxi driver.
   - (B) A flight attendant.
   - (C) A train conductor.
   - (D) A box-office clerk.

2. How much will the man pay?   Ⓐ Ⓑ Ⓒ Ⓓ
   - (A) $10.00.
   - (B) $17.00.
   - (C) $30.00.
   - (D) $70.00.

3. What time is it now?   Ⓐ Ⓑ Ⓒ Ⓓ
   - (A) 11:13.
   - (B) 11:30.
   - (C) 12:15.
   - (D) 12:45.

CONVERSATIONS **87**

CONVERSATION 2 (Questions 4–6)

4. Who is the woman talking to?   Ⓐ Ⓑ Ⓒ Ⓓ
   - (A) An airline ticket agent.
   - (B) A travel agent.
   - (C) A hotel clerk.
   - (D) A car driver.

5. What is the woman doing?   Ⓐ Ⓑ Ⓒ Ⓓ
   - (A) Making hotel reservations.
   - (B) Buying plane tickets.
   - (C) Choosing a book.
   - (D) Renting a car.

6. What will the woman do on her trip?   Ⓐ Ⓑ Ⓒ Ⓓ
   - (A) Have a business meeting.
   - (B) Get married.
   - (C) Swim at the beach.
   - (D) Attend a cousin's wedding.

CONVERSATION 3 (Questions 7–9)

7. When did the man make his reservation?   Ⓐ Ⓑ Ⓒ Ⓓ
   - (A) Today.
   - (B) Last night.
   - (C) A week ago.
   - (D) A month ago.

8. How long will he stay at the hotel?   Ⓐ Ⓑ Ⓒ Ⓓ
   - (A) Two nights.
   - (B) Until Tuesday.
   - (C) Until Wednesday.
   - (D) Seven days.

9. What did the clerk offer the man?   Ⓐ Ⓑ Ⓒ Ⓓ
   - (A) A book.
   - (B) Some free meals.
   - (C) A couch.
   - (D) Some movie tickets.

CONVERSATION 4 (Questions 10–12)

10. When is the meeting?   Ⓐ Ⓑ Ⓒ Ⓓ
   - (A) Today.
   - (B) Tuesday.
   - (C) Wednesday.
   - (D) Friday.

11. Where will it take place?
    (A) In the conference room.
    (B) In Room 4.
    (C) In the cafeteria.
    (D) In a café.

    Ⓐ Ⓑ Ⓒ Ⓓ

12. What time will it start?
    (A) Noon.
    (B) 1:00.
    (C) 1:15.
    (D) 1:50.

    Ⓐ Ⓑ Ⓒ Ⓓ

CONVERSATION 5 (Questions 13–15)

13. Why doesn't the man want to go to the seafood restaurant?
    (A) There are too many people.
    (B) The food isn't good.
    (C) It's too expensive.
    (D) It's closed midnight.

    Ⓐ Ⓑ Ⓒ Ⓓ

14. Where will the speakers go after dinner?
    (A) To a play.
    (B) To the movies.
    (C) Shopping.
    (D) Home.

    Ⓐ Ⓑ Ⓒ Ⓓ

15. When do they have to leave?
    (A) Right now.
    (B) In 15 minutes.
    (C) In 50 minutes.
    (D) In two hours.

    Ⓐ Ⓑ Ⓒ Ⓓ

GRAMMAR TIP

Going to in the Present and Future

Going to can be used for both present and future ideas.

Shirley is going to the post office now to mail this package for me.
I'm going to the cafeteria for lunch. Will you join me?
We're going to London tomorrow on business.
They're going to the conference next month.

VOCABULARY TIP

Ways to Tell Time

In the listening sections of the TOEIC, you will hear people talking about time. There are different ways to say the hour of the day.

3:10	three ten	ten past three
3:15	three fifteen	quarter past three
3:30	three thirty	half past three
3:40	three forty	twenty to four
3:45	three forty-five	quarter to four

STRATEGY PRACTICE

DIRECTIONS: Listen to the conversations and choose the appropriate answers to the questions. There will be three questions for each conversation.

1. When will the meeting be held?   (A) (B) (C) (D)
   - (A) Today.
   - (B) Tonight.
   - (C) Tomorrow morning.
   - (D) Tomorrow afternoon.

2. How many people will be at the meeting?   (A) (B) (C) (D)
   - (A) 11.
   - (B) 15.
   - (C) 16.
   - (D) 17.

3. Where does the woman want to have the meeting?   (A) (B) (C) (D)
   - (A) In the cafeteria.
   - (B) In the reading room.
   - (C) In the assistant's office.
   - (D) In the conference room.

4. How is the weather?   (A) (B) (C) (D)
   - (A) It's snowing.
   - (B) It's raining.
   - (C) It's sunny.
   - (D) It's hot.

5. When will Marina arrive?   (A) (B) (C) (D)
   - (A) 9:00 A.M.
   - (B) 10:00 A.M.
   - (C) 11:30 A.M.
   - (D) 2:30 P.M.

6. How is Marina traveling?   (A) (B) (C) (D)
   - (A) By bus.
   - (B) By car.
   - (C) By train.
   - (D) By plane.

7. When is the man leaving for his vacation?   (A) (B) (C) (D)
   - (A) On Monday.
   - (B) On the weekend.
   - (C) In two weeks.
   - (D) In a month.

CONVERSATIONS   91

8. How often does he take a vacation? Ⓐ Ⓑ Ⓒ Ⓓ
   (A) Once a month.
   (B) Once a year.
   (C) Twice a year.
   (D) Three times a year.

9. Where will he spend his vacation? Ⓐ Ⓑ Ⓒ Ⓓ
   (A) In the mountains.
   (B) On a boat.
   (C) At the beach.
   (D) By a lake.

10. Why doesn't the man order shrimp? Ⓐ Ⓑ Ⓒ Ⓓ
    (A) He doesn't like it.
    (B) He has an allergy to it.
    (C) It costs too much.
    (D) It's not on the menu.

11. How much does the tuna special cost? Ⓐ Ⓑ Ⓒ Ⓓ
    (A) $7.50.
    (B) $11.00.
    (C) $17.00.
    (D) $17.50.

12. What will the man order? Ⓐ Ⓑ Ⓒ Ⓓ
    (A) Shrimp.
    (B) Tuna.
    (C) Rice.
    (D) Spaghetti.

13. Where is the woman going? Ⓐ Ⓑ Ⓒ Ⓓ
    (A) The bank.
    (B) The post office.
    (C) The office supply store.
    (D) The supply closet.

14. What does the man want? Ⓐ Ⓑ Ⓒ Ⓓ
    (A) Paper.
    (B) Folders.
    (C) Pencils.
    (D) Pens.

15. How much money does the man give the woman? Ⓐ Ⓑ Ⓒ Ⓓ
    (A) $10.00.
    (B) $15.00.
    (C) $20.00.
    (D) $25.00.

LISTENING COMPREHENSION

16. When is the meeting?   Ⓐ Ⓑ Ⓒ Ⓓ
    (A) Today.
    (B) Tomorrow.
    (C) Tuesday.
    (D) Next week.

17. Where is the meeting?   Ⓐ Ⓑ Ⓒ Ⓓ
    (A) In a conference room.
    (B) In the man's office.
    (C) In New York.
    (D) In a hotel.

18. Why can't the man attend the meeting?   Ⓐ Ⓑ Ⓒ Ⓓ
    (A) He will be at a conference.
    (B) He will be away on a trip.
    (C) His car broke down.
    (D) He doesn't feel well.

---

19. Who is the woman talking to?   Ⓐ Ⓑ Ⓒ Ⓓ
    (A) Her doctor.
    (B) Her assistant.
    (C) A massage therapist.
    (D) A telephone operator.

20. Why was the woman late for her appointment?   Ⓐ Ⓑ Ⓒ Ⓓ
    (A) She had a hard time driving in the dark.
    (B) She couldn't find the doctor's office.
    (C) She had to make a phone call.
    (D) She couldn't park the car.

21. Where did the man put the messages?   Ⓐ Ⓑ Ⓒ Ⓓ
    (A) On the door.
    (B) In the desk.
    (C) On the floor.
    (D) In the apartment.

---

22. What is the woman's job?   Ⓐ Ⓑ Ⓒ Ⓓ
    (A) Bus driver.
    (B) Taxi driver.
    (C) Tour guide.
    (D) Train conductor.

23. Why is the fare higher than the man expected?   Ⓐ Ⓑ Ⓒ Ⓓ
    (A) It's snowing.
    (B) It's late at night.
    (C) He took a long trip.
    (D) All the prices have changed.

CONVERSATIONS   **93**

24. What is the man doing?   (A) (B) (C) (D)
    (A) Paying.
    (B) Asking directions.
    (C) Giving directions.
    (D) Asking the time.

25. Why are the speakers upset?   (A) (B) (C) (D)
    (A) The water is bad.
    (B) Their watches are broken.
    (C) The food doesn't taste good.
    (D) They've been waiting for a long time.

26. What time do they have to leave the restaurant?   (A) (B) (C) (D)
    (A) 3:00.
    (B) 4:00.
    (C) 8:00.
    (D) 9:00.

27. What will they do next?   (A) (B) (C) (D)
    (A) Go home.
    (B) Take a rest.
    (C) Hear some music.
    (D) Go to another restaurant.

28. Where are the speakers?   (A) (B) (C) (D)
    (A) At work.
    (B) At home.
    (C) At the garage.
    (D) At the bus stop.

29. Why does the woman take the bus?   (A) (B) (C) (D)
    (A) It's fast.
    (B) It's relaxing.
    (C) It's always on time.
    (D) It's cheaper than a taxi.

30. How long does the bus ride take?   (A) (B) (C) (D)
    (A) Half an hour.
    (B) Forty minutes.
    (C) Forty-five minutes.
    (D) An hour.

PART 4: TALKS

PART 4

Directions: You will hear some talks given by a single speaker. You will be asked to answer three questions about what the speaker says in each talk. Select the best response to each question and mark the letter (A), (B), (C), or (D) on your answer sheet. The talks will not be printed in your test book and will be spoken only one time.

STRATEGY OVERVIEW

The following exercises will help you develop strategies for listening to talks and choosing the best response. They will also help you improve your vocabulary in specific ways.

LANGUAGE STRATEGIES

Listen for words in the talks that are associated with these topics:

- Advertisements – Listen for information selling products or services.
- Weather – Listen for information about the weather.
- News – Listen for information about news events.
- Recorded Announcements – Listen for recorded telephone, and other, messages.
- Special Announcements – Listen for content about a variety of topics.
- Business Announcements – Listen for content about business.

TEST STRATEGIES

In Part 4, you can use the same strategies that you used in Part 3 to determine the correct answers.

- Read before listening – Read the question and answer choices before you hear the audio.
- Listen for specifics – Listen for specific answers to the questions.

TALKS   95

ADVERTISEMENTS

LANGUAGE STRATEGIES

Vocabulary Practice A

DIRECTIONS: Match the type of advertisement with its usual location.

TYPE	LOCATION
1. _____ print ads	**a.** streets, sides of buildings
2. _____ pop-up ads	**b.** radio, TV
3. _____ commercials	**c.** websites
4. _____ billboards	**d.** magazines, newspapers

Vocabulary Practice B

DIRECTIONS: Write the correct form of the word in the sentence.

for sale   sale   selling

1. The used cars will not be _____ until they have been inspected.

2. The _____ lasts until Friday.

3. We're _____ our entire inventory.

to sell   sold   on sale

4. Hurry. This offer won't last. All stock _____ for only two more days!

5. The plan is _____ everything at 50 percent off.

6. Once a product is _____, we take it off the website.

subscribes   subscriptions   subscribers

7. I have _____ for every major daily paper.

8. My office _____ to an e-newsletter.

9. Our magazine has over 3 million _____.

96   LISTENING COMPREHENSION

advertises   advertisers   advertisements

10. I want to block the pop-up _____ when I surf the Internet.

11. All _____ want to reach the largest market possible.

12. Our travel agent _____ the lowest fares to Europe.

Context

DIRECTIONS: You will hear two advertisements. They will not be repeated. Below you will read three questions about each advertisement. After you listen to the advertisement, answer the questions.

TALK 1 (Questions 1–3)

1. What is being sold?   Ⓐ Ⓑ Ⓒ Ⓓ
   - (A) Used cars.
   - (B) Ship models.
   - (C) Used televisions.
   - (D) Computers.

2. How much can a buyer save?   Ⓐ Ⓑ Ⓒ Ⓓ
   - (A) One thousand dollars.
   - (B) Over one thousand dollars.
   - (C) Five percent of the total.
   - (D) Ten percent of the total.

3. When will the sale end?   Ⓐ Ⓑ Ⓒ Ⓓ
   - (A) Today.
   - (B) Tomorrow.
   - (C) In five days.
   - (D) In two weeks.

TALK 2 (Questions 4–6)

4. How long is the sale?   Ⓐ Ⓑ Ⓒ Ⓓ
   - (A) One day.
   - (B) Two days.
   - (C) Five days.
   - (D) One week.

5. What is on sale?   Ⓐ Ⓑ Ⓒ Ⓓ
   - (A) Clothing.
   - (B) Kitchen chairs.
   - (C) Office furniture.
   - (D) Computers.

TALKS   **97**

6. What is the discount on chairs?
   (A) 15 percent.
   (B) 17 percent.
   (C) 50 percent.
   (D) 75 percent.

Ⓐ Ⓑ Ⓒ Ⓓ

WEATHER

LANGUAGE STRATEGIES

Vocabulary Practice A

DIRECTIONS: Match the synonyms.

1. _____ cool

2. _____ very breezy

3. _____ mild

4. _____ hot

5. _____ freezing

6. _____ rain

7. _____ clear

8. _____ cloudy

9. _____ typhoon

10. _____ blizzard

a. snowstorm

b. showers

c. sunny skies

d. comfortable

e. windy

f. tropical windstorm

g. chilly

h. very warm

i. not clear

j. very cold

Vocabulary Practice B

DIRECTIONS: Use the words from the lists above to complete these sentences. (There may be more than one option.)

1. It's _____ outside, so I need to dress warmly.

2. I'll take my umbrella because it looks like _____.

3. It's getting _____ out, so we should close the windows in case it rains.

98   LISTENING COMPREHENSION

4. It's too _____ to play tennis.

5. When the sky is _____, it's good weather to fly.

6. It's not too hot and it's not too cold; the weather is nice and _____ for this time of year.

7. It's colder than cold. It's _____!

8. The light snowstorm turned into a heavy _____, and now all the roads are icy.

9. I want to go to the beach when the skies are _____, not when the skies are cloudy.

10. Hurricanes, also known as _____ in Asia, can cause lots of damage to buildings and homes.

Context

DIRECTIONS: You will hear two weather reports. They will not be repeated. Below you will read three questions about each report. After you listen to the report, answer the questions.

TALK 1 (Questions 1–3)

1. What is today's weather?   Ⓐ Ⓑ Ⓒ Ⓓ
   (A) Snowy.
   (B) Cloudy.
   (C) Rainy.
   (D) Sunny.

2. What will the temperature be tomorrow?   Ⓐ Ⓑ Ⓒ Ⓓ
   (A) Warm.
   (B) Hot.
   (C) Mild.
   (D) Cold.

3. When will it rain?   Ⓐ Ⓑ Ⓒ Ⓓ
   (A) Tomorrow.
   (B) On the weekend.
   (C) Next week.
   (D) Wednesday or Thursday.

TALK 2 (Questions 4–6)

4. When will the rain begin? Ⓐ Ⓑ Ⓒ Ⓓ
   - (A) Tonight.
   - (B) Tomorrow morning.
   - (C) In the afternoon.
   - (D) By tomorrow night.

5. When will the showers stop? Ⓐ Ⓑ Ⓒ Ⓓ
   - (A) By tonight.
   - (B) By tomorrow morning.
   - (C) By tomorrow afternoon.
   - (D) By late tomorrow evening.

6. How will the weather be on the weekend? Ⓐ Ⓑ Ⓒ Ⓓ
   - (A) Warm.
   - (B) Misty.
   - (C) Rainy.
   - (D) Cold.

NEWS

LANGUAGE STRATEGIES

Vocabulary Practice A

DIRECTIONS: Cross out the word that does not belong.

1. political   government   election   vote   game

2. cultural   math   art   concert   play

3. economic   finance   realtor   money   fiscal

4. tour   travel   trip   vacation   street

5. month   day   week   year   pound

6. high-speed   fast   convenient   quick   accelerated

Vocabulary Practice B

DIRECTIONS: Complete the sentences below using the following reasons.

because it hasn't rained

in order to see the parade

because of the snowstorm

because of the increase in the sales tax

because of the holiday

because it is so light

because they finally signed the agreement

1. The laptop computer is useful for business travelers _____.

2. The participants celebrated with a dinner _____.

3. We are experiencing a drought _____.

4. The town hall was closed _____.

5. The patients received gifts _____.

6. Everyone came downtown _____.

7. People will purchase less than before _____.

Context

DIRECTIONS: You will hear two news items. They will not be repeated. Below you will read three questions about each item. After you listen to the news item, answer the questions.

TALK 1 (Questions 1–3)

1. What is the advantage of this computer?   Ⓐ   Ⓑ   Ⓒ   Ⓓ
   (A) Large memory.
   (B) Small size.
   (C) Sturdy construction.
   (D) Low price.

2. Who will find the computer most useful?   Ⓐ   Ⓑ   Ⓒ   Ⓓ
   (A) Business travelers.
   (B) Stock market brokers.
   (C) Secretaries.
   (D) Travel agents.

3. When will the new computer arrive in stores?   Ⓐ   Ⓑ   Ⓒ   Ⓓ
   (A) Today.
   (B) On Tuesday.
   (C) In two weeks.
   (D) In two months.

TALK 2 (Questions 4–6)

4. Why were public offices closed?   Ⓐ   Ⓑ   Ⓒ   Ⓓ
   (A) Because of the heavy snowfall.
   (B) Because of the holiday.
   (C) Because it was lunchtime.
   (D) Because it was a weekend.

5. When will schools reopen?   Ⓐ   Ⓑ   Ⓒ   Ⓓ
   (A) Tomorrow.
   (B) Next week.
   (C) Next month.
   (D) In the fall.

6. What are residents advised to do?   Ⓐ   Ⓑ   Ⓒ   Ⓓ
   (A) Run for public office.
   (B) Go to school.
   (C) Stay at home.
   (D) Repair the roads.

102 LISTENING COMPREHENSION

RECORDED ANNOUNCEMENTS

LANGUAGE STRATEGIES

Vocabulary Practice A

DIRECTIONS: Where do you call to find out certain information? Write the source.

YOU WANT TO KNOW:

1. the temperature _____
2. the time a film starts _____
3. the hours a reference desk is open _____
4. why you're having computer trouble _____
5. about job vacancies _____
6. how to get a driver's license _____
7. features about different office products _____

YOU CALL THIS SOURCE:

a. motor vehicles department
b. technical support
c. weather information
d. cinema hotline
e. library
f. employment helpline
g. customer service

Vocabulary Practice B

DIRECTIONS: Read the answer and write the question.

1. The museum will close at 9 P.M. on Sunday.

   When _____

2. All applicants should send an e-mail with their résumés.

   What _____

3. Guests are not permitted to play on Sunday or Monday.

   On what _____

4. The library is closed for a staff meeting.

   Why _____

5. All calls will be answered in the order they are received.

   How _____

TALKS   103

6. A caller would contact this office for information on a product.

Why —————————————————————————————

7. An adult ticket costs $9.00.

How much —————————————————————————

8. In an emergency, you should hang up and dial 911.

What —————————————————————————————

9. You should bring a photo and proof of citizenship when you apply for a license.

What —————————————————————————————

10. The store will close early because of the storm.

Why —————————————————————————————

Context

DIRECTIONS: You will hear two recorded announcements. They will not be repeated. Below you will read three questions about each announcement. After you listen to the announcement, answer the questions.

TALK 1 (Questions 1–3)

1. What time does the museum close on Tuesday? Ⓐ Ⓑ Ⓒ Ⓓ
   (A) 4 P.M.
   (B) 6 P.M.
   (C) 7 P.M.
   (D) 9 P.M.

2. What day is the museum closed? Ⓐ Ⓑ Ⓒ Ⓓ
   (A) Sunday.
   (B) Monday.
   (C) Thursday.
   (D) Friday.

3. Where should museum visitors put their coats? Ⓐ Ⓑ Ⓒ Ⓓ
   (A) Near the back door.
   (B) On the ground floor.
   (C) In the bag room.
   (D) On the fourth floor.

104 LISTENING COMPREHENSION

TALK 2 (Questions 4–6)

4. Between what hours may only parties
   of four people play?   (A) (B) (C) (D)
   - (A)   5 A.M. and 8 P.M.
   - (B)   8 A.M. and 12 P.M.
   - (C)   12 P.M. and 7 P.M.
   - (D)   5 P.M. and 8 P.M.

5. On what days may guests NOT play?   (A) (B) (C) (D)
   - (A)   Monday and Tuesday.
   - (B)   Tuesday and Wednesday.
   - (C)   Thursday and Sunday.
   - (D)   Saturday and Sunday.

6. How often does the Senior Tournament take place?   (A) (B) (C) (D)
   - (A)   Every day.
   - (B)   Every week.
   - (C)   Every month.
   - (D)   Every year.

SPECIAL ANNOUNCEMENTS

LANGUAGE STRATEGIES

Vocabulary Practice A

DIRECTIONS: Complete these sentences using these words.

main	chemistry
attentive	reviews
specialty	express
platform	guide
security guard	freight

1. I study history, but my _____ is history of ancient civilizations.

2. When I studied _____, I learned that H_2O means two parts hydrogen for one part oxygen.

3. The local train stops at every station, but the _____ train makes only one station stop.

4. Wait on _____ 9 for the train.

5. We shipped the goods with a reliable _____ company.

6. If you are not _____, you will miss important information.

7. I always read the _____ before I choose which movie to see.

8. The best _____ is one that likes people and loves to give tours.

9. You will have to show your ID to the _____ at the gate before you can be admitted.

10. Our branch office is in Miami, but our _____ office is in Madrid.

Vocabulary Practice B

DIRECTIONS: Read each sentence. Then write a new sentence using one of the following verb phrases.

taking a tour	filling out a lost-article form
working in the garden	getting off at the next stop
getting on a plane	playing golf
filling the car with gas	attending a concert
waiting for the express train	lining up for tickets

1. I enjoy planting flowers and growing vegetables.

   I'm working in the garden.

2. There will be a lot of people wanting to see this play, so I'll be at the box office early.

3. I gave my boarding pass to the gate agent and am now looking for my seat in economy class.

4. I'm new in this city, so I want to be taken to all the important sites.

5. My car is low on fuel, so I stopped at a service station.

6. I'm moving toward the door of the train so I will be ready to disembark.

7. I don't want to take the local since I'm in a hurry.

8. I enjoy all kinds of sports, especially one that keeps me outside.

9. I love watching an orchestra play.

10. I'm writing my name and address and describing what I can't find.

TALKS 107

Context

🎧 **DIRECTIONS:** You will hear two special announcements. They will not be repeated. Below you will read three questions about each announcement. After you listen to the announcement, answer the questions.

TALK 1 (Questions 1–3)

1. On what kind of train is this announcement being made?   Ⓐ Ⓑ Ⓒ Ⓓ
   - (A) Mail.
   - (B) Freight.
   - (C) Local.
   - (D) Express.

2. What is across the platform?   Ⓐ Ⓑ Ⓒ Ⓓ
   - (A) A cafeteria.
   - (B) The local train.
   - (C) The exit doors.
   - (D) Some steps.

3. Where is the next stop?   Ⓐ Ⓑ Ⓒ Ⓓ
   - (A) New York.
   - (B) Tokyo.
   - (C) Newark.
   - (D) London.

TALK 2 (Questions 4–6)

4. Where is this announcement being heard?   Ⓐ Ⓑ Ⓒ Ⓓ
   - (A) At a school.
   - (B) At a golf course.
   - (C) In a hospital.
   - (D) In a theater.

5. At what time of day is this announcement being made?   Ⓐ Ⓑ Ⓒ Ⓓ
   - (A) In the morning.
   - (B) At noon.
   - (C) In the afternoon.
   - (D) In the evening.

6. What is the problem being described?   Ⓐ Ⓑ Ⓒ Ⓓ
   - (A) Someone is sick.
   - (B) There are no more rolls.
   - (C) People are not attentive.
   - (D) Children are playing on the stairs.

108   LISTENING COMPREHENSION

BUSINESS ANNOUNCEMENTS

LANGUAGE STRATEGIES

Vocabulary Practice A

DIRECTIONS: Certain words are associated with certain activities. Look at the verb phrases below. Write two or more words associated with each of the activities these phrases describe.

1. having a company picnic *food, activities* _____

2. buying new computers _____

3. hiring new employees _____

4. attending a conference _____

5. ordering supplies _____

6. taking a vacation _____

7. using a drinking fountain _____

8. starting a small business _____

9. parking near the door _____

10. writing a list _____

Vocabulary Practice B

DIRECTIONS: Read the sentences. Then write new sentences using the activities in Vocabulary Practice A.

1. Ms. Wilson is filling out a purchase order for more pens, pencils, and paper.
   She's ordering supplies. _____

2. The Human Resources officer is reviewing the qualifications of job applicants.

   _____

3. The president himself drove his workers to the park for their annual outing.

   _____

4. We shopped for bigger monitors and faster operating systems.

   _____

TALKS 109

5. We are looking forward to hearing presentations and participating in seminars.

6. I put everyone's name and their job on a piece of paper and posted it on our company's website.

7. She's thirsty and wants some water.

8. She's reading a travel guide to find some places to visit.

9. He's looking for a space large enough for his car by the main entrance.

10. We're writing a business plan and getting financial backing before we can open our doors to our customers.

Context

DIRECTIONS: You will hear two business announcements. They will not be repeated. Below you will read three questions about each announcement. After you listen to the announcement, answer the questions.

TALK 1 (Questions 1–3)

1. What will be discussed at the meeting?   Ⓐ Ⓑ Ⓒ Ⓓ
   (A) The budget.
   (B) Vacation policy.
   (C) Buying new computers.
   (D) Firing employees.

2. What is Mrs. Lopez's job?   Ⓐ Ⓑ Ⓒ Ⓓ
   (A) Trainer.
   (B) Copywriter.
   (C) Accountant.
   (D) Meeting planner.

3. Why isn't Mrs. Lopez at the meeting?   Ⓐ Ⓑ Ⓒ Ⓓ
   (A) She's on vacation.
   (B) She's sick.
   (C) She's out of town.
   (D) She's on the train.

110   LISTENING COMPREHENSION

TALK 2 (Questions 4–6)

4. What will be opened?   Ⓐ Ⓑ Ⓒ Ⓓ
   (A) A store.
   (B) A factory.
   (C) A new company.
   (D) A management school.

5. What is this announcement about?   Ⓐ Ⓑ Ⓒ Ⓓ
   (A) Food distribution.
   (B) Asia's economy.
   (C) Job openings.
   (D) Management styles.

6. What should applicants send?   Ⓐ Ⓑ Ⓒ Ⓓ
   (A) Their financial statements.
   (B) Their college degrees.
   (C) A certified check.
   (D) A résumé.

TEST STRATEGIES

DIRECTIONS: Read the questions before you hear the conversation. Then listen for specific details that answer the questions.

TALK 1 (Questions 1–3)

1. What kind of sale is it?   Ⓐ Ⓑ Ⓒ Ⓓ
   (A) Holiday.
   (B) Back-to-school.
   (C) Damaged goods.
   (D) Weekend.

2. What is on sale?   Ⓐ Ⓑ Ⓒ Ⓓ
   (A) Notebooks.
   (B) Pens.
   (C) Paper.
   (D) A store.

3. How can you get a free notebook?   Ⓐ Ⓑ Ⓒ Ⓓ
   (A) Buy more than ten notebooks.
   (B) Buy more than ten pens.
   (C) Arrive before 10:00.
   (D) Bring ten friends.

TALK 2 (Questions 4–6)

4. When might it rain?   Ⓐ Ⓑ Ⓒ Ⓓ
   (A) This afternoon.
   (B) Late tonight.
   (C) Tomorrow morning.
   (D) Tomorrow night.

5. What might follow the rain?   Ⓐ Ⓑ Ⓒ Ⓓ
   (A) Sunny skies.
   (B) Snow.
   (C) Thundershowers.
   (D) A typhoon.

6. What will the temperature be tomorrow?   Ⓐ Ⓑ Ⓒ Ⓓ
   (A) Hot.
   (B) Warm.
   (C) Cool.
   (D) Cold.

TALK 3 (Questions 7–9)

7. What kind of agreement was signed?   Ⓐ Ⓑ Ⓒ Ⓓ
   (A) Political.
   (B) Cultural.
   (C) Economic.
   (D) Trade.

8. What took place after the signing?   Ⓐ Ⓑ Ⓒ Ⓓ
   (A) A concert.
   (B) A dinner.
   (C) A play.
   (D) A dance.

9. Which of the following groups is   Ⓐ Ⓑ Ⓒ Ⓓ
   NOT part of the agreement?
   (A) Artists.
   (B) Drama.
   (C) Orchestras.
   (D) Ballet.

TALK 4 (Questions 10–12)

10. Why would a caller contact this office?   Ⓐ Ⓑ Ⓒ Ⓓ
    (A) To make a complaint.
    (B) To order a product.
    (C) To get a job.
    (D) To talk to a consumer.

112   LISTENING COMPREHENSION

11. How will calls be answered? Ⓐ Ⓑ Ⓒ Ⓓ
    (A) Patiently.
    (B) Promptly.
    (C) In the order received.
    (D) In the order of importance.

12. What is the caller advised to do? Ⓐ Ⓑ Ⓒ Ⓓ
    (A) Hang up and try again.
    (B) Place an order.
    (C) Wait for an agent.
    (D) Talk to another agent.

TALK 5 (Questions 13–15)

13. When will the tour begin? Ⓐ Ⓑ Ⓒ Ⓓ
    (A) In 15 minutes.
    (B) In 30 minutes.
    (C) At 3:00.
    (D) At 10:00.

14. What should you do if you have a ticket? Ⓐ Ⓑ Ⓒ Ⓓ
    (A) Line up at the end of the hall.
    (B) Go to the front desk.
    (C) Tell the guide.
    (D) Wait at the front door.

15. How much are the tickets? Ⓐ Ⓑ Ⓒ Ⓓ
    (A) They're $15.00.
    (B) They're free.
    (C) They're three for the price of one.
    (D) They're $10.50.

TALK 6 (Questions 16–18)

16. Who is Mr. Thompson? Ⓐ Ⓑ Ⓒ Ⓓ
    (A) A college professor.
    (B) An administrator.
    (C) An author.
    (D) An accountant.

17. What will Mr. Thompson talk about tonight? Ⓐ Ⓑ Ⓒ Ⓓ
    (A) Taxes.
    (B) Starting a small business.
    (C) Conferences.
    (D) His twenty years of experience.

TALKS 113

18. What will happen after the talk?　　Ⓐ　Ⓑ　Ⓒ　Ⓓ
- (A) Mr. Thompson will make a call.
- (B) Tea will be served.
- (C) Mr. Thompson will answer questions.
- (D) There will be a dinner.

GRAMMAR TIP

Negative to Positive

Be careful of sentences that have negative markers. They could have a positive meaning.

Sentence:	He couldn't be more prepared.
Meaning:	He is very prepared.
Sentence:	She wasn't the most qualified person for the job.
Meaning:	She was not very qualified. Others were more qualified.
Sentence:	Don't you think we should finish this work tonight?
Meaning:	I want to finish this work tonight, and I want you to agree with me.
Sentence:	There isn't anything I'd rather do less.
Meaning:	I would prefer not to do this.

VOCABULARY TIP

Words Beginning with *re-*

We can add *re-* to a verb to form another verb. It means *again*.

Verb	Verb	Definition
do	redo	do again
read	reread	read again
paint	repaint	paint again
appear	reappear	appear again

The director didn't approve the report so we had to *redo* it.

The article was very interesting, and I *reread* it several times.

The theater lobby has been *repainted* recently.

After several days of rainy weather, the sun will *reappear* tomorrow.

STRATEGY PRACTICE

DIRECTIONS: Listen to the talks and choose the appropriate answers to the questions. There are three questions for each talk.

1. When will the snowfall begin?   Ⓐ Ⓑ Ⓒ Ⓓ
   (A) At midday.
   (B) At 4:00.
   (C) Before midnight.
   (D) Tomorrow evening.

2. How much snow will fall?   Ⓐ Ⓑ Ⓒ Ⓓ
   (A) 3 centimeters.
   (B) 13 centimeters.
   (C) 30 centimeters.
   (D) 33 centimeters.

3. What will the weather be like on Wednesday?   Ⓐ Ⓑ Ⓒ Ⓓ
   (A) Cold.
   (B) Windy.
   (C) Snowy.
   (D) Cloudy.

4. Where is the shoe store?   Ⓐ Ⓑ Ⓒ Ⓓ
   (A) In the mall.
   (B) On Maine Avenue.
   (C) Near the train station.
   (D) In the back of the school.

5. What is on sale this month?   Ⓐ Ⓑ Ⓒ Ⓓ
   (A) All styles of shoes.
   (B) Men's shoes.
   (C) Women's shoes.
   (D) Children's shoes.

6. How much is the discount?   Ⓐ Ⓑ Ⓒ Ⓓ
   (A) 5 percent.
   (B) 10 percent.
   (C) 20 percent.
   (D) 25 percent.

7. Where is Marlene Rich now?   Ⓐ Ⓑ Ⓒ Ⓓ
   (A) In the director's office.
   (B) At a conference.
   (C) Talking to another employee.
   (D) Buying a desk.

TALKS **115**

8. When will she return? Ⓐ Ⓑ Ⓒ Ⓓ
   (A)   On Sunday.
   (B)   On Monday.
   (C)   At the end of the week.
   (D)   In two weeks.

9. What happens if callers press 1? Ⓐ Ⓑ Ⓒ Ⓓ
   (A)   They can leave a message for Marlene.
   (B)   They can speak with the director.
   (C)   They can participate in a conference call.
   (D)   They can hear a list of phone numbers.

10. What will be built? Ⓐ Ⓑ Ⓒ Ⓓ
   (A)   A theater.
   (B)   A bus station.
   (C)   A concert hall.
   (D)   A sports arena.

11. What will it have on the ground floor? Ⓐ Ⓑ Ⓒ Ⓓ
   (A)   Restaurants.
   (B)   A subway stop.
   (C)   A concert hall.
   (D)   A sports arena.

12. When will construction be finished? Ⓐ Ⓑ Ⓒ Ⓓ
   (A)   Next month.
   (B)   In two months.
   (C)   Next year.
   (D)   In two years.

13. What time is the first show? Ⓐ Ⓑ Ⓒ Ⓓ
   (A)   7:00.
   (B)   7:30.
   (C)   8:00.
   (D)   9:30.

14. What is the price of a general admission ticket? Ⓐ Ⓑ Ⓒ Ⓓ
   (A) $8.00.
   (B) $9.00.
   (C) $10.00.
   (D) $12.00.

15. Who is NOT allowed inside the theater? Ⓐ Ⓑ Ⓒ Ⓓ
   (A)   Children under 12.
   (B)   Senior citizens.
   (C)   People without an ID.
   (D)   Candy sellers.

16. What kind of insurance is being sold?　Ⓐ　Ⓑ　Ⓒ　Ⓓ
    (A) Car.
    (B) Life.
    (C) Fire.
    (D) Health.

17. What must one be to get this insurance?　Ⓐ　Ⓑ　Ⓒ　Ⓓ
    (A) Sixty years old or older.
    (B) In good health.
    (C) A doctor.
    (D) Married.

18. How can one get information about this insurance?　Ⓐ　Ⓑ　Ⓒ　Ⓓ
    (A) Send an e-mail.
    (B) Visit an office.
    (C) Write a letter.
    (D) Make a phone call.

19. What was the temperature today?　Ⓐ　Ⓑ　Ⓒ　Ⓓ
    (A) Hot.
    (B) Cool.
    (C) Mild.
    (D) Average.

20. How were the winds described?　Ⓐ　Ⓑ　Ⓒ　Ⓓ
    (A) Cool.
    (B) Light.
    (C) Warm.
    (D) Strong.

21. What is the season?　Ⓐ　Ⓑ　Ⓒ　Ⓓ
    (A) Spring.
    (B) Summer.
    (C) Fall.
    (D) Winter.

22. How long will the tour last?　Ⓐ　Ⓑ　Ⓒ　Ⓓ
    (A) One week.
    (B) Two weeks.
    (C) Five weeks.
    (D) Twelve weeks.

23. Where did the president go?　Ⓐ　Ⓑ　Ⓒ　Ⓓ
    (A) To Asia.
    (B) To Malaysia.
    (C) To Indonesia.
    (D) To Australia.

TALKS 117

24. Who is traveling with the president? (A) (B) (C) (D)
    (A) His wife.
    (B) Office workers.
    (C) A tour guide.
    (D) The foreign minister.

25. What should you do in an emergency? (A) (B) (C) (D)
    (A) Call to make an appointment.
    (B) Call after 5:00 P.M.
    (C) Call tomorrow.
    (D) Call another phone number.

26. What should you do to speak with a nurse? (A) (B) (C) (D)
    (A) Hang up.
    (B) Make an appointment.
    (C) Call between 9:00 A.M. and 5:00 P.M.
    (D) Visit the office tomorrow.

27. Why is Dr. Sato out of the office? (A) (B) (C) (D)
    (A) He's on vacation.
    (B) He has an emergency.
    (C) He's at a conference.
    (D) He's sick.

28. Who is making the announcement? (A) (B) (C) (D)
    (A) An airplane pilot.
    (B) A ship's captain.
    (C) A flight attendant.
    (D) A passenger.

29. What does the announcer want people to do? (A) (B) (C) (D)
    (A) Sit on the other side.
    (B) Check the weather.
    (C) Look at the view.
    (D) Go swimming in the lake.

30. How is the weather? (A) (B) (C) (D)
    (A) Snowy.
    (B) Rainy.
    (C) Clear.
    (D) Cloudy.

118 LISTENING COMPREHENSION

LISTENING COMPREHENSION REVIEW

You will find the answer sheet for the Listening Comprehension Review on page 382. Use it to record your answers. Play the audio program for the Listening Comprehension Review when you are ready to begin.

LISTENING TEST

In the Listening test, you will be asked to demonstrate how well you understand spoken English. The entire Listening test will last approximately 45 minutes. There are four parts, and directions are given for each part. You must mark your answers on the separate answer sheet. Do not write your answers in the test book.

PART 1

Directions: For each question in this part, you will hear four statements about a picture in your test book. When you hear the statements, you must select the one statement that best describes what you see in the picture. Then find the number of the question on your answer sheet and mark your answer. The statements will not be printed in your test book and will be spoken only one time.

Example

Sample Answer

Statement (C), "They're standing near the table," is the best description of the picture, so you should select answer (C) and mark it on your answer sheet.

GO ON TO THE NEXT PAGE

LISTENING COMPREHENSION REVIEW   119

1.

2.

120 LISTENING COMPREHENSION

3.

4.

GO ON TO THE NEXT PAGE

LISTENING COMPREHENSION REVIEW 121

5.

6.

122   LISTENING COMPREHENSION

7.

8.

GO ON TO THE NEXT PAGE

LISTENING COMPREHENSION REVIEW 123

9.

10.

124 LISTENING COMPREHENSION

PART 2

Directions: You will hear a question or statement and three responses spoken in English. They will not be printed in your test book and will be spoken only one time. Select the best response to the question or statement and mark the letter (A), (B), or (C) on your answer sheet.

Example

Sample Answer
Ⓐ ⬤ Ⓒ

You will hear: Where is the meeting room?

You will also hear: (A) To meet the new director.
(B) It's the first room on the right.
(C) Yes, at two o'clock.

Your best response to the question "Where is the meeting room?" is choice (B), "It's the first room on the right," so (B) is the correct answer. You should mark answer (B) on your answer sheet.

11. Mark your answer on your answer sheet.

12. Mark your answer on your answer sheet.

13. Mark your answer on your answer sheet.

14. Mark your answer on your answer sheet.

15. Mark your answer on your answer sheet.

16. Mark your answer on your answer sheet.

17. Mark your answer on your answer sheet.

18. Mark your answer on your answer sheet.

19. Mark your answer on your answer sheet.

20. Mark your answer on your answer sheet.

21. Mark your answer on your answer sheet.

22. Mark your answer on your answer sheet.

23. Mark your answer on your answer sheet.

24. Mark your answer on your answer sheet.

25. Mark your answer on your answer sheet.

26. Mark your answer on your answer sheet.

27. Mark your answer on your answer sheet.

28. Mark your answer on your answer sheet.

29. Mark your answer on your answer sheet.

30. Mark your answer on your answer sheet.

31. Mark your answer on your answer sheet.

32. Mark your answer on your answer sheet.

33. Mark your answer on your answer sheet.

34. Mark your answer on your answer sheet.

35. Mark your answer on your answer sheet.

36. Mark your answer on your answer sheet.

37. Mark your answer on your answer sheet.

38. Mark your answer on your answer sheet.

39. Mark your answer on your answer sheet.

40. Mark your answer on your answer sheet.

GO ON TO THE NEXT PAGE ➤

LISTENING COMPREHENSION REVIEW **125**

PART 3

 Directions: You will hear some conversations between two people. You will be asked to answer three questions about what the speakers say in each conversation. Select the best response to each question and mark the letter (A), (B), (C), or (D) on your answer sheet. The conversations will not be printed in your test book and will be spoken only one time.

41. Why did the woman buy a new coat?
    (A) Her old coat was too small.
    (B) She wants to own two coats.
    (C) Her old coat wasn't a nice color.
    (D) The man didn't like his old coat.

42. What color is the new coat?
    (A) Gold.
    (B) Blue.
    (C) Green.
    (D) White.

43. How much did the new coat cost?
    (A) $70.
    (B) $700.
    (C) $740.
    (D) $1,100.

44. When will Mr. Kim's flight arrive?
    (A) At 3:00.
    (B) At 4:00.
    (C) At 5:00.
    (D) At 11:00.

45. How will Mr. Kim get downtown?
    (A) By car.
    (B) By bus.
    (C) By cab.
    (D) By subway.

46. Where will Mr. Kim probably meet the speakers tonight?
    (A) At his hotel.
    (B) At the airport.
    (C) At a restaurant.
    (D) At the subway station.

47. Where are the speakers?
    (A) At the beach.
    (B) At a fish store.
    (C) At a restaurant.
    (D) At an aquarium.

48. How much does the tuna cost?
    (A) $13.
    (B) $30.
    (C) $35.
    (D) $40.

49. What will the man get?
    (A) Tuna.
    (B) Rice.
    (C) Shrimp.
    (D) Ice cream.

50. What are the speakers waiting for?
    (A) A bus.
    (B) A car.
    (C) A train.
    (D) A plane.

51. How long has the woman been waiting?
    (A) Thirty minutes.
    (B) An hour.
    (C) Since noon.
    (D) Since 5:00.

52. Where is the woman going?
    (A) To the store.
    (B) To the park.
    (C) To work.
    (D) Home.

126 LISTENING COMPREHENSION

53. When will the woman send the envelope?
    (A) Before lunch.
    (B) In the afternoon.
    (C) Tonight.
    (D) Tomorrow morning.

54. What is the woman doing now?
    (A) Reading a letter.
    (B) Typing a report.
    (C) Eating lunch.
    (D) Addressing envelopes.

55. What is in the envelope?
    (A) A book.
    (B) A form.
    (C) A letter.
    (D) A sweater.

56. Where will the speakers meet?
    (A) At the woman's office.
    (B) At the dentist's office.
    (C) In a conference room.
    (D) In a hotel.

57. When will the speakers meet?
    (A) Tuesday morning.
    (B) Tuesday afternoon.
    (C) Wednesday morning.
    (D) Thursday afternoon.

58. What will the secretary send to the woman?
    (A) Photocopies.
    (B) Photographs.
    (C) A book.
    (D) A conference report.

59. When will Mark start his new job?
    (A) Next week.
    (B) In two weeks.
    (C) Next month.
    (D) In two months.

60. Why did Mark leave his old job?
    (A) He retired.
    (B) He was fired.
    (C) He wasn't paid enough.
    (D) He didn't get enough vacations.

61. How long did he work at his old job?
    (A) 13 years.
    (B) 14 years.
    (C) 30 years.
    (D) 40 years.

62. Where are the speakers?
    (A) In a bank.
    (B) In a post office.
    (C) In a stationery store.
    (D) In a photographer's studio.

63. What is in the envelope?
    (A) Cash.
    (B) Jewelry.
    (C) Photographs.
    (D) Press releases.

64. How much will the woman have to pay?
    (A) $3.00.
    (B) $7.00.
    (C) $9.00.
    (D) $11.00.

GO ON TO THE NEXT PAGE

LISTENING COMPREHENSION REVIEW **127**

65. Where are the speakers?
    (A) At home.
    (B) At a hotel.
    (C) At a restaurant.
    (D) At an exercise club.

66. What time does the man want to wake up?
    (A) 6:00.
    (B) 6:05.
    (C) 6:40.
    (D) 6:45.

67. What is the man going to do now?
    (A) Eat dinner.
    (B) Have breakfast.
    (C) Go swimming.
    (D) Attend a meeting.

68. When will Mrs. Davis arrive?
    (A) 1:00.
    (B) 7:00.
    (C) 8:00.
    (D) 11:00.

69. Why will Mrs. Davis be late?
    (A) Her plane is delayed.
    (B) It's raining hard.
    (C) Her train is late.
    (D) Her car won't start.

70. What does Mrs. Davis have to do this afternoon?
    (A) Write a letter.
    (B) Go to a meeting.
    (C) Read an article.
    (D) Eat lunch.

128   LISTENING COMPREHENSION

PART 4

 Directions: You will hear some talks given by a single speaker. You will be asked to answer three questions about what the speaker says in each talk. Select the best response to each question and mark the letter (A), (B), (C), or (D) on your answer sheet. The talks will not be printed in your test book and will be spoken only one time.

71. Who is speaking?
    (A) A college professor.
    (B) A book writer.
    (C) A student.
    (D) A doctor.

72. When is the exam?
    (A) Tuesday.
    (B) Wednesday.
    (C) Thursday.
    (D) Friday.

73. What should be brought to the exam?
    (A) Textbooks.
    (B) Pencils.
    (C) Notes.
    (D) Pens.

74. What will the low temperature be tonight?
    (A) 7 degrees.
    (B) 11 degrees.
    (C) 15 degrees.
    (D) 16 degrees.

75. What will the weather be like tomorrow?
    (A) Rainy.
    (B) Sunny.
    (C) Cloudy.
    (D) Windy.

76. When will the rain stop?
    (A) Saturday.
    (B) Sunday.
    (C) Monday.
    (D) Wednesday.

77. What happened at the zoo today?
    (A) New lions were bought.
    (B) Baby lions were born.
    (C) There were games for children.
    (D) A new director was hired.

78. Who made the announcement?
    (A) The lion specialist.
    (B) The zoo director.
    (C) The publicity agent.
    (D) The activities director.

79. When will there be special activities at the zoo?
    (A) In two days.
    (B) Next weekend.
    (C) Next week.
    (D) Next month.

80. Where is the speaker?
    (A) On a train.
    (B) On a boat.
    (C) On a plane.
    (D) On a tour bus.

81. When will they arrive in Los Angeles?
    (A) 5:00.
    (B) 5:30.
    (C) 12:00.
    (D) 12:30.

82. What will attendants bring to all the passengers?
    (A) Lunch.
    (B) Beverages.
    (C) Magazines.
    (D) Pillows and blankets.

GO ON TO THE NEXT PAGE

LISTENING COMPREHENSION REVIEW

83. What does the Beautiful Interiors store sell?
    (A) Office supplies.
    (B) Furniture.
    (C) Clothes.
    (D) Cars.

84. When is the last day of the sale?
    (A) Monday.
    (B) Thursday.
    (C) Friday.
    (D) Sunday.

85. Where is the store located?
    (A) In a shopping mall.
    (B) Down the street from a hotel.
    (C) In a subway station.
    (D) Next to City Hall.

86. What happens if callers press 2?
    (A) They can speak to a lawyer.
    (B) They can make an appointment.
    (C) They can speak with Ms. Stevenson.
    (D) They can find out the office hours.

87. Who can answer questions about bills?
    (A) Mr. Park.
    (B) Ms. Stevenson.
    (C) The office assistant.
    (D) The operator.

88. What should a caller do in case of an emergency when the office is closed?
    (A) Press 3.
    (B) Call back during office hours.
    (C) Dial a different phone number.
    (D) Ask for the office assistant.

89. Why was the bridge closed?
    (A) Because of an accident.
    (B) Because of the snow.
    (C) Because of heavy traffic.
    (D) Because of construction.

90. When will the bridge be reopened?
    (A) Today.
    (B) Tonight.
    (C) Tuesday.
    (D) Wednesday.

91. What will the weather be like on Tuesday?
    (A) Snowy.
    (B) Rainy.
    (C) Windy.
    (D) Sunny.

92. Who is James Jones?
    (A) A medical doctor.
    (B) A university professor.
    (C) A travel agent.
    (D) A florist.

93. What will James Jones talk about?
    (A) Chemistry.
    (B) University studies.
    (C) Hiking in the Amazon.
    (D) A train trip.

94. What will James Jones do after the talk?
    (A) He will answer questions.
    (B) He will take photographs.
    (C) He will display flowers.
    (D) He will sell photographs.

95. How much do tickets for the tour cost?
    (A) $7.00.
    (B) $8.00.
    (C) $10.00.
    (D) $11.00.

96. What will the tour participants see first?
    (A) Modern paintings.
    (B) Sculptures.
    (C) Prints.
    (D) Portraits.

97. Where are the works by local artists?
    (A) On the ground floor.
    (B) On the first floor.
    (C) On the second floor.
    (D) On the third floor.

98. Where are the passengers now?
    (A) On the train.
    (B) Waiting at the gate.
    (C) By the station exit.
    (D) At the baggage office.

99. When will the train arrive in the station?
    (A) In four minutes.
    (B) In five minutes.
    (C) In eight minutes.
    (D) In ten minutes.

100. What should passengers with checked baggage do?
    (A) Write a check to pay for it.
    (B) Wait for it by the gate.
    (C) Stay on the train.
    (D) Ask the conductor for help.

LISTENING COMPREHENSION REVIEW **131**

READING

In the second section of the TOEIC test, you will have the chance to show how well you understand written English. There are three parts to this section, with special directions for each part:

Part 5	Incomplete Sentences
Part 6	Text Completion
Part 7	Reading Comprehension
	• Single Passages
	• Double Passages

In this part of the *Intermediate Course* for the TOEIC test, you will learn strategies to help you on the Reading section. Each part begins with activities to help you develop these strategies. Each part ends with grammar or reading comprehension questions similar to those on the TOEIC test.

PART 5: INCOMPLETE SENTENCES

READING TEST

In the Reading test, you will read a variety of texts and answer several different types of reading comprehension questions. The entire Reading test will last 75 minutes. There are three parts, and directions are given for each part. You are encouraged to answer as many questions as possible within the time allowed.

You must mark your answers on the separate answer sheet. Do not write your answers in the test book.

PART 5

Directions: A word or phrase is missing in each of the sentences below. Four answer choices are given below each sentence. Select the best answer to complete the sentence. Then mark the letter (A), (B), (C), or (D) on your answer sheet.

STRATEGY OVERVIEW

In Part 5 of the TOEIC Test, you will be given a sentence that has a missing word or phrase. You will need to choose the word or phrase that best completes the sentence. Use these strategies to choose the best answer to complete each sentence.

LANGUAGE STRATEGIES

- Word Form – Decide which noun, verb, adjective, adverb, or pronoun is needed to complete the sentence.

TEST STRATEGIES

- Context – Look at the meaning of the whole sentence to choose which word or phrase best completes it.

---

134   READING

WORD FORM: NOUNS

LANGUAGE STRATEGIES

In these TOEIC test questions, you will have to choose the noun form of a word from four choices. You must understand that a noun is missing from the sentence. You must also know which of the four choices is a noun.

Example:

The buffet table has a wide _____ of food items to choose from.
(A) selectively
(B) selective
(C) select
(D) selection

The correct answer is (D) *selection*. The missing word is a noun. None of the other choices is a noun.

DIRECTIONS: Mark the choice that best completes the sentence.

1. Your signature below will represent your _____ of this contract.   Ⓐ Ⓑ Ⓒ Ⓓ
   (A) accepted
   (B) acceptance
   (C) accept
   (D) acceptable

2. The _____ on who could be hired for that position did not seem legal.   Ⓐ Ⓑ Ⓒ Ⓓ
   (A) restrictions
   (B) restricted
   (C) restricting
   (D) restricted

3. Employee _____ in this company will prove beneficial for everyone.   Ⓐ Ⓑ Ⓒ Ⓓ
   (A) invest
   (B) invested
   (C) investments
   (D) investing

INCOMPLETE SENTENCES **135**

4. The contract calls for a $1,000 _____ for every day we go over the deadline.
    (A) penalize
    (B) penalty
    (C) penal
    (D) penalizing

Ⓐ Ⓑ Ⓒ Ⓓ

5. The manager's _____ for next year's profits is very optimistic.
    (A) projection
    (B) projecting
    (C) project
    (D) projected

Ⓐ Ⓑ Ⓒ Ⓓ

6. We have no other _____ if we want to expand the company safely.
    (A) optimal
    (B) optimum
    (C) opt
    (D) option

Ⓐ Ⓑ Ⓒ Ⓓ

7. I missed breakfast and lunch, so my _____ right now is to get something to eat.
    (A) priority
    (B) prior
    (C) prioritize
    (D) priors

Ⓐ Ⓑ Ⓒ Ⓓ

8. The restaurant is due for an _____ by the Health Department next week.
    (A) inspection
    (B) inspecting
    (C) inspect
    (D) inspected

Ⓐ Ⓑ Ⓒ Ⓓ

9. Our success is based completely on the _____ of our products.
    (A) rely
    (B) reliable
    (C) reliant
    (D) reliability

Ⓐ Ⓑ Ⓒ Ⓓ

10. The low profits we've had over the last two quarters are due to the bad _____.
    (A) economical
    (B) economize
    (C) economic
    (D) economy

Ⓐ Ⓑ Ⓒ Ⓓ

136 READING

WORD FORM: VERBS

LANGUAGE STRATEGIES

In these TOEIC test questions, you will have to choose the verb form of a word from four choices. You must understand that a verb is missing from the sentence. You must also know which of the four choices is a verb.

Example:

We will _____ our operation and open two new branches.
- (A) expansion
- (B) expansive
- (C) expand
- (D) expansively

The correct answer is (C) *expand*. The missing word is a verb. None of the other choices is a verb.

DIRECTIONS: Mark the choice that best completes the sentence.

1. If you cannot _____ those accusations, I want to hear no more about it.   Ⓐ Ⓑ Ⓒ Ⓓ
   - (A) substantial
   - (B) substance
   - (C) substantiate
   - (D) substantially

2. Government experts _____ the stock market to do better in the coming months.   Ⓐ Ⓑ Ⓒ Ⓓ
   - (A) expectable
   - (B) expect
   - (C) expectation
   - (D) expectant

3. Do you _____ to increase employee benefits during the next open enrollment?   Ⓐ Ⓑ Ⓒ Ⓓ
   - (A) intend
   - (B) intent
   - (C) intention
   - (D) intently

INCOMPLETE SENTENCES **137**

4. Whenever out-of-town clients visit us, we do our best to _____ them. A B C D
   (A) entertainment
   (B) entertaining
   (C) entertainer
   (D) entertain

5. The auditors _____ that the bookkeepers send them figures every two weeks. A B C D
   (A) preference
   (B) preferable
   (C) preferential
   (D) prefer

6. My boss's wife loves to _____ antique bottles and jars. A B C D
   (A) collection
   (B) collect
   (C) collectible
   (D) collector

7. I dislike radios playing in the office because they _____ me while I try to work. A B C D
   (A) distraction
   (B) distracter
   (C) distract
   (D) distracting

8. We would like to _____ that these bonuses are a one-time only thing. A B C D
   (A) emphasize
   (B) emphatic
   (C) emphasis
   (D) emphatically

9. Management likes employees who _____ to participate in company events. A B C D
   (A) voluntary
   (B) volunteerism
   (C) volunteer
   (D) voluntarily

10. By law, we must _____ how much federal income tax to deduct from your pay. A B C D
    (A) calculable
    (B) calculation
    (C) calculate
    (D) calculator

138 READING

WORD FORM: ADJECTIVES

LANGUAGE STRATEGIES

In these TOEIC test questions, you will have to choose the adjective form of a word from four choices. You must understand that an adjective is missing from the sentence. You must also know which of the four choices is an adjective.

Example:

Please sit down and make yourself _____.
(A)   comfortable
(B)   comfort
(C)   comfortably
(D)   comforter

The correct answer is (D) *comfortable*. The missing word is an adjective. None of the other choices is an adjective.

DIRECTIONS: Mark the choice that best completes the sentence.

1. All staff members are _____ for the accuracy of their time cards.
    (A)   account
    (B)   accountant
    (C)   accountable
    (D)   accountability

    Ⓐ   Ⓑ   Ⓒ   Ⓓ

2. Everybody who works here has his/her _____ parking space in the garage.
    (A)   own
    (B)   owner
    (C)   owe
    (D)   owing

    Ⓐ   Ⓑ   Ⓒ   Ⓓ

3. Some people say the _____ power in this company lies with the boss's brother.
    (A)   reality
    (B)   realism
    (C)   really
    (D)   real

    Ⓐ   Ⓑ   Ⓒ   Ⓓ

4. We're all glad that the new CEO is a very
_____ leader.
(A) progressive
(B) progress
(C) progression
(D) progressively

5. It's so nice that your assistant is such a
_____ person.
(A) friend
(B) friendliness
(C) friendly
(D) friendship

6. The new line of cleaning products is still
in the _____ stage of development.
(A) experimenter
(B) experiment
(C) experimentation
(D) experimental

7. The loyalty she has from her staff is _____
of what a good manager she is.
(A) indicate
(B) indicative
(C) indicator
(D) indication

8. Jeanne's _____ approach to all of her work
is what makes her so valuable to us.
(A) methodical
(B) methodology
(C) method
(D) methodically

9. Before you go abroad, make sure you have a
_____ passport.
(A) validity
(B) validation
(C) validate
(D) valid

10. We are proud that our company has the most
_____ health-care plan in the state.
(A) comprehend
(B) comprehensive
(C) comprehensively
(D) comprehension

140 READING

WORD FORM: ADVERBS

LANGUAGE STRATEGIES

In these TOEIC test questions, you will have to choose the adverb form of a word from four choices. You must understand that an adverb is missing from the sentence. You must also know which of the four choices is an adverb.

Example:

This form must be completed _____.
(A) accurate
(B) accuracy
(C) accurately
(D) accurateness

The correct answer is (C) *accurately*. The missing word is an adverb. None of the other choices is an adverb.

DIRECTIONS: Mark the choice that best completes the sentence.

1. When we plan out next year's budget, let's do it _____ this time.   Ⓐ Ⓑ Ⓒ Ⓓ
   (A) really
   (B) reality
   (C) realistic
   (D) realistically

2. Our books are audited _____ by an outside agency.   Ⓐ Ⓑ Ⓒ Ⓓ
   (A) periodical
   (B) period
   (C) periodically
   (D) periodic

3. Mr. Talbot is _____ awaiting the report on his yearly evaluation.   Ⓐ Ⓑ Ⓒ Ⓓ
   (A) anxiously
   (B) anxious
   (C) anxiety
   (D) anxiousness

INCOMPLETE SENTENCES **141**

4. The CEO has been _____ advised by the board of directors.
  (A) reliably
  (B) reliable
  (C) reliability
  (D) rely

5. Ms. Yates surprised all of us at the conference with her _____ delivered speech.
  (A) impressive
  (B) impression
  (C) impressively
  (D) impress

6. We've never seen a more _____ organized presentation than the one you gave.
  (A) profess
  (B) professional
  (C) profession
  (D) professionally

7. _____ speaking, this hotel offers guests more amenities than most hotels.
  (A) Generally
  (B) Generality
  (C) General
  (D) Generalize

8. All the candy produced in our factories is _____ wrapped for safety.
  (A) individuality
  (B) individually
  (C) individual
  (D) individualize

9. The CEO's office is so _____ decorated that I feel it's embarrassing.
  (A) expend
  (B) expensive
  (C) expensively
  (D) expense

10. From now on, any employee who is _____ late for work will be dismissed.
  (A) habitually
  (B) habituate
  (C) habitual
  (D) habit

142 READING

WORD FORM: PRONOUNS

LANGUAGE STRATEGIES

In these TOEIC test questions, you will have to choose the correct form of a pronoun from four choices. You must understand what part of speech is missing. You must also know what part of speech the four pronouns are.

Example:

The customer called to cancel _____ order.
(A)　it
(B)　her
(C)　hers
(D)　she

The correct answer is (B) *her*. The missing pronoun is a possessive pronoun. None of the other choices is a possessive pronoun.

DIRECTIONS: Mark the choice that best completes the sentence.

1. The government has a responsibility to protect _____ citizens from inflation.   Ⓐ Ⓑ Ⓒ Ⓓ
   (A)　its
   (B)　it's
   (C)　it
   (D)　their

2. I see you met my assistant. _____ and I go back many years.   Ⓐ Ⓑ Ⓒ Ⓓ
   (A)　Her
   (B)　She
   (C)　Hers
   (D)　We

3. Instead of filling those orders now, take care of _____ tomorrow morning.   Ⓐ Ⓑ Ⓒ Ⓓ
   (A)　them
   (B)　they
   (C)　their
   (D)　its

INCOMPLETE SENTENCES   **143**

4. All of _____ have been invited to the boss's cocktail party this Friday evening.
   (A) we
   (B) our
   (C) us
   (D) ours

Ⓐ Ⓑ Ⓒ Ⓓ

5. The idea for the new routing system wasn't Patterson's; it was _____.
   (A) me
   (B) mine
   (C) my
   (D) I

Ⓐ Ⓑ Ⓒ Ⓓ

6. Telling somebody that _____ is laid off is a very unpleasant task.
   (A) him
   (B) his
   (C) he
   (D) they

Ⓐ Ⓑ Ⓒ Ⓓ

7. My computer has a lot of memory, but _____ has more.
   (A) she
   (B) hers
   (C) her
   (D) it

Ⓐ Ⓑ Ⓒ Ⓓ

8. _____ isn't good business practice to arrive late for meetings.
   (A) He
   (B) It
   (C) She
   (D) You

Ⓐ Ⓑ Ⓒ Ⓓ

9. When _____ probation period is up, you'll be given the full benefits package.
   (A) you
   (B) your
   (C) yours
   (D) our

Ⓐ Ⓑ Ⓒ Ⓓ

10. The police were right when _____ advised us to get a new security system.
    (A) it
    (B) she
    (C) them
    (D) they

Ⓐ Ⓑ Ⓒ Ⓓ

CONTEXT: NOUNS

TEST STRATEGIES

In these TOEIC test questions, you will have to choose the correct noun from four noun choices. You must understand the meaning of the sentence and the meaning of the noun choices.

Example:

> The _____ to the banquet were sent to all of our clients.
> (A) requests
> (B) invitations
> (C) suggestions
> (D) offers

The correct answer is (B) *invitations*. None of the other nouns fits the context of the sentence.

DIRECTIONS: Mark the choice that best completes the sentence.

1. Has anybody seen the _____ of toner that just arrived for the copy machine?
   (A) bags
   (B) envelopes
   (C) cans
   (D) boxes

   Ⓐ Ⓑ Ⓒ Ⓓ

2. There is a three-month probation _____ for all new employees.
   (A) timing
   (B) era
   (C) period
   (D) sequence

   Ⓐ Ⓑ Ⓒ Ⓓ

3. To call another company or other places, press 9 for an outside _____.
   (A) line
   (B) lane
   (C) land
   (D) lining

   Ⓐ Ⓑ Ⓒ Ⓓ

INCOMPLETE SENTENCES **145**

4. Your business card should have your contact _____. Ⓐ Ⓑ Ⓒ Ⓓ
   (A) information
   (B) report
   (C) announcement
   (D) figures

5. Tariffs are set by our federal _____ Department. Ⓐ Ⓑ Ⓒ Ⓓ
   (A) Business
   (B) Negotiation
   (C) Commerce
   (D) Deal

6. It's hard to read anything on your computer. Ⓐ Ⓑ Ⓒ Ⓓ
   You should get a new _____.
   (A) screen
   (B) television
   (C) monitor
   (D) viewer

7. Which _____ is Mr. Hashimoto arriving at Ⓐ Ⓑ Ⓒ Ⓓ
   when his plane lands?
   (A) terminal
   (B) building
   (C) house
   (D) place

8. The vending machines in the employee _____ Ⓐ Ⓑ Ⓒ Ⓓ
   are out of order again.
   (A) room
   (B) place
   (C) salon
   (D) lounge

9. To relieve work-related stress, our company Ⓐ Ⓑ Ⓒ Ⓓ
   provides free _____ for everyone.
   (A) messages
   (B) drugs
   (C) massages
   (D) sleep

10. Because Jack was injured at work, he's receiving Ⓐ Ⓑ Ⓒ Ⓓ
    workman's _____.
    (A) compensation
    (B) help
    (C) reimbursement
    (D) funds

CONTEXT: VERBS

TEST STRATEGIES

In these TOEIC test questions, you will have to choose the correct verb from four verb choices. You must understand the meaning of the sentence and the meaning of the verb choices.

Example:

The meeting room _____ 40 people.
(A) gathers
(B) carries
(C) holds
(D) waits

The correct answer is (C) *holds*. None of the other verbs fit the context of the sentence.

DIRECTIONS: Mark the choice that best completes the sentence.

1. I'm sorry to be late for the meeting, but my new secretary _____ to tell me you had scheduled it earlier.
   (A) decided
   (B) neglected
   (C) refused
   (D) thought

   Ⓐ Ⓑ Ⓒ Ⓓ

2. When you get to our main entrance, _____ a left as you enter the parking lot.
   (A) make
   (B) turn
   (C) do
   (D) throw

   Ⓐ Ⓑ Ⓒ Ⓓ

3. It's a company custom to _____ to work in casual clothes on Fridays.
   (A) come
   (B) be
   (C) dress
   (D) attend

   Ⓐ Ⓑ Ⓒ Ⓓ

INCOMPLETE SENTENCES **147**

4. If you're _____ Ms. Rogers, you'll find her in the board room.
   (A) looking to
   (B) looking at
   (C) looking for
   (D) looking into

5. Most of us in this office _____ lunch at noon.
   (A) make
   (B) have
   (C) bring
   (D) go

6. The boss doesn't _____ to playing the radio at your desk if the music is low.
   (A) mind
   (B) refuse
   (C) negate
   (D) object

7. If I criticize your work, you shouldn't _____ it personally.
   (A) make
   (B) think
   (C) believe
   (D) take

8. If you _____ long before leaving for the airport, the hotel will keep your bags for you.
   (A) exit
   (B) depart
   (C) check out
   (D) move out

9. I'm glad you enjoyed that appetizer, so I _____ the chicken for your entrée.
   (A) feel
   (B) recommend
   (C) try
   (D) refer

10. My daughter in college is _____ international business.
   (A) studying
   (B) rehearsing
   (C) revisiting
   (D) inquiring

148 READING

CONTEXT: ADJECTIVES

TEST STRATEGIES

In these TOEIC test questions, you will have to choose the correct adjective from four adjective choices. You must understand the meaning of the sentence and the meaning of the adjective choices.

Example:

We want our employees to behave in the most _____ manner.
- (A) operational
- (B) expensive
- (C) awkward
- (D) professional

The correct answer is (D) *professional*. None of the other adjectives fit the context of the sentence.

DIRECTIONS: Mark the choice that best completes the sentence.

1. Did you know that in Western culture it can be considered _____ to stare at somebody? Ⓐ Ⓑ Ⓒ Ⓓ
   - (A) assertive
   - (B) rude
   - (C) silly
   - (D) funny

2. I still think that giving a presentation in front of many strangers is _____. Ⓐ Ⓑ Ⓒ Ⓓ
   - (A) energetic
   - (B) tepid
   - (C) scary
   - (D) famous

3. The new filing clerk's smile and cute way of speaking are completely _____. Ⓐ Ⓑ Ⓒ Ⓓ
   - (A) lovable
   - (B) loving
   - (C) beloved
   - (D) loved

INCOMPLETE SENTENCES **149**

4. It was not _____ to wear a T-shirt and jeans to the boss's retirement party.
   (A) restful
   (B) appropriate
   (C) exciting
   (D) friendly

   Ⓐ Ⓑ Ⓒ Ⓓ

5. If we don't meet those deadlines, we're going to be in _____ trouble.
   (A) heavy
   (B) big
   (C) large
   (D) great

   Ⓐ Ⓑ Ⓒ Ⓓ

6. It was very _____ finding Mr. Klein's cat sitting on his desk this morning.
   (A) satisfying
   (B) rewarding
   (C) intense
   (D) odd

   Ⓐ Ⓑ Ⓒ Ⓓ

7. Helen's Web design skills are simply _____.
   (A) amazing
   (B) annoying
   (C) enveloping
   (D) encouraging

   Ⓐ Ⓑ Ⓒ Ⓓ

8. I heard that the electrician says we should have a _____ overhaul of the wiring.
   (A) complete
   (B) fair
   (C) whole
   (D) round

   Ⓐ Ⓑ Ⓒ Ⓓ

9. My sales figures this quarter are much _____ than they've been for a long time.
   (A) grander
   (B) upper
   (C) higher
   (D) larger

   Ⓐ Ⓑ Ⓒ Ⓓ

10. I hope the company has enough money to pay for these _____ renovations.
    (A) needy
    (B) late
    (C) likely
    (D) costly

    Ⓐ Ⓑ Ⓒ Ⓓ

CONTEXT: ADVERBS

TEST STRATEGIES

In these TOEIC test questions, you will have to choose the correct adverb from four adverb choices. You must understand the meaning of the sentence and the meaning of the adverb choices.

Example:

All the hotel rooms were _____ cleaned.
- (A) anxiously
- (B) thoroughly
- (C) shortly
- (D) firstly

The correct answer is (B) *thoroughly*. None of the other adverbs fit the context of the sentence.

DIRECTIONS: Mark the choice that best completes the sentence.

1. The company _____ accepts your resignation.   Ⓐ Ⓑ Ⓒ Ⓓ
   - (A) practically
   - (B) sadly
   - (C) stoically
   - (D) righteously

2. Al can copy documents so _____ that you can't   Ⓐ Ⓑ Ⓒ Ⓓ
   tell the original from the copy.
   - (A) intensely
   - (B) directly
   - (C) acutely
   - (D) skillfully

3. We've sold _____ twice the amount of giftware   Ⓐ Ⓑ Ⓒ Ⓓ
   this quarter than a year ago.
   - (A) roughly
   - (B) justly
   - (C) nicely
   - (D) equally

INCOMPLETE SENTENCES **151**

4. You _____ wouldn't object to a pay increase, would you?   (A) (B) (C) (D)
   - (A) happily
   - (B) obviously
   - (C) notably
   - (D) casually

5. _____, I'm so tired that I don't care if we're not offered any overtime.   (A) (B) (C) (D)
   - (A) Naturally
   - (B) Critically
   - (C) Frankly
   - (D) Bluntly

6. I was _____ pleased to be given such a generous pay increase.   (A) (B) (C) (D)
   - (A) extremely
   - (B) willfully
   - (C) sadly
   - (D) barely

7. The supervisor _____ wanted to change our shifts, but he's changed his mind.   (A) (B) (C) (D)
   - (A) originally
   - (B) awkwardly
   - (C) principally
   - (D) surely

8. The company _____ uses WordIt as our word processing program.   (A) (B) (C) (D)
   - (A) previously
   - (B) currently
   - (C) actively
   - (D) tightly

9. Sheila has learned her job _____ well considering how new she is here.   (A) (B) (C) (D)
   - (A) purposely
   - (B) reasonably
   - (C) sincerely
   - (D) neatly

10. Management has been thinking _____ of opening up two new branch offices.   (A) (B) (C) (D)
    - (A) additionally
    - (B) abundantly
    - (C) newly
    - (D) seriously

152   READING

CONTEXT: CONJUNCTIONS

TEST STRATEGIES

In these TOEIC test questions, you will have to choose the correct conjunction from four conjunction choices. You must understand the meaning of the sentence and the meaning of the conjunction choices.

Example:

Both the secretary _____ the file clerk left early.
(A) nor
(B) either
(C) or
(D) and

The correct answer is (D) *and*. None of the other conjunctions fit the context of the sentence.

DIRECTIONS: Mark the choice that best completes the sentence.

1. We haven't seen that memo _____ it was   Ⓐ Ⓑ Ⓒ Ⓓ
   first distributed.
   (A) since
   (B) when
   (C) while
   (D) as

2. Mr. Kendall will continue working _____ his   Ⓐ Ⓑ Ⓒ Ⓓ
   replacement has been trained.
   (A) in order that
   (B) because
   (C) until
   (D) so

3. She got not only a substantial raise _____   Ⓐ Ⓑ Ⓒ Ⓓ
   a large bonus.
   (A) because
   (B) although
   (C) and
   (D) but also

INCOMPLETE SENTENCES **153**

4. _____ you come up with a better idea, let's try out my suggestion.
   (A) If
   (B) After
   (C) Neither
   (D) Unless

   (A) (B) (C) (D)

5. _____ Genji and I are being transferred to the Mumbai office.
   (A) Both
   (B) Either
   (C) And
   (D) Also

   (A) (B) (C) (D)

6. I'll go to the convention center _____ I've checked into the hotel.
   (A) since
   (B) as soon as
   (C) though
   (D) as

   (A) (B) (C) (D)

7. Mr. Romney didn't tell us _____ he'd decided to hire new people.
   (A) but
   (B) that
   (C) as
   (D) while

   (A) (B) (C) (D)

8. Neither the boss _____ his assistant were aware the deadline had passed.
   (A) or
   (B) but
   (C) nor
   (D) either

   (A) (B) (C) (D)

9. _____ Nora has finished this work, get her started on the Findlay account.
   (A) Once
   (B) While
   (C) As
   (D) So

   (A) (B) (C) (D)

10. I'll look for another restaurant _____ Chez Michel is fully booked.
    (A) although
    (B) before
    (C) not only
    (D) if

    (A) (B) (C) (D)

154   READING

CONTEXT: PREPOSITIONS

TEST STRATEGIES

In these TOEIC test questions, you will have to choose the correct preposition from four preposition choices. You must understand the meaning of the sentence and the meaning of the four preposition choices.

Example:

Put your coat _____ the closet.
(A) in
(B) next
(C) at
(D) to

The correct answer is (A) *in*. None of the other prepositions fit the context of the sentence.

DIRECTIONS: Mark the choice that best completes the sentence.

1. Please file these invoices _____ Payment Pending.
   (A) under
   (B) over
   (C) on
   (D) inside

   Ⓐ Ⓑ Ⓒ Ⓓ

2. When did you say you were leaving _____ London?
   (A) to
   (B) at
   (C) for
   (D) towards

   Ⓐ Ⓑ Ⓒ Ⓓ

3. In a business letter, you should put a colon _____ the greeting.
   (A) before
   (B) after
   (C) in
   (D) by

   Ⓐ Ⓑ Ⓒ Ⓓ

INCOMPLETE SENTENCES **155**

4. Wang is originally from Hong Kong, but he's lived in San Francisco _____ years.
   (A) for
   (B) in
   (C) through
   (D) over

   Ⓐ Ⓑ Ⓒ Ⓓ

5. What happened to the little memo I had attached _____ this invoice?
   (A) to
   (B) on
   (C) over
   (D) at

   Ⓐ Ⓑ Ⓒ Ⓓ

6. _____ the time you read this message, I'll be halfway across the Atlantic.
   (A) In
   (B) On
   (C) By
   (D) For

   Ⓐ Ⓑ Ⓒ Ⓓ

7. Now I'll never retrieve my ten-year pin because it rolled _____ the refrigerator.
   (A) below
   (B) over
   (C) around
   (D) behind

   Ⓐ Ⓑ Ⓒ Ⓓ

8. I always get nervous driving _____ heavy traffic on the way to work.
   (A) on
   (B) by
   (C) in
   (D) with

   Ⓐ Ⓑ Ⓒ Ⓓ

9. You can come _____ for an interview next Monday at 9:30 A.M.
   (A) through
   (B) in
   (C) out
   (D) about

   Ⓐ Ⓑ Ⓒ Ⓓ

10. We were late because we had to drive _____ for twenty minutes looking for parking.
    (A) around
    (B) over
    (C) up
    (D) down

    Ⓐ Ⓑ Ⓒ Ⓓ

GRAMMAR TIP

Contractions with 's

A contraction with 's (*he's, she's, it's*) can mean *is* or *has*. It means *is* and is followed by an *-ing* verb if the meaning of the sentence requires the present continuous tense. It means *has* and is followed by a past participle verb if the meaning of the sentence requires the present perfect tense.

> He's working now.
> He's worked here all his life.
>
> She's living in New York now.
> She's lived there since last summer.
>
> It's raining now.
> It's rained everyday for the past week.

VOCABULARY TIP

Uses of *Since*

Since may be used with a time expression or time clause to designate the point in time when an action began.

> He has worked here since the day he graduated from college.
> It's been raining since early this morning.

Since may also be used to designate the reason for something.

> She put on her coat since the room was so cold.
> Since he grew up in France, he speaks French fluently.

STRATEGY PRACTICE

DIRECTIONS: Mark the choice that best completes the sentence.

1. Please call the _____ and find out if they
   have any more armchairs in stock.   Ⓐ Ⓑ Ⓒ Ⓓ
   (A) storehouse
   (B) warehouse
   (C) outhouse
   (D) stock house

2. Hotel room _____ always go up during
   the tourist season.   Ⓐ Ⓑ Ⓒ Ⓓ
   (A) tolls
   (B) invoices
   (C) monies
   (D) rates

3. You will be _____ for all your expenses
   on the trip.   Ⓐ Ⓑ Ⓒ Ⓓ
   (A) reimbursed
   (B) recompensed
   (C) restituted
   (D) reprimanded

4. Because of family problems, he's _____
   a year's leave of absence.   Ⓐ Ⓑ Ⓒ Ⓓ
   (A) taking
   (B) making
   (C) doing
   (D) fixing

5. Her speeches are much too _____ because
   she loves listening to herself speak.   Ⓐ Ⓑ Ⓒ Ⓓ
   (A) bright
   (B) large
   (C) lengthy
   (D) interesting

158 READING

6. If the lab test results are not _____, there could be dangerous consequences.   (A) (B) (C) (D)
   (A) expected
   (B) accurate
   (C) acute
   (D) expelled

7. He handled that delicate matter very _____.   (A) (B) (C) (D)
   (A) erroneously
   (B) factually
   (C) precisely
   (D) diplomatically

8. You can have a four-day work week _____ you stay two hours later each day.   (A) (B) (C) (D)
   (A) whatever
   (B) as far as
   (C) considering
   (D) as long as

9. She's still coming into work _____ she has the flu.   (A) (B) (C) (D)
   (A) however
   (B) even though
   (C) but
   (D) nonetheless

10. If you happen to drive _____ my house, stop in for a cup of coffee.   (A) (B) (C) (D)
    (A) over
    (B) by
    (C) up to
    (D) around

11. The first records of an import/export business go back _____ 3500 B.C.   (A) (B) (C) (D)
    (A) ago
    (B) for
    (C) at
    (D) to

INCOMPLETE SENTENCES **159**

12. Her _____ with accounting procedures
should be good for our office.
(A) familiarity
(B) familiar
(C) familiarize
(D) familial

Ⓐ Ⓑ Ⓒ Ⓓ

13. Your handwriting is so unclear that I can't read
this _____ you made.
(A) notate
(B) noticeable
(C) notation
(D) notable

Ⓐ Ⓑ Ⓒ Ⓓ

14. We need to _____ our expansion plans
as soon as possible.
(A) finale
(B) finality
(C) final
(D) finalize

Ⓐ Ⓑ Ⓒ Ⓓ

15. I hear the government is going to _____
some peculiar dealings on Wall Street.
(A) investigation
(B) investigate
(C) investigational
(D) investigative

Ⓐ Ⓑ Ⓒ Ⓓ

16. Mr. Kaplowitz's _____ behavior is beginning
to worry many of us.
(A) oddity
(B) oddly
(C) odd
(D) oddness

Ⓐ Ⓑ Ⓒ Ⓓ

17. That was a _____ research job you did for
the company!
(A) fantastic
(B) fantasy
(C) fantasize
(D) fantastical

Ⓐ Ⓑ Ⓒ Ⓓ

160 READING

18. Please remember to deal _____ with our competitors during the negotiations. Ⓐ Ⓑ Ⓒ Ⓓ
    - (A) cautious
    - (B) caution
    - (C) cautiously
    - (D) cautiousness

19. My friend Bruno likes everybody _____ meets. Ⓐ Ⓑ Ⓒ Ⓓ
    - (A) it
    - (B) him
    - (C) he
    - (D) its

20. I missed the news at 6:00, but I can watch _____ at 11:00. Ⓐ Ⓑ Ⓒ Ⓓ
    - (A) them
    - (B) it
    - (C) its
    - (D) they

INCOMPLETE SENTENCES 161

PART 6: TEXT COMPLETION

PART 6

Directions: Read the texts that follow. A word or phrase is missing in some of the sentences. Four answer choices are given below each of the sentences. Select the best answer to complete the text. Then mark the letter (A), (B), (C), or (D) on your answer sheet.

STRATEGY OVERVIEW

In Part 6 of the TOEIC Test you will see text with three blanks. You will be asked to choose the word or phrase that best completes each blank. Much of the grammar that you studied for Part 5 will be useful here. In addition, use these strategies to choose the correct answers in Part 6.

LANGUAGE STRATEGIES

- Verb Patterns – Understand the different forms of verb tenses and modal auxiliaries.

- Modifier Choices – Understand the different forms of adjectives and adverbs.

TEST STRATEGIES

- Context – Look at number, part of speech, pronoun type, and verb tense to choose the correct word for the context.

VERBS

LANGUAGE STRATEGIES

VERB TENSES

Verb tenses in English indicate the time or state of the action in a sentence. Here we will review these verb tenses.

✔ **Present Tense**

   Simple Present and Present Continuous

   Present Perfect

   Present Perfect Continuous

✔ **Past Tense**

   Simple Past

   Past Continuous

   Past Perfect

✔ **Future Tense**

   Simple Future

   Future Perfect

THE SIMPLE PRESENT

✔ We form the simple present by using the basic verb (*I like, they need*). The only change is adding *-s* or *-es* for the third person singular (*he likes, she needs, it passes*).

✔ We use the simple present for two main reasons:

   ➡ for a small group of verbs that deal with the senses (*see, taste, smell,* etc.) and the mind (*know, want, believe,* etc.);

      Man: *Do you understand my point?*
      Woman: *Yes, now I know what you mean.*

   ➡ to explain that something happens all the time, repeatedly, usually, or is a fact.

      Woman: *Where is Nobue?*
      Man: *At home. She sleeps late on Saturday mornings.*

THE PRESENT CONTINUOUS

✔ We form the present continuous by using the auxiliary *be* in the present before the verb and adding *-ing* to the end of the verb.

✔ We use the present continuous with actions in the real present.

      Man: *What are you doing?*
      Woman: *I'm getting dressed to go out.*

TEXT COMPLETION **163**

THE PRESENT PERFECT

✔ We form the present perfect by using the auxiliary *have* or *has* and the past participle of the verb.

✔ We use the present perfect to show that an action began in the past and continues to the general present.

⇨ *Production in our factories has increased a lot since we installed the new machinery.*

THE PRESENT PERFECT CONTINUOUS

✔ We form the present perfect continuous by using *have been* or *has been* before the verb and adding *-ing* to the end of the verb.

✔ We use the present perfect continuous to show that an action began in the past and continues to <u>this moment</u> in the present.

⇨ *I've been waiting for you for over an hour.*

In the following TOEIC test questions, you will have to choose the correct verb form from four verb choices. You must understand the meaning of the sentence and the meaning of the verb choices.

Practice: Present Tenses

DIRECTIONS: Mark the choice that best completes the sentence.

1. I only _____ to work on Monday. The rest of the week I work from home.   Ⓐ Ⓑ Ⓒ Ⓓ
   - (A) go
   - (B) am going
   - (C) have gone
   - (D) have been going

2. My boss _____ to Australia next month to open a new business.   Ⓐ Ⓑ Ⓒ Ⓓ
   - (A) travels
   - (B) is traveling
   - (C) has traveled
   - (D) has been traveling

3. My co-workers and I _____ at this restaurant once before.   Ⓐ Ⓑ Ⓒ Ⓓ
   - (A) eat
   - (B) is eating
   - (C) have eaten
   - (D) have been eating

4. Since June, Jake _____ rather than driving to the fitness center. He has more time now that he is retired.   Ⓐ Ⓑ Ⓒ Ⓓ
   - (A) walking
   - (B) is walking
   - (C) has walked
   - (D) has been walking

5. I always _____ to wish my boss a happy birthday.   Ⓐ Ⓑ Ⓒ Ⓓ
   - (A) forget
   - (B) am forgetting
   - (C) have forgotten
   - (D) have been forgetting

164   READING

6. I _____ my suitcases already. You can put them   Ⓐ   Ⓑ   Ⓒ   Ⓓ
in the car now.

(A)   pack   (C)   have packed

(B)   am packing   (D)   have been packing

7. I'm sorry. I _____ to call you all week, but we   Ⓐ   Ⓑ   Ⓒ   Ⓓ
have been so busy at work.

(A)   mean   (C)   have meant

(B)   am meaning   (D)   have been meaning

8. First we _____ the forms. After that we sign   Ⓐ   Ⓑ   Ⓒ   Ⓓ
and mail them.

(A)   print   (C)   have printed

(B)   are printing   (D)   have been printing

9. I _____ your old telephone number, but I still   Ⓐ   Ⓑ   Ⓒ   Ⓓ
need to write your new one down.

(A)   erase   (C)   have erased

(B)   am erasing   (D)   have been erasing

10. We _____ the rose bushes all day. I apologize that   Ⓐ   Ⓑ   Ⓒ   Ⓓ
the front gardens are so messy.

(A)   trim   (C)   have trimmed

(B)   are trimming   (D)   have been trimming

TEXT COMPLETION   **165**

THE SIMPLE PAST

✔ If a verb is regular, we form the simple past by putting *-ed* or *-d* on the end (*work, worked / type, typed*). If the verb is irregular, there are usually internal changes (*get, got*) or almost complete changes (*bring, brought*).

✔ We use the simple past for two main reasons:
 ➡ to show that an action happened in the past and is completely finished;
  Columbus arrived in the New World in 1492.
 ➡ to show which of two actions in the past lasted for a shorter time.
  They were having dinner when I called.

THE PAST CONTINUOUS

✔ We form the past continuous by using the auxiliary *was* or *were* before the verb and adding *-ing* to the end of the verb.

✔ We use the past continuous for two main reasons:
 ➡ to show that an action was in progress at a certain point in the past;
  I was hoping to get a call from them before now.
 ➡ to show which of two actions in the past was longer.
  They were having dinner when I called.

THE PAST PERFECT

✔ We form the past perfect by using the auxiliary *had* plus the past participle of the verb.

✔ We use the past perfect to show which of two actions in the past happened first. The past perfect represents what happened first; the simple past or past continuous represents what happened next.
  He missed his appointment because his car had broken down.

Practice: Past Tenses

DIRECTIONS: Mark the choice that best completes the sentence.

1. We _____ three new staff members last week. I'm happy with them so far.   Ⓐ Ⓑ Ⓒ Ⓓ
 (A) hired   (C) had hired
 (B) were hiring   (D) had been hiring

2. The old tenants _____ the property by the time we looked at it. There was no furniture left inside.   Ⓐ Ⓑ Ⓒ Ⓓ
 (A) vacated   (C) had vacated
 (B) were vacating   (D) had been vacating

3. Sorry for not taking your call this afternoon. I _____ up some work for tonight's meeting.   Ⓐ Ⓑ Ⓒ Ⓓ
 (A) finished   (C) had finished
 (B) was finishing   (D) had been finishing

166 READING

4. We _____ from another supplier for three months by the time James made his offer.

    (A) ordered   (C) had ordered

    (B) ordering   (D) had been ordering

5. The rent _____ by 5 percent this month. We might need to close the shop.

    (A) increased   (C) had increased

    (B) was increasing   (D) had been increasing

6. The McKenzies almost _____ their house for less than it was worth. A real estate agent helped them out.

    (A) sold   (C) had sold

    (B) were selling   (D) had been selling

7. I _____ the bus by then. In fact, I was probably at work by the time you arrived at my house.

    (A) already caught   (C) had already caught

    (B) was already catching   (D) had been already catching

8. Susan and I _____ you went home already. Do you want to come to lunch with us?

    (A) thought   (C) had thought

    (B) were thinking   (D) had been thinking

9. The mayor forgot his main point while he _____ the public.

    (A) was addressed   (C) had addressed

    (B) was addressing   (D) had been addressing

10. George and Jim _____ me to go to the conference by the time I realized what it was about.

    (A) convinced   (C) had convinced

    (B) were convincing   (D) had been convincing

TEXT COMPLETION   **167**

THE SIMPLE FUTURE

✔ With all verbs, both regular and irregular, we form the simple future by adding *will* before the verb.

✔ We use the simple future for four main reasons:

⇨ to show that an action will happen in the future;

The office will close at 5:00 P.M. tonight.

⇨ to make a prediction;

We assume she'll quit her job.

⇨ to make a promise;

I'll mail the letters for you.

⇨ to make a request.

Will you close the door, please?

THE FUTURE PERFECT

✔ We form the future perfect by using *will* plus the auxiliary *have* plus the past participle of the verb.

✔ We use the future perfect for two main reasons:

⇨ to show that an action will be completed before a time in the future;

I'll have read the article online before you find it in the newspaper.

⇨ to make a prediction about actions that are now finished.

We will have to wait in the lobby because the performance will have started by now.

Practice: Future Tenses

DIRECTIONS: Mark the choice that best completes the sentence.

1. The new course _____ by the 5th of June. It's too Ⓐ Ⓑ Ⓒ Ⓓ
   bad that you don't get back on that date.
(A)	will start	(C)	will have started
(B)	will be starting	(D)	will have been starting

2. Mr. Davidson _____ on the door when he is Ⓐ Ⓑ Ⓒ Ⓓ
   ready to see you.
(A)	will knock	(C)	will have knocked
(B)	will be knocking	(D)	will have been knocking

3. Jenny will have lots of time to spend with her parents Ⓐ Ⓑ Ⓒ Ⓓ
   in January. She _____ her job by then.
(A)	is quitting	(C)	will have quit
(B)	will be quitting	(D)	will have been quitting

4. _____ fax these documents to our client, please? Ⓐ Ⓑ Ⓒ Ⓓ
(A)	Will you	(C)	Will you have
(B)	Will you be	(D)	Will you have been

5. We will have to stand at the back of the auditorium   Ⓐ Ⓑ Ⓒ Ⓓ
   because the volunteers _____ all of the seats
   by now.
   (A) will take   (C) will have taken
   (B) will be taking   (D) will have been taking

6. Go home, Eric. I promise I _____ the lights   Ⓐ Ⓑ Ⓒ Ⓓ
   before I leave the office.
   (A) will turn off   (C) will have turned off
   (B) will be turning off   (D) will have been turning off

7. I _____ the arrangements from home. I am   Ⓐ Ⓑ Ⓒ Ⓓ
   sick today.
   (A) will be made   (C) will have made
   (B) will be making   (D) will have been making

8. The class _____ for three weeks by the time   Ⓐ Ⓑ Ⓒ Ⓓ
   you join us. I'll fill you in at that time.
   (A) will run   (C) will have run
   (B) will be running   (D) will have been running

9. _____ you $20 that Jesse gets that raise when   Ⓐ Ⓑ Ⓒ Ⓓ
   she asks for it.
   (A) I'll bet   (C) I'll have bet
   (B) I'll be betting   (D) I'll have been betting

10. I assume _____ to New York rather than drive.   Ⓐ Ⓑ Ⓒ Ⓓ
    (A) you'll fly   (C) you'll have flown
    (B) you'll be flown   (D) you'll have been flying

TEXT COMPLETION **169**

MODAL AUXILIARIES

✔ The form of a modal does not change from first person to third person:

    I can. / He can.

✔ You never put *to* after a modal:

    Incorrect: *I can to type.*

    Correct: *I can type.*

✔ We use modals to help give verbs extra meaning. Here are the modals for this practice with their extra meanings:

⇨ can   = ability (*He can type 65 words per minute.*)

           = permission [informal language] (*I can punch out early.*)

⇨ could   = possibility (*She could be late because of the heavy rain.*)

⇨ will   = future [usually for a promise or prediction] (*I'm sure they'll get raises.*)

⇨ may   = possibility (*She may be late because of the heavy rain.*)

           = permission [formal language] (*I may punch out early.*)

⇨ might   = possibility (*She might be late because of the heavy rain.*)

⇨ shall   = future [formal language, usually an offer or a suggestion] (*Shall we meet tomorrow afternoon to discuss the latest budget report?*)

⇨ should = advice, suggestion, a good idea (*You should check the books again.*)

           = expectation (*Because he works so hard, he should get promoted soon.*)

⇨ ought to = should (*You ought to call her.*)

⇨ must   = necessity (*The bookkeeper must finish doing the payroll by Thursday.*)

           = logical conclusion (*It must be very stressful being a CEO.*)

⇨ would = possibility (*I would have gotten to work on time, but my train was late.*)

           = intent (*He promised he would pick her up on time.*)

Practice: Modal Auxiliaries

DIRECTIONS: Mark the choice that best completes the sentence.

1. My receptionist _____ set you up with an appointment. Just go down the hall to your right.
    (A) can   (C) may
    (B) might   (D) ought to

    Ⓐ   Ⓑ   Ⓒ   Ⓓ

2. _____ I hang your coat while you're removing your shoes?
    (A) Shall   (C) Must
    (B) Would   (D) Ought

    Ⓐ   Ⓑ   Ⓒ   Ⓓ

3. We _____ finish this assignment by the deadline, but it's pretty unlikely.
    (A) can   (C) will
    (B) might   (D) would

    Ⓐ   Ⓑ   Ⓒ   Ⓓ

170   READING

4. You _____ bring your spouse if you wish. However, you'll have to pay for an extra ticket.
   (A) may
   (B) might
   (C) ought to
   (D) should

   Ⓐ Ⓑ Ⓒ Ⓓ

5. He _____ take a taxi to the airport, but it makes more sense for me to just drop him off.
   (A) should
   (B) could
   (C) ought to
   (D) will

   Ⓐ Ⓑ Ⓒ Ⓓ

6. I _____ have called you sooner, but our telephones weren't working.
   (A) will
   (B) would
   (C) could
   (D) must

   Ⓐ Ⓑ Ⓒ Ⓓ

7. Is there a chance you _____ lose your job this winter?
   (A) can
   (B) might
   (C) should
   (D) must

   Ⓐ Ⓑ Ⓒ Ⓓ

8. If you want, we _____ book you on an earlier flight.
   (A) should
   (B) can
   (C) must
   (D) may

   Ⓐ Ⓑ Ⓒ Ⓓ

9. The office _____ close on the day before the holiday. It all depends how busy we are next week.
   (A) will
   (B) must
   (C) might
   (D) can

   Ⓐ Ⓑ Ⓒ Ⓓ

10. _____ I take your order now, or are you still deciding?
    (A) May
    (B) Must
    (C) Would
    (D) Will

   Ⓐ Ⓑ Ⓒ Ⓓ

TEXT COMPLETION **171**

MODIFIERS

LANGUAGE STRATEGIES

ADJECTIVES: COMPARATIVE AND SUPERLATIVE FORMS

COMPARATIVES

✔ We use comparatives when we talk about two things:

> *Alexander of Macedonia was <u>greater than</u> Napoleon.*

> *Elizabeth I of England was <u>as great as</u> Catherine of Russia.*

✔ We form comparatives four ways:

⇨ If the adjective has one syllable (*great*), we add *-er* to it (*greater*) and follow the word with *than* (*greater than*).

⇨ If the adjective has two syllables and ends in *-y* (*friendly*), we change the *y* to *i* and add *-er* (*friendlier*) and follow the word with *than* (*friendlier than*).

⇨ If the adjective has two or more syllables (*interesting*), we put *more* before it (*more interesting*) and follow the word with *than* (*more interesting than*).

⇨ If two or more things are the same, we put *as* before and after the adjective (*as great as*).

SUPERLATIVES

✔ We use superlatives when we talk about three or more things:

> *Of the five bosses I've worked for in my career, Mr. Honeywell is <u>the friendliest</u>.*

✔ We form superlatives in similar ways:

⇨ If the adjective has one syllable (*great*), we put *the* before it and add *-est* to it (*the greatest*).

⇨ If the adjective has two syllables and ends in *y* (*friendly*), we put *the* before it, change the *y* to *i*, and add *-est* to it (*the friendliest*).

⇨ If the adjective has two or more syllables (*interesting*), we put *the most* before it (*the most interesting*).

✔ Some adjectives in English have irregular comparative and superlative forms:

good	*better*	*best*
bad	*worse*	*worst*
far	*farther/further*	*farthest/furthest*
little	*less (noncount)*	*least*
many/more	*more*	*most*
few (count)	*fewer*	*fewest*

172   READING

Practice: Comparative and Superlative Adjectives

DIRECTIONS: Mark the choice that best completes the sentence.

1. The size ten envelopes are _____ for sending documents than those small ones.
   - (A) better
   - (B) more better
   - (C) best
   - (D) the best

   Ⓐ Ⓑ Ⓒ Ⓓ

2. You can buy the slightly _____ pens this time. We don't need the most expensive ones.
   - (A) cheap
   - (B) cheaper
   - (C) cheapest
   - (D) the cheapest

   Ⓐ Ⓑ Ⓒ Ⓓ

3. Paul is _____ candidate for that position. He hates speaking in public.
   - (A) the bad
   - (B) worse
   - (C) worst
   - (D) the worst

   Ⓐ Ⓑ Ⓒ Ⓓ

4. Our new handbook is _____ than our old one.
   - (A) interesting
   - (B) more interesting
   - (C) the interesting
   - (D) the most interesting

   Ⓐ Ⓑ Ⓒ Ⓓ

5. _____ month of the year is usually January or February.
   - (A) More slow
   - (B) Slower
   - (C) Slowest
   - (D) The slowest

   Ⓐ Ⓑ Ⓒ Ⓓ

6. Please don't call us between noon and one. That is _____ time of day.
   - (A) busy
   - (B) a busier
   - (C) busiest
   - (D) the busiest

   Ⓐ Ⓑ Ⓒ Ⓓ

TEXT COMPLETION **173**

7. Which room is _____ one, Conference Room A or B?
(A) more quiet
(B) quieter
(C) the quieter
(D) quietest

Ⓐ Ⓑ Ⓒ Ⓓ

8. The interior lights seem _____ than they usually do.
(A) more bright
(B) brighter
(C) brightest
(D) the brightest

Ⓐ Ⓑ Ⓒ Ⓓ

9. You'll get _____ response if you call rather than e-mail the board members.
(A) the quick
(B) a quicker
(C) quickest
(D) the quickest

Ⓐ Ⓑ Ⓒ Ⓓ

10. The flower bouquet was much _____ when it was delivered on Tuesday.
(A) beautiful
(B) more beautiful
(C) the prettiest
(D) more pretty

Ⓐ Ⓑ Ⓒ Ⓓ

174   READING

ADVERBS OF FREQUENCY

SINGLE WORDS

✔ Adverbs of frequency can be single words such as *always, seldom,* or *never.*

    ⇨ We put adverbs of frequency after the verb *be.*

        They are <u>rarely</u> late for meetings.

    ⇨ We put adverbs of frequency between the subject and the verb.

        She <u>never</u> acts rude, even when she has a lot of stress.

    ⇨ We put adverbs of frequency after the first auxiliary.

        She can <u>usually</u> be reached on her cell phone.

PHRASES

✔ Adverbs of frequency can also be phrases such as *on occasion* or *from time to time.*

    <u>On occasion</u>, the whole office likes having lunch together.

    The whole office likes having lunch together <u>from time to time</u>.

Practice: Adverbs of Frequency

DIRECTIONS: Mark the choice that best completes the sentence.

1. We _____ look at résumés sent by e-mail. You must deliver it by mail or in person.
   - (A) sometimes
   - (B) rarely
   - (C) never
   - (D) always

   Ⓐ   Ⓑ   Ⓒ   Ⓓ

2. I _____ buy a cup of coffee at work, but I usually bring one from home.
   - (A) always
   - (B) sometimes
   - (C) usually
   - (D) often

   Ⓐ   Ⓑ   Ⓒ   Ⓓ

3. It is our policy to give employees at least one warning. We _____ fire a person after only one minor mistake.
   - (A) sometimes
   - (B) never
   - (C) rarely
   - (D) frequently

   Ⓐ   Ⓑ   Ⓒ   Ⓓ

TEXT COMPLETION

4. Jack _____ brings his dog Spot to work with him. On most days, he leaves Spot in his backyard.
   (A) occasionally
   (B) frequently
   (C) almost always
   (D) often

   Ⓐ Ⓑ Ⓒ Ⓓ

5. I _____ forget to date forms. I must have been really tired yesterday.
   (A) sometimes
   (B) frequently
   (C) often
   (D) rarely

   Ⓐ Ⓑ Ⓒ Ⓓ

6. We _____ invite students to come into the office for a day. Ask our receptionist when our next session is.
   (A) never
   (B) rarely
   (C) frequently
   (D) almost never

   Ⓐ Ⓑ Ⓒ Ⓓ

7. The power _____ goes out in this building at about this time. We should ask an electrician to look at the wiring.
   (A) seldom
   (B) often
   (C) rarely
   (D) sometimes

   Ⓐ Ⓑ Ⓒ Ⓓ

8. I _____ walk to work. When it's raining I take the bus, though.
   (A) never
   (B) sometimes
   (C) almost always
   (D) occasionally

   Ⓐ Ⓑ Ⓒ Ⓓ

9. The boss _____ orders pizza for us on Fridays. He's away today, so we'll have to go out to eat.
   (A) never
   (B) rarely
   (C) usually
   (D) occasionally

   Ⓐ Ⓑ Ⓒ Ⓓ

10. I _____ do my taxes on time. This is the first year I sent them in late.
    (A) frequently
    (B) often
    (C) rarely
    (D) always

    Ⓐ Ⓑ Ⓒ Ⓓ

176 READING

VERBAL ADJECTIVES: PRESENT AND PAST PARTICIPLES

PRESENT PARTICIPLE

✔ We use the present participle adjective to describe a person or thing that is responsible for doing an action or causing a feeling (*burning food / a frightening movie*).

✔ We form the present participle by adding *-ing* to a verb (*interesting*).

PAST PARTICIPLE

✔ We use the past participle adjective to describe a person or thing that receives an action or feeling (*the burned food / the frightened moviegoers*).

✔ We form the past participle in three ways:

⇨ If the verb is regular, it looks just like the simple past: we add *-d* or *-ed* to it (*boiled*).

⇨ If the verb ends in *-ay*, it looks like the simple past: we change the *y* to *i* and then add *-d* (*paid*).

⇨ If the verb is irregular, it is the third form of that verb (*see, saw, seen*).

Practice: Verbal Adjectives

DIRECTIONS: Mark the choice that best completes the sentence.

1. The _____ photocopier is sitting on the floor underneath the table.   Ⓐ Ⓑ Ⓒ Ⓓ
   - (A) break
   - (B) broken
   - (C) breaking
   - (D) broke

2. We're interested in the woman _____ in the last chair of the first row.   Ⓐ Ⓑ Ⓒ Ⓓ
   - (A) seat
   - (B) seated
   - (C) seating
   - (D) sat

3. I found this _____ piece of paper on your desk. Why did you destroy the document?   Ⓐ Ⓑ Ⓒ Ⓓ
   - (A) tearing
   - (B) tear
   - (C) torn
   - (D) to tear

TEXT COMPLETION **177**

4. Did you hear the _____ news? Anna is going to
   be the new manager!
   (A) surprise
   (B) surprised
   (C) surprising
   (D) to surprise

   Ⓐ Ⓑ Ⓒ Ⓓ

5. Our _____ candidate has at least three years
   of work experience.
   (A) preference
   (B) prefer
   (C) preferred
   (D) preferring

   Ⓐ Ⓑ Ⓒ Ⓓ

6. The speech that Mark delivered was
   well _____.
   (A) plan
   (B) planned
   (C) planning
   (D) planner

   Ⓐ Ⓑ Ⓒ Ⓓ

7. We can expect _____ costs in lumber this
   month.
   (A) rise
   (B) risen
   (C) rising
   (D) rose

   Ⓐ Ⓑ Ⓒ Ⓓ

8. The city finally removed the _____ tree from
   the sidewalk today. It's been in the way since the storm.
   (A) fall
   (B) falling
   (C) fall down
   (D) fallen

   Ⓐ Ⓑ Ⓒ Ⓓ

9. Please don't make me go to another _____ sales
   meeting.
   (A) boredom
   (B) boring
   (C) bored
   (D) bore

   Ⓐ Ⓑ Ⓒ Ⓓ

10. My eyes are sore from making these _____
    calculations.
    (A) tired
    (B) tire
    (C) tiring
    (D) tire out

   Ⓐ Ⓑ Ⓒ Ⓓ

178   READING

CONTEXT

TEST STRATEGIES

Words do not stand alone. They depend on their context for meaning. When you complete the text in Part 6, you might have to read the whole passage to understand the context. You will need to understand how one word or phrase refers to another.

CONTEXT

WORD MEANING

✔ The meaning of a word must fit the meaning of the sentence.

> *Mr. Green is earning more money at his new job. He is very happy to be earning a higher _____.*

The sentence is about the money Mr. Green earns. The word *salary* would fit the blank.

PART OF SPEECH

✔ The part of speech of a word must fit the sentence.

> *Ms. Havermeyer is an extremely _____ accountant.*

The word *efficient*, or some other adjective, would fit the blank to modify the noun *account*.

PRONOUN

✔ A pronoun must match the gender and number of the noun and the part of speech required in the sentence.

> *My brother and I started this company while _____ were still in school.*

The pronoun *we* refers to *My brother and I*. The plural verb *were* limits the choice to a plural pronoun.

VERB TENSE

✔ A verb must match time of the context of the passage.

> *Although we were unable to finish the report today, we _____ it tomorrow.*

The time marker *tomorrow* indicates the blank requires a future verb *will finish*.

TEXT COMPLETION **179**

Practice: Context

DIRECTIONS: Mark the choice that best completes the sentence.

1. We expect to finish renovations on the building by the Ⓐ Ⓑ Ⓒ Ⓓ
   end of the month. In fact, work on the first and second
   floor offices _____ completed.
   (A) has been
   (B) have been
   (C) were
   (D) are

2. We hire only qualified individuals. All applicants Ⓐ Ⓑ Ⓒ Ⓓ
   must have a college degree and relevant _____.
   (A) experientially
   (B) experiential
   (C) experienced
   (D) experience

3. All our phone center employees are trained to provide Ⓐ Ⓑ Ⓒ Ⓓ
   top-quality customer service. We can rely on _____
   to treat each customer with respect and patience.
   (A) us
   (B) him
   (C) them
   (D) you

4. We hope to finish the plans for the conference by Ⓐ Ⓑ Ⓒ Ⓓ
   Friday. We _____ on them for a month.
   (A) are working
   (B) were working
   (C) will be working
   (D) have been working

5. It is important that all your work be accurate. Please Ⓐ Ⓑ Ⓒ Ⓓ
   check all documents for _____ before submitting
   the documents to your supervisor.
   (A) signatures
   (B) dates
   (C) errors
   (D) locations

180 READING

6. You may have to go to other parts of the city on errands for the office. _____ for bus fare and other minor expenses is kept in the top file drawer.
   (A) Coins
   (B) Cash
   (C) Bills
   (D) Dollars

   (A) (B) (C) (D)

7. Our current office space is not comfortable for our growing staff. It is too _____ and crowded.
   (A) furniture
   (B) rooms
   (C) small
   (D) size

   (A) (B) (C) (D)

8. My sister worked at this company for many years. _____ often spoke of the friendly, cooperative work environment.
   (A) It
   (B) He
   (C) She
   (D) They

   (A) (B) (C) (D)

9. Mr. Park will speak at next month's conference. He _____ to this when I communicated with him last week.
   (A) agrees
   (B) agreed
   (C) has agreed
   (D) will agree

   (A) (B) (C) (D)

10. More people than we expected are coming to the banquet. We are not sure if the dining room can hold such a large _____.
    (A) menu
    (B) crowd
    (C) person
    (D) carpet

    (A) (B) (C) (D)

TEXT COMPLETION 181

GRAMMAR TIP

Adjectives and Prepositions

Certain adjectives are followed by certain prepositions.

about	for	in	of
concerned	famous	interested	afraid
excited	ready		aware
happy	responsible		capable
worried	sorry		proud
			tired

They were worried about the low sales figures.
The report is ready for printing.
She is interested in international finance.
We are aware of the poor conditions in that area.

VOCABULARY TIP

Prefix –un

We can add –un to an adjective to form another adjective. It means *not*.

Adjective	Adjective	Definition
happy	unhappy	not happy
able	unable	not able
interesting	uninteresting	not interesting
comfortable	uncomfortable	not comfortable

If you are *unhappy* at your job, it is time to start looking for a new one.
They were *unable* to be at the meeting so they didn't hear the news.
No one wants to read an *uninteresting* article.
The hotel room was *uncomfortable* so we won't stay there again.

STRATEGY PRACTICE

DIRECTIONS: Read the following passages and choose the word or phrase that best completes the blanks.

Questions 1–3 refer to the following announcement.

Please welcome our newest _____, Claire Peterson. Ms. Peterson

1. (A) employ
    (B) employer
    (C) employee
    (D) employment

began working in the Accounting Department at the beginning of this week. Prior to joining our staff, she worked for the Simpson Group for eight years. While she _____ there, she wrote a

2. (A) is working
    (B) has worked
    (C) will work
    (D) was working

financial advice column for their monthly newsletter. We are very pleased that she has agreed to do the same for us. Ms. Peterson is enjoying her new position. "I _____ so many wonderful people

3. (A) have met
    (B) will have met
    (C) had met
    (D) meet

this week, " she says. "This seems like a fantastic place to work." We think so, too.

TEXT COMPLETION **183**

Questions 4–6 refer to the following e-mail.

To: Rita Marconi
From: Frank Howard
Subject: Company picnic

Rita,

The weather forecast for tomorrow is rain, so I think we _____

4. (A) can
   (B) might
   (C) would
   (D) should

postpone the company picnic. Of course, we could move it to an indoor location, but that wouldn't be the same. Please notify everyone that the picnic _____ place Friday of next week. Then call to change our

5. (A) will have taken
   (B) will take
   (C) takes
   (D) took

picnic site reservation. Mr. James, head of Park Reservations, has always been very helpful, so try to speak with him about it. When I _____ with him last time about the possibilities of changing dates

6. (A) speak
   (B) spoke
   (C) was speaking
   (D) have spoken

or locations, he was very accommodating, so I don't think there will be any problem. Thanks.

Frank

Questions 7–9 refer to the following memo.

To All Employees:

Mr. Sachimoto of the Tokyo office will be visiting our offices next week. This will be his first visit with us. Since he has _____ been here before, please do all you can to make sure

7. (A) never
   (B) often
   (C) seldom
   (D) occasionally

he leaves here with a good impression. While we plan to keep our guest very busy during the work day, we also want him to enjoy some _____ times with us. A reception is

8. (A) relax
   (B) relaxed
   (C) relaxing
   (D) relaxation

planned for Friday evening, and all staff are strongly encouraged to attend. While each of you may have other occasions to meet and talk with Mr. Sachimoto during the week, we consider Friday's event _____ of his visit. We hope to see all of you there.

9. (A) important
   (B) more important
   (C) the more important
   (D) the most important

TEXT COMPLETION **185**

Questions 10–12 refer to the following e-mail.

From: Rosemary Hall
To: Luis Vasquez
Subject: San Francisco Trip

Hi Rosemary,

I am traveling to San Francisco next week on company business, and I'd like your advice. I know you _____ travel there; in

10. (A) never
(B) rarely
(C) occasionally
(D) often

fact, you were in San Francisco five or six times last year, weren't you? I have a lot of recommendations for hotels and don't know how to choose. Which do you think is _____ hotel? I'm looking for something

11. (A) good
(B) better than
(C) best
(D) the best

comfortable and affordable. It doesn't have to be right downtown. Also, I'm thinking about taking the train instead of flying. Because of budget restraints, I need to find the least _____ way to

12. (A) cheap
(B) price
(C) expensive
(D) cost

travel, and plane tickets cost a great deal more. Have you ever taken the train? Is it comfortable? Reliable? Thanks for your help.

Luis

186 READING

Questions 13–15 refer to the following article.

Last night, the Mayor's Office _____ plans to start construction

13. (A) announce
(B) announces
(C) announced
(D) will announce

of a new soccer stadium early next year. "The condition of the current stadium is very dangerous," Mayor Wilson stated at last night's press conference. "The structure is falling apart, and renovation will be very costly. It's _____ to go ahead and build a new

14. (A) efficient
(B) more efficient
(C) more efficient than
(D) the most efficient

stadium than to try to repair the old one." The mayor said that construction of the new stadium should be completed in two years and expressed confidence that _____ would draw many new

15. (A) it
(B) he
(C) they
(D) we

businesses to the city.

TEXT COMPLETION **187**

Part 7:
Reading Comprehension

PART 7

Directions: In this part, you will read a selection of texts, such as magazine and newspaper articles, letters, and advertisements. Each text is followed by several questions. Select the best answer for each question and mark the letter (A), (B), (C), or (D) on your answer sheet.

Part 7 of the TOEIC test has two parts. In the first part (Questions 153–180) you will read a variety of passages, such as advertisements, forms, letters, e-mails, faxes, memos, graphs, charts, instructions, or notices, and answer two to five questions about each passage. In the second part (Questions 181–200), you will read sets of two passages each and then answer five questions about them. You will need to understand both passages in the set and the relationship between them in order to answer the questions.

A good reader uses a variety of strategies to understand any one passage or set of passages. In this section of the *Intermediate Course*, you will have the opportunity to practice applying your reading strategies to a variety of passage types. Each type of reading will illustrate how to use all the strategies efficiently together.

STRATEGY OVERVIEW

LANGUAGE STRATEGIES

- Words in Context – Use the context to determine the meanings of new words and answer vocabulary questions. Look at other words in the sentence or even the whole paragraph to understand what a word means.

TEST STRATEGIES

- Skimming – Move your eyes quickly over the whole passage looking for general information. This will help you figure out the main idea and answer general information questions. For the double passages, it will help you get an idea of the relationship between the two passages and how they might be the same or different.

- Scanning – Move your eyes quickly over the passage to find specific information. This will help you answer detail questions. For the double passages, use scanning to check whether the information in one passage contradicts or negates the information in the other passage.

- Reading Fast – Read fast to get the whole idea of the passage. Reading fast will help you finish the passages faster, retain all the new information, and have more time to answer the questions.

---

188   READING

ADVERTISEMENTS

READING STRATEGIES

- **Skimming** and **scanning** are good strategies for reading advertisements. You will quickly look for the answers to these questions:

    What is being advertised?
    Who is it for?

- **Reading fast** is a very important skill to develop. Reading every word in an advertisement is not necessary. When you skim advertisements for the general idea and scan them for specific information, you will learn to read them faster.

Practice these reading strategies with the advertisements on the following pages. (Note that the short form of *advertisement* is *ad*.)

Advertisement 1

Sale! Sale! Sale!

McGruder's Department Store announces its biggest sale
of the year. You'll find fantastic savings throughout the store.

25% off all men's and women's business suits

25% off all men's and women's shoes

50% off all women's summer clothes

Don't miss out on this great opportunity to get
stylish designer items at bargain prices. With prices like these,
you can't afford not to shop.

Now through Saturday at all McGruder's locations:

**Park Avenue Mall   Springfield Center   Downtown
Manchester Depot**

Open Monday–Saturday, 8:30 A.M.–9:00 P.M.
Closed Sunday

SKIMMING Look quickly at the advertisement to answer these questions.

1. What is on sale?   (A) (B)
   (A) Business supplies
   (B) Clothes

2. Who is the sale for?   (A) (B) (C)
   (A) Men
   (B) Women
   (C) Both men and women

SCANNING Mark the words that appear in the ad, and circle them in the ad.

3. (A) bathing suit   (A) (B)
   (B) business suit

4. (A) summer   (A) (B)
   (B) winter

190   READING

5. (A) department   Ⓐ   Ⓑ
    (B) apartment

6. Find and circle these days in the ad. Some may appear more than once.
Monday   Saturday   Sunday

CONTEXT Find these words and phrases, and guess their meanings in this advertisement.

7. What does "25% off" mean?   Ⓐ   Ⓑ
    (A) It costs $25.
    (B) It costs one quarter less than the usual price.

8. What does "Now through Saturday" mean?   Ⓐ   Ⓑ
    (A) Beginning today and ending on Saturday
    (B) Beginning on Saturday

READING FAST

Read the letter as fast as you can. How long did it take?

_____ minutes _____ seconds

READING COMPREHENSION Mark the best answer.

9. What is not on sale?   Ⓐ   Ⓑ   Ⓒ   Ⓓ
    (A) Men's shoes
    (B) Women's business suits
    (C) Men's summer clothes
    (D) Women's shoes

10. What is the first day of the sale?   Ⓐ   Ⓑ   Ⓒ   Ⓓ
    (A) Today
    (B) On Saturday
    (C) On Sunday
    (D) Next week

11. How much do women's summer clothes cost?   Ⓐ   Ⓑ   Ⓒ   Ⓓ
    (A) $50 each
    (B) $50 less than the usual price
    (C) Half the usual price
    (D) One quarter of the usual price

12. The word "Mall" in line 12 is closest in meaning to   Ⓐ   Ⓑ   Ⓒ   Ⓓ
    (A) Shopping area
    (B) Parking lot
    (C) Food stall
    (D) Pedestrian track

Advertisement 2

Grand Opening!

For your convenience,

The State Street Bank

is opening a new full-service branch at the City Airport. Now it will be easier than ever to take care of all your banking needs as you leave or return from your trips.

Join us at our new location for our

Grand Opening

next

Saturday, September 15, from 1:00–4:00 P.M.

FOOD!

ENTERTAINMENT ACTIVITIES FOR THE WHOLE FAMILY

MUSIC

There will be food, music, and a variety of entertainment activities for the whole family. Representatives of local TV station WXYZ will be there to report on the event. So come on by and bring the whole family. Customer service specialists will be on hand to explain all the services our bank has to offer.

Find out about:
- The special benefits of opening a State Street checking or savings account
- How to qualify for our special low-interest loans
- State Street's custom-designed financial planning services

Prizes! Prizes! Prizes!

There will be prizes for the first 50 customers to open a checking or savings account at the new branch. In addition, all Grand Opening guests will be automatically entered in our Grand Prize Drawing. You could win a Caribbean Cruise for two!

See you there!

SKIMMING Look quickly at the advertisement to answer this question.

1. What kind of information does this advertisement give? (A) (B)
   (A) A list of things for sale
   (B) An explanation of an event

SCANNING Look quickly at the advertisement to answer these questions.

2. What is the name of the bank? (A) (B)
   (A) State Street Bank
   (B) City Bank

3. What is the name of the airport? (A) (B)
   (A) City Airport
   (B) Bank Street Airport

4. What hours do you see in the advertisement? (A) (B)
   (A) 1:00–4:00 A.M.
   (B) 1:00–4:00 P.M.

CONTEXT Find these words and phrases, and guess their meanings in this advertisement.

5. branch (A) (B)
   (A) part of a tree
   (B) a business location

6. grand opening (A) (B)
   (A) a special celebration for a new business
   (B) the hours that a bank does business

READING FAST

Read the letter as fast as you can. How long did it take?

_____ minutes _____ seconds

READING COMPREHENSION Mark the best answer.

7. What is being advertised? (A) (B) (C) (D)
   (A) A bank
   (B) A restaurant
   (C) A concert
   (D) A travel agency

8. Where will the grand opening take place? (A) (B) (C) (D)
   (A) On State Street
   (B) At the airport
   (C) At a TV station
   (D) In a park

9. The word "Representatives" in paragraph 2, line 2, is closest in meaning to   Ⓐ Ⓑ Ⓒ Ⓓ
   (A)   Legislators
   (B)   Staff
   (C)   Siblings
   (D)   Specialists

10. When will the grand opening take place?   Ⓐ Ⓑ Ⓒ Ⓓ
    (A)   In the morning
    (B)   In the afternoon
    (C)   In the evening
    (D)   At night

Advertisement 3

Busy downtown law firm seeks administrative assistant with 3–5 years' experience working in a law office. Must be proficient in the use of word processing and database programs and be familiar with common legal documents. Must have a good telephone manner and a pleasant appearance. Working knowledge of Spanish a plus. Duties include word processing, management of client database, maintaining files, directing phone calls, and assisting clients who come to our office. We offer a competitive salary, health insurance, and paid vacation, as well as opportunity for advancement. To apply, call Ms. Ortiz, Director of Human Resources, between 10 and 4. Must be able to provide three references and proof of employment eligibility.

SKIMMING Look quickly at the advertisement to answer this question.

1. What is this advertisement for?   Ⓐ Ⓑ
    (A)   A job opening
    (B)   An office for rent

SCANNING Look quickly at the advertisement to complete these questions.

2. Find and circle these numbers in the ad.
    3–5   10 and 4

3. What is 3–5?   (A) (B)
  - (A) The number of people who work in the office
  - (B) The years of experience required for the job

4. What is 10 and 4?   (A) (B)
  - (A) The daily hours of the job
  - (B) The hours to apply for the job

CONTEXT Find these words and phrases, and guess their meanings in this advertisement.

5. legal documents   (A) (B)
  - (A) papers that lawyers write
  - (B) job application forms

6. telephone manner   (A) (B)
  - (A) a way to speak on the phone
  - (B) a type of phone

7. paid vacation   (A) (B)
  - (A) your job pays all your vacation expenses
  - (B) you continue to receive your salary while on vacation

8. firm   (A) (B)
  - (A) hard
  - (B) a business or company

> **READING FAST**
>
> Read the letter as fast as you can. How long did it take?
>
> _____ minutes _____ seconds

READING COMPREHENSION Mark the best answer.

9. What kind of position is advertised?   (A) (B) (C) (D)
  - (A) Director of Human Resources
  - (B) Lawyer
  - (C) Administrative assistant
  - (D) Computer programmer

10. What is one skill required for this job?   (A) (B) (C) (D)
  - (A) The ability to talk pleasantly on the telephone
  - (B) The ability to write legal documents
  - (C) The ability to develop computer programs
  - (D) The ability to find new clients

11. What is a benefit of this job? Ⓐ Ⓑ Ⓒ Ⓓ
   (A) They will pay for your vacation expenses.
   (B) You can make all the phone calls you want.
   (C) You only have to work from 10–4.
   (D) They will pay for your health insurance.

12. The word "Duties" in line 8 is closest in meaning to Ⓐ Ⓑ Ⓒ Ⓓ
   (A) Taxes
   (B) Benefits
   (C) Classes
   (D) Responsibilities

FORMS

READING STRATEGIES

- **Skimming** is an important strategy to use when you read different forms.

  You want to know right away:

Who wrote it	*What* is it for?
Who is it for?	*Why* do I need to read it?
What kind of form is it?	

- **Scanning** helps you look for specific information. Use the Reading Comprehension questions to guide your scanning.

- **Using context** is a way to find the meanings of new words. Look at the other words on the form. Then look at the new word in its context and try to guess what it means.

- **Reading fast** is very helpful. Just like advertisements, forms are often short readings. Good readers skim and scan quickly to learn the most important information on the form.

Practice these reading strategies with the forms on the following pages.

Form 1

OUR TOWN SPORTS CLUB

Membership Application

Name _____

Address _____

_____

E-mail _____

Home phone _____ Work phone _____ Cell phone _____

Occupation _____

Type of membership (check one) Individual ($500) ___ Family ($1,200) ___

Student ($375) ___ Trial (one month only) ($100) ___

Method of payment (check one)   Cash ___   Check ___   Credit card ___

Credit card number _____ Expiration date _____

Signature (for credit card payments only) _____

Please check any of the following activities that you may wish to participate in. We will forward the necessary information to you.

Teams:
___ Tennis   ___ Squash   ___ Swimming

Classes:
___ Aerobics   ___ Water Aerobics   ___ Swimming   ___ Squash
___ School vacation camps for kids

SKIMMING Mark the words you see at the top of the form.

1. (A) Membership application   Ⓐ   Ⓑ
   (B) Job application

2. (A) Sports equipment   Ⓐ   Ⓑ
   (B) Sports club

SCANNING Look quickly at the application to complete these questions.

3. Look at the form. Circle the names of the different types of membership.

4. Look at the form. Which type of payment is not   Ⓐ   Ⓑ   Ⓒ   Ⓓ
   mentioned?
   (A) Cash
   (B) Credit card
   (C) Money order
   (D) Check

CONTEXT Find these words, and guess their meanings on this form.

5. occupation   Ⓐ   Ⓑ
   (A) job or profession
   (B) an activity to pass the time

6. trial   Ⓐ   Ⓑ
   (A) try doing something to see if you like it
   (B) a legal process

READING FAST

Read the letter as fast as you can. How long did it take?

_____ minutes _____ seconds

READING COMPREHENSION Mark the best answer.

7. What is this form for?   Ⓐ   Ⓑ   Ⓒ   Ⓓ
   (A) Getting a new telephone number
   (B) Joining a club
   (C) Applying for a job
   (D) Ordering sports equipment

8. Which is the least expensive type of membership?   Ⓐ   Ⓑ   Ⓒ   Ⓓ
   (A) Individual
   (B) Family
   (C) Student
   (D) Trial

READING COMPREHENSION **199**

9. How many different types of payment are accepted? Ⓐ Ⓑ Ⓒ Ⓓ
   (A) One
   (B) Two
   (C) Three
   (D) Four

10. Who has to sign the form? Ⓐ Ⓑ Ⓒ Ⓓ
   (A) Everybody
   (B) People who pay by credit card
   (C) People who pay by check
   (D) The whole family

11. The word "Method" in line 11 is closest in meaning to Ⓐ Ⓑ Ⓒ Ⓓ
   (A) Technique
   (B) System
   (C) Process
   (D) Type

Form 2

How did you enjoy your stay?

Help us serve you better by filling out this form and leaving it in your room.

	good	*fair*	*poor*
1. Your room			
Cleanliness of room	☐	☐	☐
Comfort of beds	☐	☐	☐
Maid service	☐	☐	☐
2. Room service			
Menu selection	☐	☐	☐
Speed of service	☐	☐	☐
Prices	☐	☐	☐
3. Front desk			
Helpfulness of staff	☐	☐	☐
4. Fitness room and pool			
Types of exercise machines	☐	☐	☐
Pool hours	☐	☐	☐
Cleanliness of lockers	☐	☐	☐

How can we improve? Please write your comments or suggestions here.

_____

_____

Thank you for your time.
We hope to see you again soon!

SKIMMING Look quickly at the form to answer this question.

1. What kind of form is this? Ⓐ Ⓑ
   - (A) An application
   - (B) A questionnaire

SCANNING Mark the words and phrases that appear in the form, and circle them on the form.

2. (A) men Ⓐ Ⓑ
   - (B) menu

3. (A) maid   Ⓐ   Ⓑ
    (B) made

4. (A) front desk   Ⓐ   Ⓑ
    (B) office desk

5. (A) customer service   Ⓐ   Ⓑ
    (B) room service

CONTEXT Find these words and phrases, and guess their meanings on this form.

6. room service   Ⓐ   Ⓑ
    (A) fixing broken things in a hotel room
    (B) delivering meals to a hotel room

7. stay   Ⓐ   Ⓑ
    (A) a visit to a hotel
    (B) remain in one place

READING FAST

Read the letter as fast as you can. How long did it take?

_____ minutes _____ seconds

READING COMPREHENSION Mark the best answer.

8. Where would you see this form?   Ⓐ   Ⓑ   Ⓒ   Ⓓ
    (A) At a restaurant
    (B) At an office
    (C) At a furniture store
    (D) At a hotel

9. What should you do with this form?   Ⓐ   Ⓑ   Ⓒ   Ⓓ
    (A) Leave it in your room
    (B) Put it on the front desk
    (C) Give it to the maid
    (D) Send it by mail

10. What is one thing that is not asked about?   Ⓐ   Ⓑ   Ⓒ   Ⓓ
    (A) Menu selection
    (B) Comfort of beds
    (C) Cleanliness of front desk
    (D) Speed of room service

11. The word "selection" in line 9 is closest in meaning to   Ⓐ   Ⓑ   Ⓒ   Ⓓ
    (A) collection
    (B) mixture
    (C) selectivity
    (D) choice

202 READING

Form 3

Vacation Leave Request Form

TickTackSystems, Inc.

Vacation Leave Request Form

Date: *April 1*

Name: *Daniel Greenwood*

Position: *Research Assistant*

Department: *Marketing*

Supervisor: *Samantha Smith*

Dates you are requesting: *May 16–20*

Type of leave you are requesting: _X_ paid ___ unpaid

Please turn this form in to the Human Resources Director
at least 3 weeks before requested leave date.

SKIMMING Find and circle these words on the form. Some may appear more than once.

1. vacation   leave   request

SCANNING Find and circle the following.

2. Find and circle these names.
   Daniel Greenwood   Samantha Smith

3. Find and circle these job titles.
   Research Assistant   Human Resources Director

4. Find and circle these dates.
   April 1   May 16–20

CONTEXT Find these words, and guess their meanings on this form.

5. leave   (A)   (B)
   (A) exit a room
   (B) time off from work

READING COMPREHENSION   203

6. request   Ⓐ   Ⓑ
   (A) ask for something
   (B) do something again

READING FAST

Read the letter as fast as you can. How long did it take?

_____ minutes _____ seconds

READING COMPREHENSION Mark the best answer.

7. What is this form for?   Ⓐ   Ⓑ   Ⓒ   Ⓓ
   (A) Asking for days off from work
   (B) Getting travel information
   (C) Making plane reservations
   (D) Paying for a trip

8. What is Mr. Greenwood's job?   Ⓐ   Ⓑ   Ⓒ   Ⓓ
   (A) Marketing supervisor
   (B) Human resources officer
   (C) Research assistant
   (D) Travel agent

9. When did Mr. Greenwood fill out this form?   Ⓐ   Ⓑ   Ⓒ   Ⓓ
   (A) Three weeks ago
   (B) Between May 16 and May 23
   (C) On April 1
   (D) On May 16

10. Who should Mr. Greenwood give this form to?   Ⓐ   Ⓑ   Ⓒ   Ⓓ
    (A) Samantha Smith
    (B) His assistant
    (C) A marketing researcher
    (D) The human resources director

11. The word "Leave" in line 1 is closest in meaning to   Ⓐ   Ⓑ   Ⓒ   Ⓓ
    (A) Exit
    (B) Time off
    (C) Removal
    (D) Project

204 READING

LETTERS, E-MAIL, FAXES, AND MEMOS

READING STRATEGIES

- **Skimming** is the way to quickly find information.

  Who is the information for?   *When* was it sent?
  Who sent it?

- **Scanning** helps you find specific information. Always check the Reading Comprehension questions and answer choices first. Scan for specific information.

  Why did they send the   *What* do they want?
     information?

- **Using context** helps you find the meanings of new words by looking at the other words and sentences surrounding the words. Business letters may have more unfamiliar words than letters from friends.

- **Reading fast** is very helpful. Written forms of communication can be short and simple or long and complicated. When you practice the reading strategies, you will improve your speed and get the necessary information at the same time.

Practice these reading strategies with the letters, e-mail, faxes, and memos on the following pages.

Letters, E-mail, Faxes, and Memos 1

Merry Marketing Company
244 Merry Way
Boston, MA 01106

July 17, 20__

To whom it may concern:

Alice Newbold has worked for the Merry Marketing Company for the past five years. She started as an administrative assistant and worked her way up to Assistant Director of Research, in which position she has been working for two years.

Ms. Newbold is a highly motivated and industrious worker. She is willing to put in long hours if necessary to get the job done. She is also a skilled manager and works well with those she supervises.

Ms. Newbold has contributed a great deal to this company. We will be sorry to lose her. I can highly recommend her for any position requiring independence, creativity, and supervisory skills.

Sincerely,

James Jones

James Jones, Director

SKIMMING Look quickly at the letter to answer these questions.

1. Who signed this letter?   Ⓐ Ⓑ
   (A) Alice Newbold
   (B) James Jones

2. Who is the letter about?   Ⓐ Ⓑ
   (A) Alice Newbold
   (B) James Jones

SCANNING Mark the words and phrases that appear in the form, and circle them on the form.

3. (A) nursing assistant   Ⓐ Ⓑ
   (B) administrative assistant

4. (A) Assistant Director   Ⓐ Ⓑ
   (B) Movie Director

5. (A) worker
   (B) walker   Ⓐ Ⓑ

6. (A) request
   (B) recommend   Ⓐ Ⓑ

CONTEXT Find these words and phrases, and guess their meanings in this letter.

7. To whom it may concern   Ⓐ Ⓑ
   (A) This letter is for a specific person.
   (B) This letter is for any person who is interested in it.

8. worked her way up   Ⓐ Ⓑ
   (A) She worked hard and got a higher job position.
   (B) She went upstairs.

9. contributed   Ⓐ Ⓑ
   (A) given
   (B) taken

READING FAST

Read the letter as fast as you can. How long did it take?

_____ minutes _____ seconds

READING COMPREHENSION Mark the best answer.

10. What is the purpose of this letter?   Ⓐ Ⓑ Ⓒ Ⓓ
    (A) To ask for a job
    (B) To describe a company
    (C) To recommend an employee for a new job
    (D) To advertise a position

11. The word "motivated" in paragraph 2, line 1, is   Ⓐ Ⓑ Ⓒ Ⓓ
    closest in meaning to
    (A) committed
    (B) irritated
    (C) intelligent
    (D) mobile

12. What has Alice Newbold done for the past five years?   Ⓐ Ⓑ Ⓒ Ⓓ
    (A) She has been an administrative assistant.
    (B) She has worked for a marketing company.
    (C) She has looked for a job.
    (D) She has supervised James Jones.

READING COMPREHENSION   **207**

Letters, E-mail, Faxes, and Memos 2

To: Bob Smith
From: Joyce Miller
Subject: meeting change
Date: March 20, 20__

Bob,
The time for the meeting tomorrow has been changed from 9:00 to 12:30. I'm sorry about this, but it turns out it's the only time everyone can meet. I know you have another meeting later in the afternoon, but I expect ours won't last more than one hour, so it shouldn't interfere with that schedule. The good news is that since it's a lunchtime meeting, the office will provide sandwiches and coffee for everyone. I'll make sure that we order from the Garden House since I know that's your favorite sandwich shop. We'll meet in the training room on the fifth floor. Please don't forget to bring ten copies of your budget report. Thanks. See you tomorrow.

Joyce

SKIMMING Look quickly at the e-mail to answer these questions.

1. Who is the e-mail for?
   To: _____

2. Who sent the e-mail?
   From: _____

3. What is the e-mail about?
   Subject: _____

SCANNING Find these words and phrases about time in the e-mail, and circle them. Some may appear more than once.

4. March 20   tomorrow   9:00   12:30   one hour   lunchtime

CONTEXT Find these words, and guess their meanings in this e-mail.

5. change   (A) (B)
   (A) make different
   (B) coins

6. last   (A) (B)
   (A) opposite of first
   (B) take time

7. budget   (A) (B)
   (A) a plan for spending money
   (B) a form of transportation

READING FAST

Read the letter as fast as you can. How long did it take?

_____ minutes _____ seconds

READING COMPREHENSION Mark the best answer.

8. When is the meeting?   (A) (B) (C) (D)
   (A) On March 20 from 9–12:30
   (B) On March 20 at 12:30
   (C) On March 21 from 9–12:30
   (D) On March 21 from 12:30–1:30

9. What should Bob bring to the meeting?   (A) (B) (C) (D)
   (A) Sandwiches
   (B) Coffee
   (C) Copies of his report
   (D) Training material

10. What will they probably discuss at the meeting?   (A) (B) (C) (D)
    (A) The budget
    (B) Lunch
    (C) Training programs
    (D) Schedules

11. The word "provide" in paragraph 1, line 6, is closest in meaning to   (A) (B) (C) (D)
    (A) warm
    (B) sell
    (C) make
    (D) supply

READING COMPREHENSION **209**

Letters, E-mail, Faxes, and Memos 3

> To: All staff
> From: Sharon Lee, Office Manager
> Re: Office supplies
>
> In order to better manage the office supplies, I have developed a new system. From now on, the supply closet will remain locked at all times. The only people authorized to have keys to the closet are myself and my assistant, Mr. Whitehead. If you wish to request supplies, please get a supply request form from Mr. Whitehead. Please submit your form 24 hours in advance of when you need your supplies. We promise to get your supplies to you within 24 hours as long as we have them on hand. It may take up to a week to get supplies that need to be ordered.
>
> I am sure you will understand the necessity of this new system. In the past we have run out of essential supplies too often. This system will help me keep track of our supplies, and I will know when to order more. By following this system, you will always have what you need when you need it. Thank you for your cooperation.

SKIMMING Look quickly at the memo to answer these questions.

1. Who is this memo for?   Ⓐ   Ⓑ
   (A) All staff
   (B) Sharon Lee

2. Who is it from?   Ⓐ   Ⓑ
   (A) The company director
   (B) The office manager

3. What is it about?   Ⓐ   Ⓑ
   (A) Office supplies
   (B) Office schedules

SCANNING Mark the words and phrases that appear in the form, and circle them on the form. Some may appear more than once.

4. (A) resistant   Ⓐ   Ⓑ
   (B) assistant

5. (A) myself   Ⓐ   Ⓑ
   (B) yourself

6. (A) manage   Ⓐ   Ⓑ
   (B) damage

7. (A) require   Ⓐ   Ⓑ
   (B) request

CONTEXT Find these words and phrases, and guess their meanings in this memo.

8. authorized   Ⓐ   Ⓑ
   - (A) have permission
   - (B) wrote a book

9. submit   Ⓐ   Ⓑ
   - (A) give
   - (B) tell about

10. in advance   Ⓐ   Ⓑ
   - (A) very skilled
   - (B) before

11. keep track of   Ⓐ   Ⓑ
   - (A) ride a train
   - (B) know about

READING FAST

Read the letter as fast as you can. How long did it take?

_____ minutes _____ seconds

READING COMPREHENSION Mark the best answer.

12. What is the purpose of this memo?   Ⓐ   Ⓑ   Ⓒ   Ⓓ
   - (A) To order new supplies
   - (B) To explain a new system
   - (C) To introduce Mr. Whitehead
   - (D) To describe where supplies are kept

13. Who has keys to the supply closet?   Ⓐ   Ⓑ   Ⓒ   Ⓓ
   - (A) Only Ms. Lee
   - (B) Only Mr. Whitehead
   - (C) Both Ms. Lee and her assistant
   - (D) All office staff

14. The word "essential" in paragraph 2, line 2,   Ⓐ   Ⓑ   Ⓒ   Ⓓ
    is closest in meaning to
   - (A) dispensable
   - (B) expensive
   - (C) forgotten
   - (D) necessary

15. How can a staff member get office supplies?   Ⓐ   Ⓑ   Ⓒ   Ⓓ
   - (A) By filling out a form
   - (B) By asking for the key to the supply closet
   - (C) By ordering them from the supply company
   - (D) By calling Ms. Lee

READING COMPREHENSION   **211**

TABLES, INDEXES, AND CHARTS

READING STRATEGIES

- **Skimming** helps you find out generally:

  What kind of a table, index, or chart is it?
  What is the title of this table or chart?
  How is the information arranged?

- **Scanning** helps you find specific information:

  Where is the number/word I need?
  What is the page I need?
  What is the relationship of the table headings?

- **Using context** is a way to find the meanings of new words by looking at and comparing categories. Remember to look at the selection as a whole. Don't worry if you don't understand every word. When you finish the exercises, you will understand many new words.

- **Reading fast** is the best way to read and understand tables, indexes, and charts. It is not necessary to read every word and number in a table, index, or chart. Therefore, these selections make excellent practice for skimming and scanning.

Practice these reading strategies with the tables, indexes, and charts on the following pages.

Tables, Indexes, and Charts 1

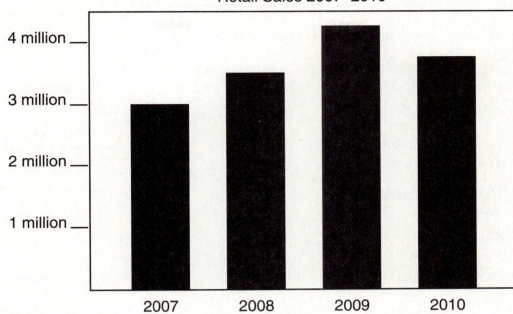

Please note: This graph represents domestic retail sales only. For figures regarding overseas retail sales for the years 2007–2010, please see page 12.

SKIMMING Look quickly at the graph to answer these questions.

1. What is this graph about? Ⓐ Ⓑ
   - (A) How much a company sold
   - (B) How much a company spent

2. How many years does it cover? Ⓐ Ⓑ Ⓒ Ⓓ
   - (A) One
   - (B) Two
   - (C) Three
   - (D) Four

SCANNING Find and circle the following.

3. Find and circle all the numbers that tell an amount of money.

4. Find and circle all the years.

CONTEXT Find this word, and guess its meaning in this graph.

5. retail Ⓐ Ⓑ
   - (A) sold in a store
   - (B) sold twice

READING COMPREHENSION 213

> **READING FAST**
>
> Read the letter as fast as you can. How long did it take?
>
> _____ minutes _____ seconds

READING COMPREHENSION Mark the best answer.

6. How many dollars in sales did the company
   make in 2008?   Ⓐ   Ⓑ   Ⓒ   Ⓓ
   (A) 3 million
   (B) 3.5 million
   (C) 3.75 million
   (D) 4.25 million

7. Which year had the highest sales?   Ⓐ   Ⓑ   Ⓒ   Ⓓ
   (A) 2007
   (B) 2008
   (C) 2009
   (D) 2010

8. In which year did the company have 3.5 million
   dollars in sales?   Ⓐ   Ⓑ   Ⓒ   Ⓓ
   (A) 2007
   (B) 2008
   (C) 2009
   (D) 2010

Tables, Indexes, and Charts 2

FREEDONIA ISLAND
Average Temperatures (Fahrenheit)
You may find the following information useful when planning your trip to
Freedonia. Please keep in mind that these are average temperatures only
and that the weather can vary a great deal.

	January		July	
	high	low	high	low
Mountain region	32	18	75	51
Coast	70	55	85	61
Capital city	57	32	75	58

214   READING

SKIMMING Look quickly at the chart to answer these questions.

1. What is the highest temperature you see? _____

2. What is the lowest temperature you see? _____

3. How many different places are mentioned? _____

SCANNING Find these words on the chart, and circle them.

4. temperature   high   low   January   July

CONTEXT Find these words, and guess their meanings in this chart.

5. average   (A) (B)
   (A) normal
   (B) something to drink

6. region   (A) (B)
   (A) a type of church
   (B) an area

READING FAST

Read the letter as fast as you can. How long did it take?

_____ minutes _____ seconds

READING COMPREHENSION Mark the best answer.

7. Where is the average high temperature 75 degrees
   in July?   (A) (B) (C) (D)
   (A)   In the mountain region only
   (B)   On the coast only
   (C)   In the capital city only
   (D)   In both the mountains and the capital city

8. What is the average high temperature on the
   coast in January?   (A) (B) (C) (D)
   (A)   55
   (B)   61
   (C)   70
   (D)   85

9. What is the coldest temperature in the
   mountain region?   (A) (B) (C) (D)
   (A)   18
   (B)   32
   (C)   51
   (D)   55

READING COMPREHENSION   **215**

10. Which is the warmest region of the island? Ⓐ Ⓑ Ⓒ Ⓓ
    (A) The mountains
    (B) The coast
    (C) The capital city
    (D) They are all the same

11. The word "Coast" in column 1, row 4, is closest in Ⓐ Ⓑ Ⓒ Ⓓ
    meaning to
    (A) Pond
    (B) Seaside
    (C) Rural
    (D) Riverbed

Tables, Indexes, and Charts 3

> ### *Emerald Airlines*
> Sale prices* between this city and:
>
> | | |
> |---|---|
> | Vancouver | $375 |
> | Los Angeles | $350 |
> | San Francisco | $225 |
> | Tokyo | $600 |
> | Seoul | $725 |
> | Honolulu | $525 |
>
> *Prices are good until June 30 and are for one-way
> economy class tickets. Round-trip tickets are twice
> the one-way fare.
>
> *Sale does not apply to business and first class tickets.*
> Make your reservation by visiting our website. All major
> credit cards are accepted. Tickets can also be reserved by
> calling 1-800-555-9942. A 5% surcharge applies to all
> reservations made by phone.

SKIMMING Look quickly at the chart to answer these questions.

1. What are the numbers about? Ⓐ Ⓑ Ⓒ
   (A) Distances
   (B) Prices
   (C) Time

2. What company's name is on the chart? _____

3. How many city names are on the chart? _____

SCANNING Find the following.

4. Look for the asterisks (*), and circle them. There are two.

5. Find these different ticket types, and circle them.

one-way   round-trip   economy class   business   first class

CONTEXT Find these words, and guess their meanings in this chart.

6. good   Ⓐ   Ⓑ
   (A)   the opposite of bad
   (B)   can be used

7. fare   Ⓐ   Ⓑ
   (A)   price
   (B)   food

8. apply   Ⓐ   Ⓑ
   (A)   be related to
   (B)   complete a form

READING FAST

Read the letter as fast as you can. How long did it take?

_____ minutes _____ seconds

READING COMPREHENSION Mark the best answer.

9. What is on sale?   Ⓐ   Ⓑ   Ⓒ   Ⓓ
   (A)   Economy class tickets only
   (B)   Business class tickets only
   (C)   Business and first class tickets
   (D)   All classes of tickets

10. Which city has a fare of $725?   Ⓐ   Ⓑ   Ⓒ   Ⓓ
   (A)   Los Angeles
   (B)   Tokyo
   (C)   Seoul
   (D)   Honolulu

11. Which is the cheapest city to travel to?   Ⓐ   Ⓑ   Ⓒ   Ⓓ
   (A)   Vancouver
   (B)   Los Angeles
   (C)   San Francisco
   (D)   Honolulu

12. How much is a round-trip ticket to Tokyo? (A) (B) (C) (D)
    (A) $225
    (B) $600
    (C) $725
    (D) $1,200

13. The word "good" in line 9, is closest in (A) (B) (C) (D)
meaning to
    (A) changing
    (B) valuable
    (C) excellent
    (D) valid

INSTRUCTIONS AND NOTICES

READING STRATEGIES

- **Skimming** is the way to find general information quickly.

  What are the instructions or notices for?
  How many steps are there in the instructions?
  Do they seem easy or complicated? Could I follow them myself?
  What kind of information do the notices give me?

- **Scanning** helps you find specific information quickly.

  Will I need any tools to follow the instructions?
  Are all the parts accounted for? Is anything missing?
  What kinds of items or places do the notices mention?
  What locations should I look for?

- **Using context** helps you find the meanings of new words by looking at them in context. Instructions and notices may have more unfamiliar words than letters from friends.

- **Reading fast** is very helpful. Instructions and notices can be short and simple or long and complicated. When you practice the reading strategies, you will improve your speed and get the necessary information at the same time.

Practice these reading strategies with the instructions and notices on the following pages.

READING COMPREHENSION **219**

Instructions and Notices 1

The Acme Guarantee

Our products are fully guaranteed for one year from the date of purchase. If you are not satisfied for any reason, you can return the product directly to us for a complete refund. Simply mail it back to us at:

Acme Corporation
1500 State Street
Big Falls, CA 12345

Make sure you include the receipt with the date and place of purchase. You will receive a refund check in 8–12 weeks.
If you would like to exchange your product for another similar one of equal value, please contact our Customer Service office at 800-555-8765 for instructions. Customer Service representatives are available to serve you 24 hours a day.

SKIMMING Look quickly at the instructions to answer these questions.

1. Do these instructions include a street address? (A) (B)
   (A) Yes
   (B) No

2. Do these instructions include an e-mail address? (A) (B)
   (A) Yes
   (B) No

3. Do these instructions include a telephone number? (A) (B)
   (A) Yes
   (B) No

SCANNING Find the following.

4. Underline all the numbers you see in the instructions.

5. Find these words and phrases in the instructions, and circle them.
   mail   receive   check   Customer Service

CONTEXT Find these words, and guess their meanings in these instructions.

6. refund (A) (B)
   (A) repayment
   (B) gift

7. satisfied   (A) (B)
    (A) happy with
    (B) not hungry

8. receipt   (A) (B)
    (A) instructions for cooking
    (B) paper with information about a purchase

READING FAST

Read the letter as fast as you can. How long did it take?

_____ minutes _____ seconds

READING COMPREHENSION Mark the best answer.

9. If a customer is not satisfied with the product, what
should he or she do?   (A) (B) (C) (D)
    (A) Return it to the place of purchase
    (B) Send it to the Acme Corporation
    (C) Call Customer Service
    (D) Write a letter to the Acme Corporation

10. What information has to be included on
the receipt?   (A) (B) (C) (D)
    (A) The customer's home address
    (B) The color and size of the product
    (C) The telephone number of the store
    (D) The name of the store where the product was bought

11. What will happen in 8 to 12 weeks?   (A) (B) (C) (D)
    (A) You will get your money back.
    (B) A Customer Service representative will call you.
    (C) The Acme Corporation will send you a new product.
    (D) You will get a receipt.

12. The word "refund" in paragraph 1, line 4, is closest in
meaning to   (A) (B) (C) (D)
    (A) credit
    (B) new
    (C) reimbursement
    (D) blank

READING COMPREHENSION **221**

Instructions and Notices 2

> Tickets for all shows at the White River Theater may be ordered by calling the box office between 8:30 A.M. and 4:30 P.M. Tuesday through Saturday. Please have the following information ready when you call: the number of tickets you wish to purchase, the time and date of the performance you want to see, and your credit card number. Tickets ordered at least a week in advance of the performance can be mailed to your home. Otherwise, you can pick up your tickets in person at the box office one hour before the performance begins. A 15% discount is available on blocks of tickets for groups of ten or more when orders are made at least two weeks in advance of the performance date. Call the box office for details.

SKIMMING Look quickly at the instructions to answer this question.

1. Look at the first sentence of the instructions. What are
   the instructions about?   Ⓐ   Ⓑ
   (A) How to use tickets
   (B) How to buy tickets

SCANNING Find the following.

2. Find these times in the instructions, and circle them.
   8:30   4:30

Mark the words and phrases that appear in the notice, and circle them on the notice. Some may appear more than once.

3. (A) number   Ⓐ   Ⓑ
   (B) numeral

4. (A) sailed   Ⓐ   Ⓑ
   (B) mailed

5. (A) fall   Ⓐ   Ⓑ
   (B) call

6. (A) purchase   Ⓐ   Ⓑ
   (B) chase

CONTEXT Find these words and phrases, and guess their meanings in these instructions.

7. box office   (A) (B)
   (A) a place that sells boxes
   (B) a place that sells theater tickets

8. performance   (A) (B)
   (A) a show in a theater
   (B) quality of work

READING FAST

Read the letter as fast as you can. How long did it take?

_____ minutes _____ seconds

READING COMPREHENSION Mark the best answer.

9. What are these tickets for?   (A) (B) (C) (D)
   (A) A theater
   (B) An airplane trip
   (C) A museum
   (D) A boat ride

10. How can tickets be ordered?   (A) (B) (C) (D)
    (A) By going to the box office
    (B) By sending the order by mail
    (C) By calling the box office
    (D) By calling the credit card company

11. What information is required for ordering tickets?   (A) (B) (C) (D)
    (A) A telephone number
    (B) A credit card number
    (C) A house number
    (D) A fax number

12. When can tickets be picked up?   (A) (B) (C) (D)
    (A) Before 8:30
    (B) Between 8:30 and 4:30
    (C) After 4:30
    (D) One hour prior to the start of the event

13. The phrase "in person" in line 8 is closest in meaning to   (A) (B) (C) (D)
    (A) anyone
    (B) selfishly
    (C) one by one
    (D) personally

READING COMPREHENSION 223

Instructions and Notices 3

To all employees of the Rosings Company:

Please be advised that as part of the office remodeling project, all conference rooms are scheduled for painting this month. Conference rooms on the second floor will be painted next week, and conference rooms on the fourth floor will be painted the following week. During this time, the cafeteria will be available for meetings every morning before 12:00 and every afternoon after 2:00. Please see Ms. Smith in the engineering office to reserve your meeting times in the cafeteria. Since this is less meeting space than we usually have available, we will have to schedule carefully to make sure everyone's needs are met. To this end, we ask that you reserve your meeting time at least a week in advance and give Ms. Smith several alternative times if possible.

We apologize for the inconvenience and thank you in advance for your cooperation. Please see me if you have any questions.

Matilde Romero
Office Manager

SKIMMING Look quickly at the notice to answer this question.

1. Look at the first sentence of the notice. What will happen to the conference rooms?   Ⓐ   Ⓑ
   (A) They will be painted.
   (B) They will be scheduled for meetings.

SCANNING Find the following.

2. Underline all the numbers in the notice.

3. Find these time expressions, and underline them.
   this month   next week   the following week
   every morning   every afternoon

4. Find this name, and circle it.
   Ms. Smith

CONTEXT Find these words and phrases, and guess their meanings in this notice.

5. remodeling   Ⓐ   Ⓑ
   (A) taking away
   (B) improvement

224   READING

6. available   Ⓐ   Ⓑ
  (A) open
  (B) closed

7. reserve   Ⓐ   Ⓑ
  (A) serve again
  (B) keep for a particular person or group

READING FAST

Read the letter as fast as you can. How long did it take?

_____ minutes _____ seconds

READING COMPREHENSION Mark the best answer.

8. When will conference rooms on the fourth floor
   be painted?   Ⓐ   Ⓑ   Ⓒ   Ⓓ
  (A) Next week
  (B) Next month
  (C) In two weeks
  (D) In two months

9. Why should people see Ms. Smith?   Ⓐ   Ⓑ   Ⓒ   Ⓓ
  (A) To plan lunch in the cafeteria
  (B) To schedule painting
  (C) To reserve the cafeteria for meetings
  (D) To plan a conference

10. When will the cafeteria be available for meetings?   Ⓐ   Ⓑ   Ⓒ   Ⓓ
  (A) Only in the mornings
  (B) Between 12:00 and 2:00
  (C) Every morning and afternoon
  (D) Only in the afternoon

11. Where does Ms. Smith work?   Ⓐ   Ⓑ   Ⓒ   Ⓓ
  (A) On the second floor
  (B) In the conference department
  (C) In the cafeteria
  (D) In the engineering office

12. What word is closest in meaning to "scheduled"
   in paragraph 1, line 2?   Ⓐ   Ⓑ   Ⓒ   Ⓓ
  (A) calendar
  (B) planned
  (C) timed
  (D) closed

READING COMPREHENSION   225

GRAMMAR TIP

Present Perfect Tense and the Indefinite Past

Often the present perfect tense is used to express an action that happened at an indefinite time in the past. The action was completed in the past, but the time when it was completed is not specified.

I have read that book, and I think it's excellent.
She has made reservations at the Hotel Benwick.
The package has arrived.
I have written to you about this problem before.

VOCABULARY TIP

Expressing Necessity

Some words and phrases express the necessity of doing something. They are all similar in meaning and usage:

Must
Have to
Have got to
Had better

You must dress professionally if you want to be treated as a professional.
We have to make our reservations soon.
He has got to improve his work or he may lose his job.
You had better not be late for your job interview.

226 READING

STRATEGY PRACTICE

Questions 1–3 refer to the following advertisement.

Global World Airlines
Special airfares for the week of September 1

Vancouver – Montreal	$225
Montreal – Miami	$199
New York – Los Angeles	$255
Los Angeles – Tokyo	$575
Los Angeles – Sydney	$610

* All fares are one-way, economy class.
* Round-trip fares are double the one-way fare.
* Prices guaranteed through September 15.

For information on first-class fares and fares to other
destinations, visit our website:
www.globalworldair.com

---

1. Who would be interested in these fares?
   (A) People who travel to Europe.
   (B) People who like to save money.
   (C) People who travel first class.
   (D) People who live in South America.

2. How much would a round-trip ticket between Montreal and Miami cost?
   (A) $199
   (B) $225
   (C) $398
   (D) $450

3. What should someone who wants a first-class ticket to Sydney do?
   (A) Pay $610 for a one-way ticket.
   (B) Travel with a different airline.
   (C) Buy a ticket by September 15.
   (D) Visit the website for more information.

Questions 4–6 refer to the following form.

You enjoy *Business World News Journal*. Why not share it with a friend or colleague? Just fill out the form below and return it to us with your check or credit card information. Pay just $35 for a one-year subscription, or $60 for two years.

Send to:
Name: *Marvin Pytrowski*
Address: *756 Orford Road, Apt. 12*
City: *Williamston, MA*
Country: *USA*

From: *Rita Finklestein*
Address: *356 Route 14*
City: *Upper Newport, OH*
Country: *USA*

_____ Please enclose a gift card with the first issue.

___*X*___ Check enclosed.

Credit card number: _____
Your signature: _____

Send to:
Subscription Manager
Business World News Journal
PO Box 694932982
Sykesville, MT
USA

---

4. What is the purpose of this form?
   (A) To submit an article to a newspaper
   (B) To request a gift catalog
   (C) To order a gift subscription
   (D) To request extra copies of a journal

5. Who is Marvin Pytrowski?
   (A) A friend of Rita Finklestein
   (B) The editor of *Business World News Journal*
   (C) The subscription manager
   (D) A journalist

6. What did Ms. Finklestein include with the form?
   (A) A check
   (B) A gift card
   (C) A credit card number
   (D) A journal article

Questions 7–9 refer to the following memo.

To: All staff members
From: George Hollinger
Subject: Client Parking
Date: April 10, 20—

It has come to our attention that recently several of our clients have had their cars towed from the building parking garage for violation of parking regulations. Obviously this is very bad for client relations, and we cannot allow this to happen again. When you arrange to have clients meet you at our offices, please make the parking regulations very clear. Clients may park in spaces marked "Visitor" only. There is no time limit on these spaces, but a parking pass is required. This is available from our receptionist at no charge. The pass must be displayed in the right front windshield of the visitor's car. Clients' cars that are parked in spaces not designated for visitors or that do not have a properly displayed pass are subject to towing. This is embarrassing for us and inconvenient for the client, not to mention very expensive. Please make your clients aware of the parking regulations so that we can avoid any further problems in the future.

7. What problem is Mr. Hollinger concerned about?
   (A) There aren't enough parking spaces in the garage.
   (B) Clients do not understand the parking regulations.
   (C) Staff members' cars have been towed.
   (D) Parking passes are difficult to get.

8. What is expensive?
   (A) Parking passes
   (B) Visitor spaces
   (C) Receptionist services
   (D) Towing fees

9. What might cause a client's car to be towed?
   (A) Parking in a space marked "Visitor"
   (B) Displaying the pass in the wrong place
   (C) Not paying for a parking pass
   (D) Parking for too long

Questions 10–14 refer to the following notice and e-mail.

Notice to all building staff

Next Tuesday, May 15, the elevators will be repaired. This means that they will be out of service between the hours of 9:00 and 5:00. During this time you will have to use the stairs. We are sorry for any inconvenience this may cause. Please don't hesitate to contact the Building Cleaning and Maintenance Office if you have any questions.

Jason Podryhula
Manager, Building Cleaning and Maintenance Staff

To: Lilya Yemchuk
From: Shirley Smith
Subject: Tuesday meeting

Lilya,

I assume you saw the notice about the repairs next Tuesday. This poses a problem for our lunch meeting. How can we get all that food up to the fifth floor conference room without an elevator? I think we'd do better to change the date. Please call the head of the cleaning and maintenance staff to see if the conference room is available for the next day. If he gives the OK, then go ahead and call the restaurant to change the day of our lunch order. Ask for Mr. Cho. He took our order last time.

You and I also need to get together to go over the Jones proposal before the lunch meeting. Let's meet first thing Tuesday. I plan to be here early enough to take the elevator up to the office. No stairs for me! I'll see you then.

Shirley

230   READING

10. What will happen next Tuesday?
    (A) The elevators will be repaired.
    (B) The building will be cleaned.
    (C) The stairs will be painted.
    (D) The restaurant will be closed.

11. Why does Ms. Smith want to change the date of the meeting?
    (A) The conference room will not be available on Tuesday.
    (B) She doesn't want to carry food up the stairs.
    (C) Ms. Yemchuk can't attend on Tuesday.
    (D) The conference room won't be clean.

12. What day does Ms. Smith want to have the meeting?
    (A) Monday
    (B) Wednesday
    (C) Thursday
    (D) Friday

13. Who gives permission to use the conference room?
    (A) Ms. Smith
    (B) Ms. Yemchuk
    (C) Mr. Podryhula
    (D) Mr. Cho

14. What time does Ms. Smith plan to arrive on Tuesday?
    (A) Before 9:00
    (B) At 9:00
    (C) At 5:00
    (D) After 5:00

READING COMPREHENSION 231

Questions 15–19 refer to the following letters.

October 25, 20___

Mr. William Prince
1785 Honeycutt Boulevard
Marysville, IL 53028

Dear Mr. Prince:

We are pleased to offer you the position of Budget Assistant at Systems, Inc. We would like you to start work on Monday, November 10. You will report to your supervisor, Ms. Chen, in room 44. We are happy to offer you the salary that we discussed in your interview. Other benefits include health insurance for you and your family. We are sorry that we cannot offer life or dental insurance at this time, but we may be able to in the future. You will also get 20 vacation days and 5 sick days per year. Stock options and a pension plan are also available. I would suggest that you make an appointment to come in and speak with Emma Park, our benefits expert, very soon, and she can explain the full benefits package to you. At the same time you can fill out some paperwork for us.

Welcome to Systems, Inc. We look forward to working with you.

Sincerely,

Ivan Katz

Ivan Katz

October 31, 20___

Mr. Ivan Katz
Human Resources Director
Systems, Inc.
1700 Main Avenue
Chicago, IL 53147

Dear Mr. Katz:

Thank you for your offer of a position at Systems, Inc. Unfortunately, I have decided to take another position. I say this with real regret as I am sure that I would enjoy working at Systems, Inc., and the benefits are very attractive. However, I believe my new position at the Horizon Company will be better for me. Systems, Inc. has offered me a higher salary and twice as many vacation days as Horizon, but Horizon has offered me the same type of job and it's closer to my home. I find that location is very important. It would take me over an hour just to get to work if I had the job at Systems, Inc. Because of my family and other commitments, I cannot agree to put myself in such a situation. Thank you again for the offer.

Sincerely,

William Prince

William Prince

15. What insurance benefit does Systems, Inc. offer?
    (A) Life insurance
    (B) Health insurance
    (C) Dental insurance
    (D) Automobile insurance

16. Who is the benefits expert at Systems, Inc.?
    (A) Ms. Chen
    (B) Ms. Park
    (C) Mr. Katz
    (D) Mr. Prince

17. Why did Mr. Prince NOT accept a new position at Systems, Inc.?
    (A) The salary is too low.
    (B) The benefits are not good.
    (C) The location is inconvenient.
    (D) The job isn't interesting.

18. What job did Mr. Prince take with Horizon?
    (A) Budget Assistant
    (B) Human Resources Director
    (C) Budget Supervisor
    (D) Insurance Salesman

19. How many vacation days a year will he get at Horizon?
    (A) 5
    (B) 10
    (C) 20
    (D) 40

READING REVIEW

You will find the answer sheet for the Reading Review on page 382. Use it to record your answers. On the TOEIC test, you will have one hour and fifteen minutes to complete Parts 5, 6, and 7.

READING TEST

In the Reading test, you will read a variety of texts and answer several different types of reading comprehension questions. The entire Reading test will last 75 minutes. There are three parts, and directions are given for each part. You are encouraged to answer as many questions as possible within the time allowed.

You must mark your answers on the separate answer sheet. Do not write your answers in the test book.

PART 5

Directions: A word or phrase is missing in each of the sentences below. Four answer choices are given below each sentence. Select the best answer to complete the sentence. Then mark the letter (A), (B), (C), or (D) on your answer sheet.

---

101. If the client _____ dissatisfied, please have him write a letter.

(A) am
(B) is
(C) are
(D) be

102. My acquaintance with Mr. Broughton started as a business relationship and became a _____.

(A) friends
(B) friendly
(C) friendless
(D) friendship

103. The train from Osaka will be arriving _____ Tokyo in ten minutes.

(A) before
(B) in
(C) around
(D) at

104. The meeting was postponed because the typists weren't able to get the work _____ in time.

(A) do
(B) done
(C) did
(D) does

105. If the receptionist is unable to answer your question, Ms. Takai _____ help you.

(A) can
(B) did
(C) could not
(D) would not

106. We rely on Ms. Lee for her experience, sensitivity, and _____ advice.

(A) wisdom
(B) wisely
(C) wise
(D) wiser

234 READING

107. Mr. Moore is doing very well at his job and expects to _____ over $100,000 next year.
    (A) salary
    (B) earn
    (C) worth
    (D) income

108. The secretary asked a clerk to check the report for typing _____.
    (A) errands
    (B) errs
    (C) errors
    (D) errant

109. Mr. Kim is considered one of the most honest _____ most hardworking members of the finance team.
    (A) but
    (B) or
    (C) and
    (D) with

110. The retirement luncheon has been changed from 12:00 _____ 12:30 because the speaker will arrive late.
    (A) at
    (B) to
    (C) until
    (D) by

111. The president of the company _____ to Korea for an important conference.
    (A) went
    (B) gone
    (C) go
    (D) going

112. Since Mr. Takahashi attends afternoon classes, he _____ the night shift.
    (A) will be always working
    (B) will always be working
    (C) will be working always
    (D) always will be working

113. We just bought a new copy machine and will install it _____ the two offices.
    (A) among
    (B) around
    (C) between
    (D) from

114. The student intern needs permission to take time off for a _____ interview.
    (A) job
    (B) worker
    (C) chore
    (D) golf

115. We asked Ms. Jones to _____ us for coffee after the workshop was over.
    (A) together
    (B) with
    (C) addition
    (D) join

116. Employees must turn off the lights _____ they leave the office.
    (A) afterward
    (B) before
    (C) while
    (D) because

117. _____ it was the office manager's birthday, the secretaries sent her roses.
    (A) But
    (B) Even though
    (C) Since
    (D) While

118. Employees of the Kita Corporation are encouraged to do exercises _____ during their breaks.
    (A) oftentimes
    (B) every day
    (C) monthly
    (D) day by day

119. The operator was not able to find the address _____ telephone number.
    (A) or
    (B) although
    (C) but
    (D) even though

120. Mrs. Gonzalez has been here for a long time, and she _____ one of the best workers we have.
    (A) always has considered been
    (B) has been always considered
    (C) has been considered always
    (D) has always been considered

121. Do you know if the _____ for last week's order has been sent?

(A) pay
(B) payment
(C) payable
(D) pays

122. The board of directors proposed that an outside consultant be _____ in.

(A) will be brought
(B) bring
(C) brought
(D) will be bringing

123. The company requires that all employees have a physical examination _____.

(A) rarely
(B) never
(C) annually
(D) seldom

124. Files in the accounting department need to be _____ according to date.

(A) organizing
(B) organize
(C) organization
(D) organized

125. The elevators are located _____ the water fountain at the end of the hall.

(A) into
(B) across
(C) near
(D) between

126. The company policy states that when they _____ late, employees must be paid at the overtime rate.

(A) working
(B) worker
(C) will work
(D) work

127. The advertising manager is _____ that the telegram that just arrived will give him a new account.

(A) hoping
(B) hopeless
(C) hopelessness
(D) hope

128. Employees are reminded that the first parking space in each row of the lot _____ open for visitors.

(A) left
(B) leave
(C) is left
(D) is leaving

129. When Mr. Storer retires, the office is going to _____ a small party for him.

(A) do
(B) get
(C) make
(D) have

130. The company director has decided to hire an interior decorator to _____ the lobby.

(A) decorating
(B) decor
(C) decorate
(D) decoration

131. If our department _____ another typist, we'd get this report done quickly.

(A) have
(B) had
(C) will have
(D) have had

132. Mr. Johnson's daughter left home last year, and now she _____ in the city.

(A) house
(B) inhabits
(C) lives
(D) resident

133. If Mr. Wong arrives before noon, the committee members _____ very surprised.

(A) would be
(B) will be
(C) is
(D) was

134. This van is not mine; it _____ to the company I work for.

(A) belongs
(B) owns
(C) possesses
(D) properties

236 READING

135. Mr. Gomez decided to _____ from his position on the board of directors after having served on it for 15 years.

(A) apply
(B) resign
(C) attend
(D) remove

136. _____ Ms. Hogan was on the phone, her client could not see her right away.

(A) Although
(B) During
(C) Before
(D) Because

137. Unfortunately, the doctor was not able to see _____ without his glasses.

(A) clearly
(B) carefully
(C) finely
(D) nearly

138. We didn't notice that the package was already damaged when it _____.

(A) arrived
(B) has arrived
(C) was arriving
(D) had arrived

139. Ms. Smith was very _____ when she received the wrong letter.

(A) confuse
(B) confusing
(C) confused
(D) confuses

140. The store is open Monday through Saturday _____ not on Sunday.

(A) either
(B) or
(C) but
(D) so

GO ON TO THE NEXT PAGE

PART 6

Directions: Read the texts that follow. A word or phrase is missing in some of the sentences. Four answer choices are given below each of the sentences. Select the best answer to complete the text. Then mark the letter (A), (B), (C), or (D) on your answer sheet.

Questions 141–143 refer to the following article.

Coffee has become the most popular drink in offices. This information is the result of a recent _____ of office workers across the country. According to the results

141. (A) conference
(B) dismissal
(C) training
(D) survey

of the study, 55 percent of office workers choose coffee as their favorite beverage. The second most popular drink is tea, chosen by 30 percent of office workers in the study. The remaining 15 percent _____ soda, water, or other drinks.

142. (A) choose
(B) chosen
(C) choice
(D) choosing

During the workday, most coffee drinkers get their coffee from a machine in the office. In fact, 70 percent of coffee drinkers get their coffee in this way. Another 20 percent get their coffee "to go" at a coffee shop or restaurant. Ten percent make their coffee at home and take it to work in a thermos. The members of this last group, more than others, believe that there is nothing like the taste of _____ coffee.

143. (A) hot
(B) fresh
(C) sweet
(D) homemade

238　READING

Questions 144–146 refer to the following notice.

NOTICE
Skyline Telephone Company

Customer Account #: 05827716494-HJ0784922
Date: May 31, 20__

This is to notify you that your _____ of $155 for phone service during

144.   (A) pay
       (B) payer
       (C) paying
       (D) payment

the month of March is overdue. The amount owed must be paid in full by June 30 or your phone service may be _____.

145.   (A) increased
       (B) extended
       (C) lowered
       (D) cut off

If you have trouble paying your bill, please contact our customer service office to find out if _____ qualify for financial assistance.

146.   (A) he
       (B) she
       (C) you
       (D) they

GO ON TO THE NEXT PAGE

READING REVIEW   **239**

Questions 147–149 refer to the following notice.

Spend the weekend in luxury at the Continental Hotel.

Take advantage of our special low weekend rates:

One night — $100
Two nights — $175

Prices include breakfast and _____ of the pool and exercise room.

147. (A) use
     (B) uses
     (C) user
     (D) using

_____! Call now. To take advantage of this offer, you must

148. (A) No wait
     (B) Don't wait
     (C) Can't wait
     (D) Doesn't wait

_____ your room two weeks in advance.

149. (A) prepare
     (B) inspect
     (C) reserve
     (D) consider

240   READING

Questions 150–152 refer to the following article.

Are you unhappy at work? _____ of sleep may be the reason. Recent studies

150. (A) Like
(B) Luck
(C) Lack
(D) Look

show that people who get fewer than six hours of sleep a night on average tend to feel less satisfied with their jobs. They report feeling angry, fatigued, unhappy, and irritable during the work day. Most of them also report difficulty in _____ their assignments. "Your coworker who always seems to be behind and

151. (A) completing
(B) completion
(C) completed
(D) complete

tends to have a large pile of undone projects on her desk may well be suffering from sleep deprivation," says Dr. Jocelyn Bush of the Sleep Studies Institute. "Naturally, there are many reasons why someone may not be able to keep _____ with a

152. (A) at
(B) of
(C) in
(D) up

normal workload," says Dr. Bush, "but until now we never considered that sleep, or not enough of it, could be a common cause for such problems." So, before sending your staff to expensive work efficiency training sessions, try suggesting that they get a little more sleep. Not on the job, of course.

GO ON TO THE NEXT PAGE

READING REVIEW **241**

PART 7

Directions: In this part you will read a selection of texts, such as magazine and newspaper articles, letters, and advertisements. Each text is followed by several questions. Select the best answer for each question and mark the letter (A), (B), (C), or (D) on your answer sheet.

Questions 153–155 refer to the following e-mail message.

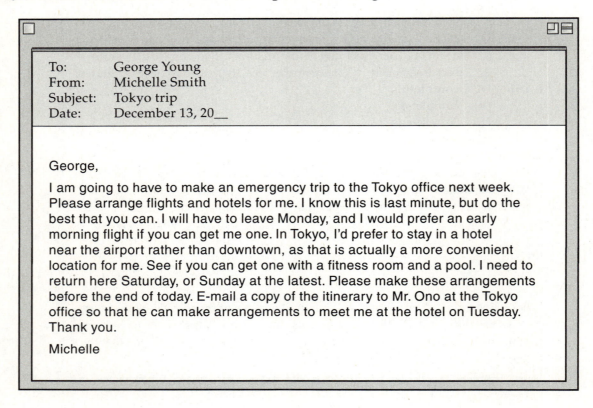

To: George Young
From: Michelle Smith
Subject: Tokyo trip
Date: December 13, 20__

George,

I am going to have to make an emergency trip to the Tokyo office next week. Please arrange flights and hotels for me. I know this is last minute, but do the best that you can. I will have to leave Monday, and I would prefer an early morning flight if you can get me one. In Tokyo, I'd prefer to stay in a hotel near the airport rather than downtown, as that is actually a more convenient location for me. See if you can get one with a fitness room and a pool. I need to return here Saturday, or Sunday at the latest. Please make these arrangements before the end of today. E-mail a copy of the itinerary to Mr. Ono at the Tokyo office so that he can make arrangements to meet me at the hotel on Tuesday. Thank you.

Michelle

153. What does Michelle want George to do?
 (A) Go to Tokyo with her
 (B) Make plane and hotel reservations
 (C) Give her travel advice
 (D) Take her to the airport

154. When will Michelle begin her trip?
 (A) Today
 (B) Monday
 (C) Saturday
 (D) December 13

155. Where will Michelle stay in Tokyo?
 (A) Downtown
 (B) At the office
 (C) Near the airport
 (D) At George's house

Questions 156–159 refer to the following advertisement.

> A small computer software company seeking to expand into the Asian market seeks an experienced sales representative. We are looking for an energetic self-starter with a minimum of three years' experience in sales, preferably with computer-related products. Must be able to work independently. Must be fluent in English and have good Japanese language skills. Must be familiar with most common office software packages. Job involves travel 1 to 2 weeks per month. We offer a competitive salary and excellent benefits, including 4 weeks paid vacation, health and life insurance, and computer training as needed. To apply, call Mr. Rogers at 555-6983 between 1 and 4. Or fax résumé and references to 555-6988. Closing date: March 31.

156. What kind of job is advertised?
(A) Computer programmer
(B) Salesperson
(C) Software developer
(D) Travel agent

157. How much experience is required?
(A) No more than 3 years
(B) 3 years or more
(C) 1 to 4 years
(D) At least 4 years

158. The word "involves" in line 9 is closest in meaning to
(A) prohibits
(B) includes
(C) prevents
(D) allows

159. How can you apply for the job?
(A) Make a phone call
(B) Take a computer training course
(C) Send an e-mail
(D) Write a letter

GO ON TO THE NEXT PAGE

Questions 160–161 refer to the following letter.

April 1, 20___

Ralph Johnson
President
Computers, Inc.
1334 Maple Avenue
Suite 10
Mapleville, MI 02148

Dear Mr. Johnson:

On behalf of Steven Reynolds, owner of the building at 1334 Maple Avenue, I am writing this letter to inform you that the rent on your office is overdue. As of today, April 1st, you owe three months' back rent. According to the lease agreement signed by you, we are permitted to request that you vacate the premises following three months of nonpayment of rent. Therefore, you are hereby notified that you are required to pay in full by April 15th, or we will have to ask you to leave the building at the end of the month. Payment must be made in the form of a cashier's check and must be received by this office on or before April 15th. We sincerely hope that we can resolve this matter in a manner satisfactory to all concerned. Please call me if you have any questions.

Sincerely,

Miriam Hopewell

Miriam Hopewell
Building Manager

160. Who wrote this letter?
  (A) A computer programmer
  (B) The president of a company
  (C) The building supervisor
  (D) The owner of the building

161. What does Mr. Johnson have to do by April 15th?
  (A) Pay rent for April only
  (B) Leave the building
  (C) Pay three months' rent
  (D) Call Miriam Hopewell

Questions 162–165 refer to the following form.

SNYDER'S STORE

Mail Order Form

Name: *Richard Robles*

Address: *185 Broad Street, Apt. 212*

quantity	item	color	price
1	sweater	blue	$75
3	tennis shirts	white	$42
1	sweater	red	$90
5	pairs socks	black	$25
1	winter coat	green	$250
		add 5% tax	$24
		shipping	$15
		Total	$521

(Returns must be made within 30 days and will be charged a 15% handling fee.)

Method of payment: _X_ check ___ money order ___ credit card ___ gift certificate

To order by phone, dial 1-800-555-0983 Monday through Friday, 8:30 A.M. until 8:30 P.M. You can use this form to plan your order before calling. Please have your credit card ready when you call.

Fax your order by dialing 1-800-555-0977.

To order online and see our latest catalog listings, visit our website.

162. What kind of store is Snyder's?
(A) A tennis store
(B) A shoe store
(C) A sports store
(D) A clothing store

163. What costs $15?
(A) A blue sweater
(B) Sending the order
(C) Sales tax
(D) Returning an item

164. How much does one pair of socks cost?
(A) $2.50
(B) $5.00
(C) $25.00
(D) $50.00

165. How will Mr. Robles pay for his order?
(A) Check
(B) Money order
(C) Credit card
(D) Gift certificate

GO ON TO THE NEXT PAGE

Questions 166–169 refer to the following instructions.

To order by mail

Complete the form below and mail it to:

Garden Supply, Inc.
4869 Wilmer Avenue
Petersburg, VA 21278

Don't forget to enclose a check or money order with your order. Credit cards are not accepted when you order by mail. You will receive your order in 4–6 weeks.

- -

First Name: _____

Last Name: _____

Company/Organization: _____

Address: _____

_____

_____

Telephone: _____

E-mail: _____

To order by phone: Call 800-555-9364   M–F   9–5
Please have the following information ready: the name, page number, and catalog number for all items you plan to order, and your credit card number. You will receive your order within 5 days.

To order online:
Go to our website and complete the form there. You must have a credit card to order online. You will receive your order in 1–2 weeks.

Substitutes
We do our best to fill each order as made. However, during the busy spring gardening season, we cannot avoid running out of items from time to time. In this case, if you would like us to select an alternate item of similar value for you, please check here: ___

---

166. When can someone order by phone?
(A) Anytime
(B) Monday through Friday only
(C) On the weekend
(D) In the evening

167. If someone wanted to pay by credit card, how would he or she order?
(A) By mail
(B) By phone only
(C) Online only
(D) Either by phone or online

168. To get an order the fastest, which way should one order?
(A) By mail
(B) By phone
(C) Online
(D) Either by phone or online

169. Which of the following is NOT needed for phone orders?
(A) A catalog number
(B) A page number
(C) A credit card
(D) An e-mail address

Questions 170–171 refer to the following notice.

NOTICE

All building visitors and tenants are hereby notified that smoking is prohibited in most areas of this office building by order of the City Chief of Police. Smoking is allowed only in the employee lounge on the second floor or on the sidewalk outside the building. Outside smokers must stand at least 10 feet away from all building entrances. Please report any violations to the Security Office in room 105. There is a $50 fine for violation of this order. Repeated violations may incur higher fines.

170. What is the punishment for people who smoke in the building?
(A) Pay $50
(B) Go to the police station
(C) Lose their employment
(D) Stay outside

171. Where is smoking allowed?
(A) On the entire second floor
(B) In most areas of the building
(C) In the office
(D) On the sidewalk

GO ON TO THE NEXT PAGE

READING REVIEW   247

Questions 172–174 refer to the following memo.

MEMORANDUM

To: All company personnel
From: Milton Freeman, Office Manager
Date: September 22, 20__
Re: Photocopier issues

The photocopier has broken down again. This is the third time this month. We are all frustrated by the loss of valuable time this causes, not to mention the costs of the repairs. Part of the problem results from attempts at repairs made by persons who don't completely understand the operation of the machine. Even a simple problem like a paper jam can become exacerbated if not dealt with properly. In order to avoid problems in the future, please observe the following guidelines:

1. If you are unsure how to operate the photocopy machine, please ask Sally Garfield, my assistant, to show you how to use it.

2. If you have any problem at all with the photocopy machine, do not attempt to fix it yourself.

3. Please report all problems with the photocopy machine to Ms. Garfield. She has been trained to fix most common problems with the machine and is always ready to assist you with all photocopier issues.

4. Do not call a repairperson yourself. This is the responsibility of Ms. Garfield.

Thank you for your patience and cooperation.

---

172. How many times has the photocopier been broken this month?
    (A) One
    (B) Two
    (C) Three
    (D) We don't know.

173. What should people do when the photocopier breaks?
    (A) Fix it
    (B) Call a repairperson
    (C) Send a memo to the office manager
    (D) Tell Sally Garfield

174. The word "observe" in paragraph 1, line 7, is closest in meaning to
    (A) view
    (B) state
    (C) follow
    (D) comment

Questions 175–177 refer to the following notice.

NORTHERN RAILROAD
Notice of Schedule Change

Date posted: March 28th

As of April 15th, there will be a new train schedule as follows.
Trains leaving for:

Marysville	10:00 A.M.	12:35 P.M.	2:50 P.M.	6:15 P.M.
Summerside	9:15 A.M.	11:45 A.M.	3:10 P.M.	5:50 P.M.
Woodmont	8:45 A.M.	12:15 P.M.	3:25 P.M.	6:40 P.M.

There will also be a fare increase starting April 15th:
Adult, one-way.........$15
Child, one-way............$9
Station office hours will remain the same (7 A.M.–8 P.M. daily)

The 15% surcharge on tickets purchased on board the train during hours that the station is open remains in effect.

Monthly train passes are available for purchase at the station or online.

Please be advised that as of January of next year, there will be an increase in station parking fees. The new fee schedule will be posted four weeks in advance of the change.

---

175. When will the train schedule change?
(A) Today
(B) March 28th
(C) April 5th
(D) April 15th

176. What time will the latest train leave for Woodmont?
(A) 8:45 A.M.
(B) 5:50 P.M.
(C) 6:15 P.M.
(D) 6:40 P.M.

177. What will NOT change?
(A) The price of adult tickets
(B) The train schedule
(C) The station office hours
(D) The fare for children

GO ON TO THE NEXT PAGE ▶

Questions 178–180 refer to the following e-mail.

To: Dan Reynolds
From: Cynthia See
Subject: Vacation schedule
Date: April 3, 20__

Dan,

I wanted to bring you up to date on the vacation schedule for next month since several people are requesting leave then. Lora Johnson wants to take off from the 1st through the 7th. Kyle Roberts asked for the following week, the 8th through the 14th. Both Sandy Greene and Tiffany Andrews asked to take off the week of the 22nd through the 28th. I have already approved all four of these requests. Do you think we could ask Philippa Conte to cover for Sandy and Tiffany during that week?

Kevin Kim also wants to take off during the last week of the month, but I haven't approved his request yet. If he's off then, we will be seriously understaffed. I don't think we can ask Philippa to cover for three people, do you? I will suggest to Kevin that he move his vacation to the first week of June. I don't want to approve any more vacations for next month. I will wait to take my vacation in July when, I hope, the schedule here will be back to normal. You were smart to plan your vacation for this month before everybody else starts taking off. You are leaving next week, right?

Let me know if you have any comments about next month's vacation schedule. Have a good time on your vacation, and I will see you when you return.
Cynthia

178. How many people want to take a vacation next month?
(A) One
(B) Two
(C) Four
(D) Five

179. Who will take a vacation during the last week of May?
(A) Philippa
(B) Kevin
(C) Sandy and Tiffany
(D) Sandy, Tiffany, and Kevin

180. When will Dan take his vacation?
(A) April
(B) May
(C) June
(D) July

250 READING

Questions 181–185 refer to the following two e-mail messages.

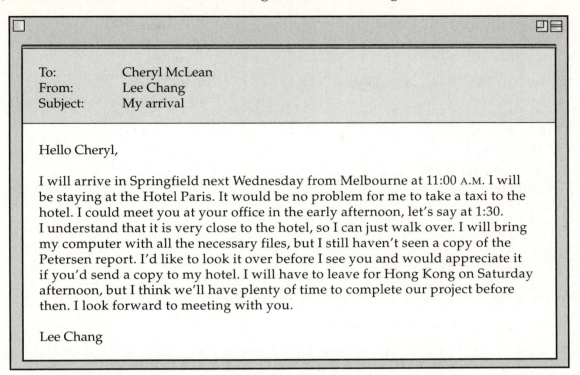

To: Cheryl McLean
From: Lee Chang
Subject: My arrival

Hello Cheryl,

I will arrive in Springfield next Wednesday from Melbourne at 11:00 A.M. I will be staying at the Hotel Paris. It would be no problem for me to take a taxi to the hotel. I could meet you at your office in the early afternoon, let's say at 1:30. I understand that it is very close to the hotel, so I can just walk over. I will bring my computer with all the necessary files, but I still haven't seen a copy of the Petersen report. I'd like to look it over before I see you and would appreciate it if you'd send a copy to my hotel. I will have to leave for Hong Kong on Saturday afternoon, but I think we'll have plenty of time to complete our project before then. I look forward to meeting with you.

Lee Chang

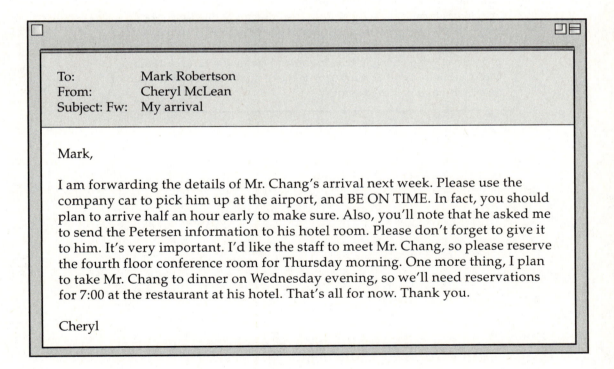

To: Mark Robertson
From: Cheryl McLean
Subject: Fw: My arrival

Mark,

I am forwarding the details of Mr. Chang's arrival next week. Please use the company car to pick him up at the airport, and BE ON TIME. In fact, you should plan to arrive half an hour early to make sure. Also, you'll note that he asked me to send the Petersen information to his hotel room. Please don't forget to give it to him. It's very important. I'd like the staff to meet Mr. Chang, so please reserve the fourth floor conference room for Thursday morning. One more thing, I plan to take Mr. Chang to dinner on Wednesday evening, so we'll need reservations for 7:00 at the restaurant at his hotel. That's all for now. Thank you.

Cheryl

181. Where is Mr. Chang arriving from?
- (A) Springfield
- (B) Melbourne
- (C) Paris
- (D) Hong Kong

182. How will Mr. Chang get to his hotel?
- (A) By taxi
- (B) By car
- (C) By foot
- (D) By bus

183. What time should Mr. Robertson arrive at the airport?
- (A) 10:30 A.M.
- (B) 11:00 A.M.
- (C) 1:00 P.M.
- (D) 1:30 P.M.

184. What should Mr. Robertson give to Mr. Chang?
- (A) A computer
- (B) Some files
- (C) A report
- (D) His hotel room key

185. Where will Mr. Chang have dinner on Wednesday evening?
- (A) In Ms. McLean's office
- (B) In a conference room
- (C) In a restaurant
- (D) In his hotel room

Questions 186–190 refer to the following article and letter.

The Playtime Corporation announced yesterday that Mai Le has been promoted to CEO of the company. Mai Le has been with Playtime for ten years. She formerly worked for the Trellis Mail Order Company and graduated from Western University School of Business 25 years ago. In her former capacity as Resource Director at Playtime, Ms. Le was noted for the innovative programs she brought to the company, including employee-of-the-month incentives and parent-friendly programs such as flexible scheduling and onsite daycare. Outgoing CEO Caroline Overall is retiring from the company and plans to open an executive consulting business.

May 15, 20___

Dear Mai,

I saw the article in today's newspaper and would like to extend my warmest congratulations to you. You deserve this more than anyone I know. From the moment I met you those many years ago on our first day of high school, I knew that you would go far. You were the smartest and most ambitious of all our classmates.

You deserve a special celebration, and I would like to invite you to dinner at the Spring Seasons Hotel. I've already spoken to your former boss, and she plans to join us. I asked some of your old coworkers, Violet Smith and Harry Wong, and I also called Lee Kim, but all three of them are out of town. So it will just be the three of us, but that will be fine. Let me know if this weekend or next weekend is better for you. I look forward to seeing you. It's been too long.

Your buddy,
Alice

---

186. Where does Mai Le currently work?
(A) At the Trellis Mail Order Company
(B) At the Playtime Corporation
(C) At the School of Business
(D) At Western University

187. When did Mai graduate from the university?
(A) 10 years ago
(B) 15 years ago
(C) 20 years ago
(D) 25 years ago

188. Why is Alice congratulating Mai?
(A) She got a promotion.
(B) She graduated from high school.
(C) She opened a consulting business.
(D) She won an employee-of-the-month award.

189. What is Alice's relationship to Mai?
(A) She is her boss.
(B) She is her parent.
(C) She is her employee.
(D) She is her former classmate.

190. Who will attend the dinner?
(A) Caroline Overall
(B) Violet Smith
(C) Harry Wong
(D) Lee Kim

GO ON TO THE NEXT PAGE

Questions 191–195 refer to the following memo and schedule.

To: Jeffrey Caldwell
From: Jose Amadeo
Re: Meeting follow-up

We agreed in our meeting that you need to improve your office skills in order to perform your job duties adequately. I have attached a schedule of classes from the Business Training Institute. A number of your co-workers have taken classes there, and it has a fine reputation. Take a look at the 105 courses. I think you should sign up for 105A. Even though you have a little experience here, it never hurts to start again from the beginning. Word Processing would also be useful, and I think you would qualify for the 101B course. Bookkeeping might be a good idea, too, but I'd prefer you sign up for just two courses now. There's no sense in overburdening yourself. So in addition to 105A, you can choose between 101B and 106A. The company will take care of the entire tuition for you, so you need have no worries there.

BUSINESS TRAINING INSTITUTE

Schedule of Classes

Course #	Course Title	Hours	Cost
101A	Word Processing—Beginning	Mon/Wed 7–9	$450
101B	Word Processing—Advanced	Tue/Thur 7–9	$450
105A	Introduction to Database Part I	Mon/Wed 5–7	$450
105B	Introduction to Database Part II	Mon/Wed 7–9	$450
105C	Advanced Database	Tue/Thur 5–7	$450
106A	Basic Bookkeeping	Tue/Thur 7–9	$450
106B	Intermediate Bookkeeping	Mon/Wed 7–9	$450
110A	Introduction to Business Writing	Tue 5:30–8:00	$425

254 READING

191. Why does Mr. Caldwell need to take classes at the Business Training Institute?
(A) To get a promotion
(B) To earn a university degree
(C) To be able to train his co-workers
(D) To do better in his current position

192. Which database course does Mr. Amadeo recommend?
(A) Introduction to Database Part I
(B) Introduction to Database Part II
(C) Intermediate Database
(D) Advanced Database

193. How many nights a week will Mr. Caldwell study?
(A) One
(B) Two
(C) Three
(D) Four

194. How much is the tuition for the Introduction to Business Writing class?
(A) $400
(B) $425
(C) $450
(D) $475

195. How many business writing courses are offered at the Business Training Institute?
(A) One
(B) Two
(C) Three
(D) Four

GO ON TO THE NEXT PAGE

Questions 196–200 refer to the following instructions and e-mail.

New Century Office Machines, Inc.
Product Guarantee

Your printer is completely guaranteed for one year from the date of purchase. If you are dissatisfied with your printer for any reason, you can return it for a complete refund within 30 days of the purchase date. After 30 days, please call our customer service number at 800-555-9927. If we cannot solve your problem over the phone, you will be asked to mail the printer back to us for repairs. For this purpose, please save the original box and packing material that your printer came with, as well as the return mailing label contained in the enclosed envelope. We are not responsible for the cost of postage.

To: Mary Jones
From: Peter Andrews
Subject: Printer

Mary,

It looks like we'll have to send the printer back to the factory. I spent two hours on the phone with customer service, but it still prints too light. Changing the ink cartridge didn't solve the problem. Unfortunately, it's too late for a complete refund. We've missed the last return date by just five days. Could you please pack up the printer and ship it to the company? I think you'll find everything you need in the storage closet. If you need money, take it out of petty cash. This is very annoying. This is the third New Century printer we've bought that's had problems. I won't buy anything from that company again. Their prices are great, but their products always break down.

Peter

196. When did they buy the printer?
- (A) Five days ago
- (B) Twenty-five days ago
- (C) Thirty days ago
- (D) Thirty-five days ago

197. What is the problem with the printer?
- (A) It takes two hours to print something.
- (B) It needs a new ink cartridge.
- (C) The printing is too light.
- (D) It's very old.

198. How will the company solve the problem?
- (A) By fixing the printer
- (B) By giving a complete refund
- (C) By exchanging the old printer for a new one
- (D) By sending a customer service representative to Peter's office

199. In order to return the printer, what will Mary have to pay for?
- (A) A box
- (B) Shipping
- (C) An envelope
- (D) Packing material

200. Why is Peter annoyed?
- (A) The printer was too expensive.
- (B) The company won't fix the printer.
- (C) New Century printers always break down.
- (D) It will cost a lot of money to return the printer.

READING REVIEW   257

PRACTICE TEST ONE

You will find the Answer Sheet for Practice Test One on page 383. Detach it from the book and use it to record your answers. Play the audio for Practice Test One when you are ready to begin.

LISTENING TEST

In the Listening test, you will be asked to demonstrate how well you understand spoken English. The entire Listening test will last approximately 45 minutes. There are four parts, and directions are given for each part. You must mark your answers on the separate answer sheet. Do not write your answers in the test book.

PART 1

Directions: For each question in this part, you will hear four statements about a picture in your test book. When you hear the statements, you must select the one statement that best describes what you see in the picture. Then find the number of the question on your answer sheet and mark your answer. The statements will not be printed in your test book and will be spoken only one time.

Example

Sample Answer

Statement (C), "They're standing near the table," is the best description of the picture, so you should select answer (C) and mark it on your answer sheet.

260 PRACTICE TEST ONE

1.

2.

3.
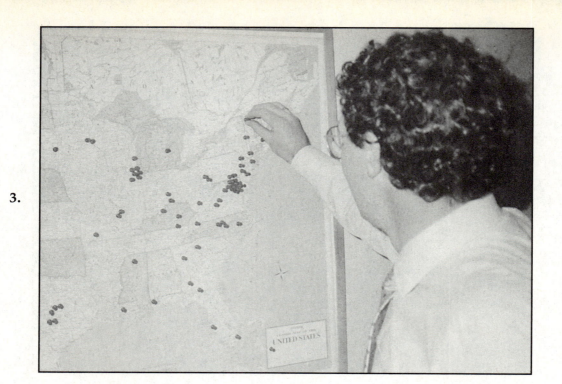

4.
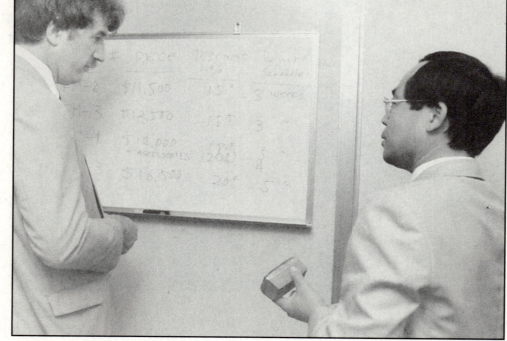

5.

6.

7.

8.

9.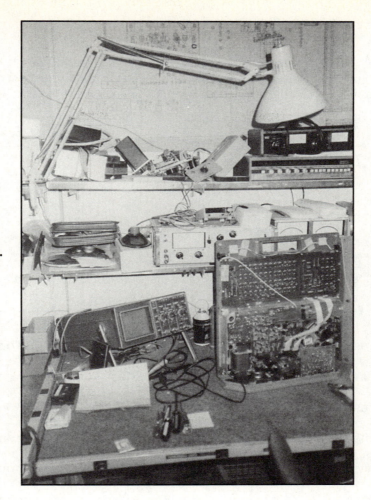

10.

GO ON TO THE NEXT PAGE

PRACTICE TEST ONE 265

PART 2

Directions: You will hear a question or statement and three responses spoken in English. They will not be printed in your test book and will be spoken only one time. Select the best response to the question or statement and mark the letter (A), (B), or (C) on your answer sheet.

Example

Sample Answer

You will hear: Where is the meeting room?

You will also hear:
(A) To meet the new director.
(B) It's the first room on the right.
(C) Yes, at two o'clock.

Your best response to the question "Where is the meeting room?" is choice (B), "It's the first room on the right," so (B) is the correct answer. You should mark answer (B) on your answer sheet.

11. Mark your answer on your answer sheet.
12. Mark your answer on your answer sheet.
13. Mark your answer on your answer sheet.
14. Mark your answer on your answer sheet.
15. Mark your answer on your answer sheet.
16. Mark your answer on your answer sheet.
17. Mark your answer on your answer sheet.
18. Mark your answer on your answer sheet.
19. Mark your answer on your answer sheet.
20. Mark your answer on your answer sheet.
21. Mark your answer on your answer sheet.
22. Mark your answer on your answer sheet.
23. Mark your answer on your answer sheet.
24. Mark your answer on your answer sheet.
25. Mark your answer on your answer sheet.
26. Mark your answer on your answer sheet.
27. Mark your answer on your answer sheet.
28. Mark your answer on your answer sheet.
29. Mark your answer on your answer sheet.
30. Mark your answer on your answer sheet.
31. Mark your answer on your answer sheet.
32. Mark your answer on your answer sheet.
33. Mark your answer on your answer sheet.
34. Mark your answer on your answer sheet.
35. Mark your answer on your answer sheet.
36. Mark your answer on your answer sheet.
37. Mark your answer on your answer sheet.
38. Mark your answer on your answer sheet.
39. Mark your answer on your answer sheet.
40. Mark your answer on your answer sheet.

PART 3

 Directions: You will hear some conversations between two people. You will be asked to answer three questions about what the speakers say in each conversation. Select the best response to each question and mark the letter (A), (B), (C), or (D) on your answer sheet. The conversations will not be printed in your test book and will be spoken only one time.

41. What is the man buying?
    (A) Shoes.
    (B) Pears.
    (C) A book.
    (D) A newspaper.

42. How much does he have to pay?
    (A) $7.75.
    (B) $17.75.
    (C) $70.75.
    (D) $75.

43. How will he pay?
    (A) With cash.
    (B) With a credit card.
    (C) With a traveler's check.
    (D) With a personal check.

44. How long will it take for the package to arrive?
    (A) Six days.
    (B) Eight days.
    (C) Ten days.
    (D) Twelve days.

45. What is inside the package?
    (A) China.
    (B) Checks.
    (C) Jewelry.
    (D) Class work.

46. How much will the man pay?
    (A) $6.00.
    (B) $9.00.
    (C) $15.00.
    (D) $1,000.00.

47. When will the repairperson come?
    (A) This morning.
    (B) Tomorrow.
    (C) At 4:00.
    (D) In four days.

48. What does the woman have to copy?
    (A) Reports.
    (B) Photographs.
    (C) A repair bill.
    (D) A meeting agenda.

49. Where is the photocopy store?
    (A) On the first floor.
    (B) On the fourth floor.
    (C) Across the street.
    (D) Next door.

50. What are the speakers waiting for?
    (A) A car.
    (B) A bus.
    (C) A train.
    (D) A plane.

51. What is the weather like?
    (A) It's raining.
    (B) It's cloudy.
    (C) It's cold.
    (D) It's hot.

52. How long has the man been waiting?
    (A) 15 minutes.
    (B) 16 minutes.
    (C) 50 minutes.
    (D) 60 minutes.

GO ON TO THE NEXT PAGE

53. When does the woman's vacation begin?

    (A) On Monday.
    (B) On Tuesday.
    (C) On Wednesday.
    (D) On Thursday.

54. How long will her vacation last?

    (A) Two days.
    (B) One week.
    (C) Eight days.
    (D) Two weeks.

55. Where will she spend her vacation?

    (A) At a lake.
    (B) At the beach.
    (C) In the mountains.
    (D) In New York.

56. Why wasn't Mr. Kim at the meeting?

    (A) He is sick.
    (B) He went downtown.
    (C) He arrived too late.
    (D) He is away on a trip.

57. How many people were at the meeting?

    (A) Two.
    (B) Seven.
    (C) Eleven.
    (D) Fifteen.

58. When is the next meeting?

    (A) Tomorrow morning.
    (B) In two days.
    (C) Next week.
    (D) Next month.

59. Where are the speakers?

    (A) In a bank.
    (B) In a store.
    (C) In a doctor's office.
    (D) In an accountant's office.

60. How much money is the check for?

    (A) $400.
    (B) $500.
    (C) $800.
    (D) $900.

61. What does the woman have to sign?

    (A) A deposit slip.
    (B) A letter.
    (C) A check.
    (D) A form.

62. What is the weather like?

    (A) It's snowing.
    (B) It's raining.
    (C) It's hot.
    (D) It's windy.

63. How will the speakers get to work?

    (A) By car.
    (B) By train.
    (C) By walking.
    (D) By taxi.

64. What does the man have to do at 10:00?

    (A) Attend a meeting.
    (B) Clean the conference room.
    (C) Talk on the telephone.
    (D) Get on the train.

268 PRACTICE TEST ONE

65. Where is the hotel?

    (A) On another street.
    (B) To the left.
    (C) Across the street.
    (D) To the right.

66. What is the woman buying?

    (A) A newspaper.
    (B) A magazine.
    (C) Candy.
    (D) Gum.

67. How much does the woman have to pay?

    (A) $4.15.
    (B) $4.16.
    (C) $4.50.
    (D) $4.60.

68. Where are the speakers?

    (A) At home.
    (B) At a bakery.
    (C) At a grocery store.
    (D) At a restaurant.

69. How often does the man go to this place?

    (A) Every day.
    (B) Every two days.
    (C) Once a week.
    (D) Once a month.

70. What will the man get?

    (A) Soup.
    (B) Rice.
    (C) Chicken.
    (D) Sandwiches.

GO ON TO THE NEXT PAGE

PART 4

 Directions: You will hear some talks given by a single speaker. You will be asked to answer three questions about what the speaker says in each talk. Select the best response to each question and mark the letter (A), (B), (C), or (D) on your answer sheet. The talks will not be printed in your test book and will be spoken only one time.

71. Who is listening to this announcement?

    (A) Company employees.
    (B) Doctors.
    (C) Parents of schoolchildren.
    (D) Police officers.

72. What has been revised?

    (A) Doctors' excuses.
    (B) Insurance regulations.
    (C) Company policy.
    (D) Employees' records.

73. When is a note required?

    (A) Within forty-eight hours.
    (B) After four days.
    (C) After a week.
    (D) Never.

74. What is happening?

    (A) Some people need a hotel room.
    (B) Some people are going home.
    (C) The personnel office is closing.
    (D) A building is on fire.

75. Who must get through?

    (A) Office personnel.
    (B) Emergency personnel.
    (C) Clerical workers.
    (D) File clerks.

76. Where should people stay?

    (A) Next to a room.
    (B) Across the street.
    (C) Beside the building.
    (D) In the emergency room.

77. What kind of program is mentioned?

    (A) Race.
    (B) Space.
    (C) Tasting.
    (D) Waste.

78. Which of the following animals is mentioned?

    (A) A dog.
    (B) A cat.
    (C) A sheep.
    (D) A rat.

79. How many times has this program been done before?

    (A) None.
    (B) Once.
    (C) Twice.
    (D) Several times.

80. How is the president described in the news report?

    (A) As a mother.
    (B) As a doctor.
    (C) As a father.
    (D) As a general.

81. How many children does the president have?

    (A) Two.
    (B) Three.
    (C) Four.
    (D) Five.

82. When did the event happen?

    (A) Yesterday.
    (B) This morning.
    (C) At noon.
    (D) In the early evening.

83. What is being sold?

    (A) A watch.
    (B) A television.
    (C) A calendar.
    (D) A guide.

84. How long does the subscription last?

    (A) Ten days.
    (B) One month.
    (C) Ten months.
    (D) One year.

85. How many people can get the special offer?

    (A) One.
    (B) The first ten.
    (C) The first one hundred.
    (D) There is no limit.

---

86. What is the problem?

    (A) No one is home.
    (B) The line is busy.
    (C) It's a nonworking number.
    (D) The caller hung up.

87. What is the listener advised to do?

    (A) Give up.
    (B) Get another job.
    (C) Not to hang up.
    (D) Try again.

88. What can a caller do by dialing 411?

    (A) Check the number he is dialing.
    (B) Ask for a refund check.
    (C) Get assistance with dialing the number.
    (D) Ask to have his phone number changed.

---

89. What is the weather like now?

    (A) Rainy.
    (B) Cool.
    (C) Warm.
    (D) Windy.

90. When will the weather change?

    (A) Sunday.
    (B) Monday.
    (C) Tuesday.
    (D) Friday.

91. How much rain is expected?

    (A) Two inches.
    (B) Three inches.
    (C) Four inches.
    (D) Twenty-four inches.

---

92. What is on sale?

    (A) Chairs.
    (B) Desks.
    (C) Paper.
    (D) Pencils.

93. What color is NOT available?

    (A) Blue.
    (B) Yellow.
    (C) Green.
    (D) White.

94. When will the sale end?

    (A) Sunday.
    (B) Tuesday.
    (C) Friday.
    (D) Saturday.

GO ON TO THE NEXT PAGE

PRACTICE TEST ONE **271**

95. What was robbed?

   (A) A clothing store.
   (B) A jewelry store.
   (C) A computer store.
   (D) A watch store.

96. What time did the robbery happen?

   (A) 8:05.
   (B) 8:15.
   (C) 8:50.
   (D) 8:55.

97. Who was in the store at the time of the robbery?

   (A) Police.
   (B) Customers.
   (C) The store staff.
   (D) The store owner.

98. When is the Sidewalk Café closed?

   (A) Monday.
   (B) Tuesday.
   (C) Saturday.
   (D) Sunday.

99. What can you get for $6.00 at the café?

   (A) Birthday cake.
   (B) Pancakes.
   (C) Steak.
   (D) Pans.

100. Where is the café located?

   (A) By a river.
   (B) In back of a park.
   (C) Near a bus station.
   (D) Close to a subway station.

Stop! This is the end of the Listening test. Turn to Part 5 in your test book.

272   PRACTICE TEST ONE

READING TEST

In the Reading test, you will read a variety of texts and answer several different types of reading comprehension questions. The entire Reading test will last 75 minutes. There are three parts, and directions are given for each part. You are encouraged to answer as many questions as possible within the time allowed.

You must mark your answers on the separate answer sheet. Do not write your answers in the test book.

PART 5

Directions: A word or phrase is missing in each of the sentences below. Four answer choices are given below each sentence. Select the best answer to complete the sentence. Then mark the letter (A), (B), (C), or (D) on your answer sheet.

101. East Coast Airlines flight number 15 from New York _____ Chicago has been canceled.

    (A) to
    (B) in
    (C) by
    (D) at

102. Beginning the first of next month, lunch breaks will be _____ by fifteen minutes.

    (A) short
    (B) shortened
    (C) shortening
    (D) shortage

103. The computer programmer realized he had forgotten to turn off the office lights _____ he had left the premises.

    (A) after
    (B) because
    (C) since
    (D) and

104. Most employees have requested that their paychecks be _____ to their homes.

    (A) mail
    (B) mails
    (C) mailed
    (D) mailing

105. The error was noticed after Ms. Radice _____ the order to the supply company.

    (A) had sent in
    (B) sends in
    (C) has sent
    (D) is sending

106. Mr. Richards, the president of Capo Electronics, has had a very _____ year.

    (A) successfully
    (B) successful
    (C) success
    (D) successes

107. Since Dr. Yamoto is always busy, it is best to call _____ make an appointment before coming to her office.

    (A) while
    (B) before
    (C) nor
    (D) and

108. After working fifteen hours at the office, the new lawyer is finally putting away his papers and heading _____.

    (A) homely
    (B) homey
    (C) home
    (D) homeless

PRACTICE TEST ONE 273

109. The photographer that we hired to take pictures of the banquet will be accompanied _____ his assistant.

(A) with
(B) by
(C) to
(D) from

110. Ms. Ueki has never made any _____ decisions regarding the operation of her company.

(A) foolish
(B) fool
(C) foolishness
(D) fooled

111. As soon as we _____ the cause of the problem, we will be able to solve it.

(A) assign
(B) determine
(C) signify
(D) confer

112. In order to provide her customers with the finest meals, the restaurant owner _____ her produce fresh daily.

(A) buy
(B) buys
(C) buying
(D) bought

113. The personnel manager needs someone to _____ her with the presentation to the board.

(A) attend
(B) assume
(C) assign
(D) assist

114. Our departmental staff meetings are held _____ in the conference room on the third floor.

(A) rarely
(B) every week
(C) always
(D) sometimes

115. The building is equipped with a sophisticated security system which turns on automatically _____ midnight.

(A) to
(B) from
(C) at
(D) for

116. The project _____ to require more time than the contractors have available.

(A) had seemed
(B) seems
(C) is seeming
(D) will seem

117. Staff members _____ ready to help out new employees and explain the office procedures.

(A) should always be
(B) being always should
(C) always be should
(D) always should being

118. The new schedules are _____ with the second shift workers at the factory.

(A) popularized
(B) popular
(C) populated
(D) popularity

119. It was agreed that the committee meet again _____ the tenth of April.

(A) for
(B) on
(C) to
(D) from

120. The travel agent said she would know the flight number and the precise arrival time _____ the airlines confirmed the reservation.

(A) during
(B) because
(C) when
(D) while

274 PRACTICE TEST ONE

121. You will have to _____ an operator's manual from the library because I don't think we have one here.

(A) loan
(B) borrow
(C) lend
(D) send

122. The height of this chair is _____, so you can change it if it's not high enough for you.

(A) adjustable
(B) reliable
(C) suitable
(D) comfortable

123. The assistant does not recall receiving a telex from the Mexico office _____ from the South American office.

(A) either
(B) and
(C) or
(D) but

124. _____ this kind of machine before, or should we call in a repairperson?

(A) Have ever you repaired
(B) Have you repaired ever
(C) Ever have you repaired
(D) Have you ever repaired

125. If our office _____ a coffee machine, Mr. Perkins said he would make coffee every morning.

(A) had
(B) have
(C) will have
(D) would have

126. The time sheets are to be filled out twice _____—in the morning when the staff arrives and in the evening when they leave.

(A) usually
(B) sometimes
(C) daily
(D) frequently

127. Because of the _____ in the value of local real estate, investors are looking for other ways to invest their money.

(A) diminish
(B) decline
(C) down
(D) weaker

128. The goal of our meetings is to make the directors _____ our problem.

(A) understanding
(B) understood
(C) understand
(D) be understanding

129. _____ Mr. Park was the only one who knew the way to the conference, he drove the car.

(A) Although
(B) Since
(C) But
(D) Therefore

130. Ms. Wang did not want her check automatically _____ into her account.

(A) deposit
(B) deposits
(C) depositing
(D) deposited

131. If this package is sent by the express mail service, it _____ California by Friday.

(A) reaches
(B) will reach
(C) reached
(D) is reaching

132. All delivery persons are asked to use the side _____ to make their deliveries.

(A) enter
(B) entered
(C) entering
(D) entrance

GO ON TO THE NEXT PAGE

PRACTICE TEST ONE **275**

133. Hotel guests who _____ checking out after 1:00 P.M. should contact the front desk.

    (A) will
    (B) were
    (C) are going
    (D) will be

134. Mr. Davis, my lawyer, was a _____ by the time he was thirty.

    (A) millions
    (B) millionaire
    (C) million
    (D) millionfold

135. If the accountant _____ a mistake, she will not charge us for her time.

    (A) makes
    (B) will make
    (C) had made
    (D) make

136. That position has been _____ for over a month, but we've finally hired someone to fill it.

    (A) taken
    (B) required
    (C) dismissed
    (D) vacant

137. We are fortunate to have a company president who is quite _____ about computers.

    (A) knowing
    (B) knowledge
    (C) knowledgeable
    (D) knows

138. Yasmin is one of our best employees and _____ working here for two years.

    (A) has
    (B) has been
    (C) is
    (D) will

139. The receptionist _____ the vice president if he knew where she was.

    (A) will call
    (B) call
    (C) called
    (D) would call

140. Because we are unusually busy right now, the department head has asked everyone to _____ their vacations until later in the year.

    (A) defer
    (B) confer
    (C) refer
    (D) infer

PART 6

Directions: Read the texts that follow. A word or phrase is missing in some of the sentences. Four answer choices are given below each of the sentences. Select the best answer to complete the text. Then mark the letter (A), (B), (C), or (D) on your answer sheet.

Questions 141–143 refer to the following letter.

February 22, 20___

Dear Samuel,

I have good news for you. I have taken a new job in Sydney. My family and I will move _____ next month. Since you have lived in Sydney for so long, I would like to

141. (A) there
(B) that
(C) here
(D) it

ask for your advice. We would like to rent a small house in a nice _____

        142. (A) industrial
(B) residential
(C) influential
(D) commercial

neighborhood. My children are small, so we would like to be in a quiet place away from businesses and traffic. We would like to live close to good schools, and I also want to be near public transportation so that I can get to work easily. Can you recommend some good neighborhoods to me?

I plan to visit your city in two weeks _____ for a house. Please send me your

        143. (A) look
(B) looking
(C) to look
(D) will look

recommendations before then if you can. I hope we can get together while I am in town.

Your friend,

Boris

GO ON TO THE NEXT PAGE

PRACTICE TEST ONE **277**

Questions 144–146 refer to the following notice.

Welcome to the Sleepwell Motel. We hope _____ stay is a

144. (A) our
(B) his
(C) your
(D) their

pleasant one. If you need assistance, please _____ 09 to speak to

145. (A) mark
(B) dial
(C) count
(D) register

someone at the front desk.

Please take note of the following local services:

Transportation
Taxi   985-555-9965
City buses   985-555-0924
Airport   985-555-9321

Entertainment
Deluxe Movie Theater   985-555-9654
Restaurant Guide   985-555-8723
Black Cat Night Club   985-555-7342

Emergency
Police 985-555-9111
Fire   985-555-2233

A _____ breakfast is available to all motel guests in the lobby

146. (A) compliment
(B) complimented
(C) complimenting
(D) complimentary

from 6:00 A.M. to 9:00 A.M.

278   PRACTICE TEST ONE

Questions 147–149 refer to the following letter.

Office Works
544 Hudson Street
Boston, MA 03291

March 29, 20___

Mary Braddock
Banquet Director
Garden Hotel
219 Center Circle
Boston, MA 03299

Dear Ms. Braddock:

Office Works is seeking a place to host our first awards banquet.

The evening will include dinner, speeches and an awards presentation. The exact date is flexible, but we would like to hold it on a Friday or Saturday evening in June.

We expect approximately 200 guests. We would like a room with a good sound system so that the guests will be able to hear the speeches _____.

147. (A) ease
(B) easy
(C) easier
(D) easily

Also, we would like to have elegant decorations that are suitable for the occasion. Does your hotel provide assistance with decorating, or will we need _____ a separate decorator?

148. (A) hire
(B) hires
(C) to hire
(D) hiring

We would like to serve a simple but elegant meal with both a meat and a vegetarian choice.

Would the Garden Hotel be able to provide suitable accommodations for this event? If so, please send me a price list including rental _____ for

149. (A) fees
(B) dates
(C) leases
(D) agents

the room, menu choices and prices, and any other charges. Thank you for your help.

Sincerely,

Lynn Osaman

Events Coordinator

GO ON TO THE NEXT PAGE

PRACTICE TEST ONE   279

Questions 150–152 refer to the following advertisement.

Ready to buy a NEW CAR?
LOOK NO FURTHER

Cango Cars is holding the biggest sale in its history of selling cars. For over ten years, Cango has been the leading _____ of new and used cars in the Canmore area.

150. (A) retailer
(B) insurer
(C) automobiles
(D) mechanic

That's because Cango has the best reputation for selling reliable, affordable vehicles in all of Alberta. We at Cango care about the drivers and passengers of Canmore. We pride _____ in doing all we can to prevent dangerous cars

151. (A) ourselves
(B) yourself
(C) yourselves
(D) itself

from getting back onto our roads and making sure our customers feel secure with the cars they choose. There is nothing more important to us than _____.

152. (A) upholstery
(B) safety
(C) earnings
(D) collision

Come to Cango Cars between August 5th and 10th, and enter to win a gently used 5-seat family sedan.

DON'T FORGET! Cango Cars is the home of the free one-year warranty. All of our vehicles, both new and used, come with a one-year money back guarantee for parts and labor.

280   PRACTICE TEST ONE

PART 7

Directions: In this part, you will read a selection of texts, such as magazine and newspaper articles, letters, and advertisements. Each text is followed by several questions. Select the best answer for each question and mark the letter (A), (B), (C), or (D) on your answer sheet.

Questions 153–155 refer to the following newspaper report.

Tomorrow, bus service on Orchard Road will be changed between the hours of 9 A.M. and 12:30 P.M. The Chingay Parade will take place from 10:00 A.M. to 12:00 P.M.

Number 7, 13, 14, 16, and 23 buses will turn left onto Scotts Road, right onto Clemenceau Avenue, and left onto Orchard Road below the parade route.

In the event of rain, the diversion will take place at 3:00 P.M. and the parade shortly after.

153. For whom is this report important?

(A) Weather reporters
(B) Bus riders
(C) City workers
(D) Bus repair people

154. At 10:00 A.M., what will happen to certain buses?

(A) They will be used in the parade.
(B) They will take a different route.
(C) They will have no riders.
(D) They will be taken out of service.

155. When will the parade take place if it rains?

(A) In the morning
(B) In the afternoon
(C) The next morning
(D) The following afternoon

GO ON TO THE NEXT PAGE

PRACTICE TEST ONE **281**

Questions 156–159 refer to the following memo.

To: All employees
From: R. Wettimuny
Re: Ordering Supplies

There has been a great deal of confusion regarding the correct procedures for ordering office supplies. Therefore, I will explain the proper steps to follow here. First, all requests for supplies must be typed and signed. Only typed requests will be accepted because I am tired of trying to decipher illegible handwriting. Second, all requests must be on my desk by the fifteenth of every month. I make out the order once each month and do not want to have to make addendums or extra orders. From now on, late requests will be put on hold until the following month. Requests that are received on time and approved by me will be sent on to the Accounting Department for processing.

Please be aware that it takes from two to six weeks for supplies to arrive once the order has been made, so it is important to plan ahead and make your requests accordingly.

Your cooperation is appreciated.

---

156. What does the memo concern?

(A) Overdue accounts
(B) Office furniture
(C) Supply requests
(D) Computers

157. What will happen to handwritten requests?

(A) They will not be accepted.
(B) They will be approved quickly.
(C) They will be read carefully.
(D) They will be sent to Accounting.

158. The word "approved" in paragraph 1, line 11, is closest in meaning to

(A) urgent
(B) valid
(C) signed
(D) accepted

159. What will happen to approved requests?

(A) They will be returned to the employee.
(B) They will be sent to Purchasing.
(C) They will be forwarded to Accounting.
(D) They will be returned to R. Wettimuny.

Questions 160–162 refer to the following chart.

Destination		Zone 1 Asia, Marshall Is., Guam, Midway, and others	Zone 2 North America, Central America, Oceania, Middle East, Europe	Zone 3 Africa, South America
Classification	Weight			
Letters*	Up to 25 g Up to 50 g	90 yen 160 yen	110 yen 190 yen	130 yen 230 yen
Postcard	Uniform rate of 70 yen to anywhere in the world			
Aerogramme	Uniform rate of 90 yen to anywhere in the world			
*Standard-sized item: 14–23.5 cm length, 9–12 cm width, thickness of within 1 cm				

160. What is the cost of sending a twelve-gram letter to South Africa?

(A) ¥70
(B) ¥90
(C) ¥130
(D) ¥230

161. How much would an aerogramme to Asia cost?

(A) ¥70
(B) ¥90
(C) ¥110
(D) ¥160

162. How much will a ¥110 letter to Europe weigh?

(A) 25 grams or less
(B) Between 25 and 50 grams
(C) More than 50 grams
(D) Unknown

GO ON TO THE NEXT PAGE

Questions 163–166 refer to the following bulletin.

RESERVATIONS: Reservations are required for all first-class compartments. Second- and third-class coaches do not require reservations.

DINING: Trains that do not have first-class cars will not have a dining car. Sandwich and beverage carts will be on all trains.

BAGGAGE: Passengers may carry up to four pieces of luggage on the train. Additional baggage may be checked.

---

163. A passenger traveling in which of the following would read this bulletin?

   (A) Plane
   (B) Car
   (C) Bus
   (D) Train

164. For which of the following are reservations required?

   (A) The dining car
   (B) First-class car
   (C) Second-class car
   (D) Third-class car

165. According to the passage, which of the following have dining cars?

   (A) All trains
   (B) Trains with first-class cars
   (C) Trains with second-class cars
   (D) Trains with third-class cars

166. The word "Additional" in paragraph 3, line 2, is closest in meaning to

   (A) Most
   (B) Extra
   (C) Overweight
   (D) Large

284   PRACTICE TEST ONE

Questions 167–171 refer to the following letter.

Lovely Lady Fashions
32 Elizabeth Bay Road
Sydney, Australia

December 15, 20__

Mrs. R.S.W. Mangala
Jewelry Export Ltd.
40 Galle Face Road
Colombo 1, Sri Lanka

Dear Mrs. Mangala:

I am interested in information regarding your company's new line of jewelry. I have seen the samples on your website, and I am interested in the possibility of importing your jewelry into Australia. I think it would sell very well here, especially among the younger women who make up the majority of my company's clientele.

I will be making a trip to Malaysia, India, and Sri Lanka next summer. I would like to arrange to meet with you then to discuss setting up a business relationship. Please let me know when you will be available for a meeting. In the meantime, I would appreciate your sending a list of your wholesale prices and information about ordering and shipping.

My associates in London have been very pleased with the quality of the gems you have sent them, and they have had a great deal of success with them. I look forward to doing business with you in the near future.

Sincerely,

James Goodwin
Import Manager

---

167. Where does Mr. Goodwin probably live?

   (A) India
   (B) Sri Lanka
   (C) Australia
   (D) Malaysia

168. What does Mrs. Mangala manufacture?

   (A) Jewelry
   (B) Fashions
   (C) Textiles
   (D) Toys

169. The word "line" in paragraph 1, line 1, is closest in meaning to

   (A) bag
   (B) straight
   (C) design
   (D) type

170. Where will the jewelry be exported from?

   (A) India
   (B) Australia
   (C) Malaysia
   (D) Sri Lanka

171. Which of the following best describes Mrs. Mangala's gems?

   (A) High-quality
   (B) Inexpensive
   (C) Uncut
   (D) Tax-free

Questions 172–174 refer to the following label.

TO WATERPROOF SHOES AND BOOTS:

Before applying, remove all dust, mud, and dirt from shoes. Make sure shoes are completely dry. Hold spray can 6–8 inches from clean, dry shoes. Let product saturate leather, covering all surfaces evenly. Allow to dry for one hour. Repeat application one more time. Allow to dry before use. The protection will last for six months under average climatic conditions. This product can also be used to protect leather handbags and briefcases. Do not use on suede. May cause discoloration of some leather products. Test on a small area first.

Caution

- Can cause damage to the respiratory system. Use in a well-ventilated area only, away from children and pets.

- Highly flammable. Use away from stoves, ovens, radiators, portable heaters, open flames, and other heat sources.

---

172. From what will this spray protect shoes?

   (A) Dirt
   (B) Dust
   (C) Water
   (D) Drying out

173. How many times must the shoes be sprayed?

   (A) One time
   (B) Two times
   (C) Six times
   (D) Eight times

174. How long will the application last?

   (A) One hour
   (B) One week
   (C) A couple of months
   (D) Half a year

286 PRACTICE TEST ONE

Questions 175–177 refer to the following table.

Introduction: While computer skills are becoming more and more necessary in everyday life, not enough children are receiving proper computer education in schools. This is the most serious educational issue facing our society today. A team of researchers looked into this issue in our local schools. See their results below.

SURVEY OF ELEMENTARY SCHOOL TEACHERS

Reasons for lack of computer education programs in public schools

	Respondents	
	Number	Percent
1. Not enough computers in school	14	32.6
2. Teachers fear computers	8	18.8
3. Not enough time in curriculum	14	32.6
4. Too expensive	20	46.5
5. Poor-quality software	16	37.2

Total Number of Teachers in Survey 43*
   (* Some teachers responded to
       more than one reason.)

175. How many teachers responded to the survey?

   (A) 20
   (B) 40
   (C) 43
   (D) 76

176. What was the reason given most often for the lack of computer education in schools?

   (A) Poor-quality software
   (B) Not enough computers
   (C) Fear of computers
   (D) Expense

177. Which of the following do teachers consider the least problematic?

   (A) Cost of computers
   (B) Quality of software
   (C) Fear of computers
   (D) Time in curriculum

GO ON TO THE NEXT PAGE

PRACTICE TEST ONE   287

Questions 178–180 refer to the following report.

The Hotel Manager of the Year Award Essay Competition winner was announced last night by the County Association of Hotel Managers. The winning essay was written by Mr. Randolph Ng of the Henry Street Historic Hotel. Mr. Ng wins a prize of $2,500 for his essay titled "The Hotel Family." "I believe that a hotel manager must be like a parent to his or her staff," said Mr. Ng at the awards ceremony banquet last night. "A good manager concentrates on helping others to be successful." The second and third prize winners were Gina Becke of the Woodside Gardens Hotel and Yoko Lee of the Hotel at Riverton, respectively. The annual essay competition was started by the County Association of Hotel Managers six years ago as a means of recognizing the hard work of hotel managers and encouraging them to reflect on what they do and share it with their colleagues. "It has become a very popular contest," says Jim Wilkerson, president of the association. "We get hundreds of entries every year." Following the awards presentation at last night's ceremony, Mr. Wilkerson announced that he will be retiring from his position as association president next year. A replacement has not yet been announced.

178. What did Mr. Ng do?

    (A) Wrote an essay
    (B) Asked for more money
    (C) Turned down a prize
    (D) Announced his retirement

179. When was the award winner announced?

    (A) Last year
    (B) Last night
    (C) This morning
    (D) This afternoon

180. What is Mr. Ng's advice?

    (A) Get your own promotion first
    (B) Have more children
    (C) Be a better parent
    (D) Help others be successful

GO ON TO THE NEXT PAGE

Questions 181–185 refer to the following advertisement and e-mail.

The National Theater presents
a live performance of
Romeo and Juliet
the third in our Festival of Shakespeare series

March 12–29
Thursday, Friday, and Saturday evenings
Saturday and Sunday matinees

Ticket prices
Matinee: orchestra—$45   balcony—$35
Evening: orchestra—$75   balcony—$55

Special group discounts are available. Groups of 15 or more receive 10% off the regular price. Groups of 25 or more receive 20% off the regular price. Call the box office for details.

Getting there:
The National Theater is conveniently located downtown, within easy walking distance of the Center City subway station and near major bus lines. A parking garage is located near the theater.

To: Maya Berg
From: Morris Stein
Subject: Shakespeare tickets

Maya,
I'd like to get tickets for our entire department to see *Romeo and Juliet*. If everyone goes, there will be just enough people for a 10% discount on the ticket price. Call the box office to find out how to order the group discount tickets, and see if you can get tickets for opening night. Make sure they are orchestra seats. I think this will be an enjoyable and convenient outing for everyone. We can all take the subway to the theater together after work.
Thanks,
Morris

290   PRACTICE TEST ONE

181. How many shows are there at the theater on Saturday?

(A) One
(B) Two
(C) Four
(D) Five

182. What does Mr. Stein want tickets for?

(A) A play
(B) A movie
(C) A lecture
(D) A concert

183. How many people work in Mr. Stein's department?

(A) 10
(B) 15
(C) 20
(D) 25

184. When does Mr. Stein want to go to the theater?

(A) March 12
(B) March 13
(C) March 21
(D) March 29

185. How does Mr. Stein plan to get to the theater?

(A) By bus
(B) By car
(C) By foot
(D) By subway

PRACTICE TEST ONE **291**

Questions 186–190 refer to the following two letters.

Customer Service Office
Union Bank
135 Main Street
Home, AK 99999

Dear Customer Service:

I received a debit card from your bank last week, and I have some questions regarding its use. Specifically, I am concerned about liability. If a thief steals my card and makes charges to my account, am I responsible for paying for them, or do I have protection like I have with my credit card? I looked in the booklet *Rules for Personal Accounts at Union Bank,* but I didn't see the information there.

I have been a customer at your bank for over 15 years and have always been happy with the service I have received there. I hope you can answer my question satisfactorily.

Sincerely,

Arthur Schmidt

Arthur Schmidt

Mr. Arthur Schmidt
1705 Oak Boulevard
Home, AK 99999

Dear Mr. Schmidt:

You recently sent a letter to our office asking about the Union Bank debit card. You wanted to know about liability. Our policy is the following: If you report a lost or stolen card within 48 hours, you are not responsible for any charges made on it. If you report it after 48 hours, you will be responsible for charges up to $50. So you see, the debit card has similar protection to a credit card. The information is actually in the document you mentioned. It appears on page 39. I am enclosing a photocopy of it for your convenience. Please let me know if I can be of any further assistance to you.

Sincerely,

Elena Ugarte

Elena Ugarte

186. Why did Mr. Schmidt write the letter?

    (A) To open a new bank account
    (B) To report a stolen credit card
    (C) To find out his account balance
    (D) To get information about his debit card

187. How long has Mr. Schmidt been banking at Union Bank?

    (A) For 48 hours
    (B) For one week
    (C) For a little less than 15 years
    (D) For more than 15 years

188. Where can Mr. Schmidt find the information he needs?

    (A) On the back of his debit card
    (B) In a booklet of bank rules
    (C) On his account statement
    (D) In his checkbook

189. What is probably Elena Ugarte's job?

    (A) Customer service representative
    (B) Credit card specialist
    (C) Loan officer
    (D) Teller

190. What did Ms. Ugarte enclose in the letter?

    (A) A new debit card
    (B) A copy of a page
    (C) A bill for $50
    (D) A photograph

GO ON TO THE NEXT PAGE

Questions 191–195 refer to the following two e-mail messages.

To: M. Takubo
From: J. H. Choi
Subject: Office rental

Mr. Takubo,
As we discussed on the phone, I am interested in renting an office for my accounting firm. We are a small business, so the space doesn't need to be large, but a convenient location is important. We need to be downtown and close to subway and bus lines. I hope you can find something reasonably priced for us in that area. We hope to spend no more than $2,000 a month. We have to leave our current office soon, so we need something that will be available by the end of the month. Thank you for your help.
Jung Choi

To: J. H. Choi
From: M. Takubo
Subject: Downtown office

Ms. Choi,
I have an office to show you that I think you'll like. It is right downtown on State Street. Since it is on the small side, the rent is somewhat lower than other offices in the area, although it's $500 more than the price you mentioned. I don't think you'll find a better price in such a convenient location. The building is very clean, and the landlord keeps it well maintained. The office will be available by the time you need it. I would like to show it to you soon. Will tomorrow morning suit you? I can meet you at the office at 11:00. The address is 730 State Street, Suite 900. Please let me know if this works for you.
M. Takubo

191. What is Mr. Takubo's job?

   (A) Landlord
   (B) Accountant
   (C) Real estate agent
   (D) Personal assistant

192. What kind of office does Ms. Choi want?

   (A) Large
   (B) Quiet
   (C) Expensive
   (D) Convenient

193. What is the rent on the State Street office?

   (A) $500
   (B) $1,500
   (C) $2,000
   (D) $2,500

194. When will the State Street office be available?

   (A) Right now
   (B) Tomorrow
   (C) By the end of this month
   (D) At the end of next month

195. What time does Mr. Takubo want to meet with Ms. Choi?

   (A) 7:30
   (B) 9:00
   (C) 11:00
   (D) 11:30

GO ON TO THE NEXT PAGE

Questions 196–200 refer to the following advertisement and letter.

Local cable television provider has an opening in its accounting department for a customer account representative. Responsibilities include answering customer telephone inquiries about billing and resolving billing disputes. Must have at least two years experience in customer service. Experience with accounting, billing, or collections desirable. Proficiency with word processing and spreadsheet software required. College degree in accounting or related field desirable. The right candidate will also have excellent communication and organization skills. Send résumé and cover letter to: Ms. Ahmad, Human Resources Director, Universal Cable Company, 1123 25th Street, Putnam, OH 44408.

June 25, 20___

Ms. Ahmad
Human Resources Director
Universal Cable Company
1123 25th Street
Putnam, OH 44408

Dear Ms. Ahmad:

I am interested in applying for the position you advertised in the Sunday edition of the Local Times. I have all the qualifications for the job, and more. I have worked for several years as a customer service representative for a mail order company—in fact, for three more years than you require. Prior to that, I worked for four years in the billing department of a local magazine. Though my college degree is in French, I took two semesters of accounting classes. I also have experience using the computer software your ad mentioned.

I hope you will consider me as a candidate for the position. I look forward to hearing from you.

Sincerely,

Joe Butler

Joe Butler

196. What kind of job is Joe applying for?

(A) Accountant
(B) Software engineer
(C) Human resources director
(D) Customer account representative

197. What should job applicants send to Ms. Ahmad?

(A) A résumé
(B) A billing statement
(C) A letter of recommendation
(D) A copy of their college diploma

198. Where does Joe work now?

(A) For a magazine
(B) For a French company
(C) For a mail order company
(D) For a cable television provider

199. How long has Joe had his current job?

(A) Two years
(B) Three years
(C) Four years
(D) Five years

200. What field is Joe's college degree in?

(A) Computer science
(B) Communications
(C) Accounting
(D) French

Stop! This is the end of the test. If you finish before time is called, you may go back to Parts 5, 6, and 7 and check your work.

PRACTICE TEST TWO

You will find the Answer Sheet for Practice Test Two on page 384. Detach it from the book and use it to record your answers. Play the audio program for Practice Test Two when you are ready to begin.

LISTENING TEST

 In the Listening test, you will be asked to demonstrate how well you understand spoken English. The entire Listening test will last approximately 45 minutes. There are four parts, and directions are given for each part. You must mark your answers on the separate sheet. Do not write your answers in the test book.

PART 1

Directions: For each question in this part, you will hear four statements about a picture in your test book. When you hear the statements, you must select the one statement that best describes what you see in the picture. Then find the number of the question on your answer sheet and mark your answer. The statements will not be printed in your test book and will be spoken only one time.

Example

Sample Answer

Statement (C), "They're standing near the table," is the best description of the picture, so you should select answer (C) and mark it on your answer sheet.

300 PRACTICE TEST TWO

1.

2.

GO ON TO THE NEXT PAGE

PRACTICE TEST TWO 301

3.

4.

5.

6.

7.
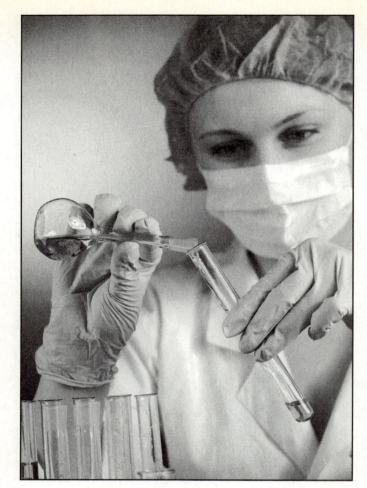

8.

9.

10.

PART 2

Directions: You will hear a question or statement and three responses spoken in English. They will not be printed in your test book and will be spoken only one time. Select the best response to the question or statement and mark the letter (A), (B), or (C) on your answer sheet.

Example

Sample Answer

You will hear: Where is the meeting room?

You will also hear: (A) To meet the new director.
                  (B) It's the first room on the right.
                  (C) Yes, at two o'clock.

Your best response to the question "Where is the meeting room?" is choice (B), "It's the first room on the right," so (B) is the correct answer. You should mark answer (B) on your answer sheet.

11. Mark your answer on your answer sheet.
12. Mark your answer on your answer sheet.
13. Mark your answer on your answer sheet.
14. Mark your answer on your answer sheet.
15. Mark your answer on your answer sheet.
16. Mark your answer on your answer sheet.
17. Mark your answer on your answer sheet.
18. Mark your answer on your answer sheet.
19. Mark your answer on your answer sheet.
20. Mark your answer on your answer sheet.
21. Mark your answer on your answer sheet.
22. Mark your answer on your answer sheet.
23. Mark your answer on your answer sheet.
24. Mark your answer on your answer sheet.
25. Mark your answer on your answer sheet.
26. Mark your answer on your answer sheet.
27. Mark your answer on your answer sheet.
28. Mark your answer on your answer sheet.
29. Mark your answer on your answer sheet.
30. Mark your answer on your answer sheet.
31. Mark your answer on your answer sheet.
32. Mark your answer on your answer sheet.
33. Mark your answer on your answer sheet.
34. Mark your answer on your answer sheet.
35. Mark your answer on your answer sheet.
36. Mark your answer on your answer sheet.
37. Mark your answer on your answer sheet.
38. Mark your answer on your answer sheet.
39. Mark your answer on your answer sheet.
40. Mark your answer on your answer sheet.

PART 3

Directions: You will hear some conversations between two people. You will be asked to answer three questions about what the speakers say in each conversation. Select the best response to each question and mark the letter (A), (B), (C), or (D) on your answer sheet. The conversations will not be printed in your test book and will be spoken only one time.

41. What are the speakers planning to do?
    (A) Sightsee downtown.
    (B) Go to a movie.
    (C) See a play.
    (D) Tell jokes.

42. How does the man feel?
    (A) Sick.
    (B) Good.
    (C) Bored.
    (D) Worried.

43. What time will the speakers leave?
    (A) 6:15.
    (B) 6:30.
    (C) 7:00.
    (D) 11:00.

44. What is Mrs. Kowalski doing?
    (A) Eating.
    (B) Sleeping.
    (C) Reading a report.
    (D) Attending a meeting.

45. What is the receptionist NOT going to do?
    (A) Take a message.
    (B) Answer the telephone.
    (C) Answer the caller's questions.
    (D) Transfer the call to Mrs. Kowalski.

46. When will the caller call again?
    (A) At noon.
    (B) Later this afternoon.
    (C) Tomorrow morning.
    (D) Tomorrow afternoon.

47. According to the man, how many wedding guests will there be?
    (A) Less than 100.
    (B) At least 100.
    (C) 300.
    (D) More than 400.

48. What does the man ask the woman to do?
    (A) Invite more people to their wedding.
    (B) Marry him.
    (C) Cater his wedding.
    (D) Have the caterer plan for extra guests.

49. What kind of food does the man want at the wedding?
    (A) Fish.
    (B) Chicken.
    (C) Vegetarian.
    (D) Steak.

50. When will the woman return?
    (A) In one hour.
    (B) Before lunch.
    (C) In the afternoon.
    (D) Tomorrow.

51. What will she pick up?
    (A) Ice.
    (B) A suit.
    (C) A sweater.
    (D) Photographs.

52. How much does she have to pay?
    (A) $7.00.
    (B) $11.00.
    (C) $17.00.
    (D) $36.00.

53. When did the woman go to the library?

   (A) Sunday.
   (B) Monday.
   (C) Tuesday.
   (D) Friday.

54. What did she do at the library?

   (A) Wrote a report.
   (B) Used the Internet.
   (C) Searched for books.
   (D) Read fashion magazines.

55. How does the man feel?

   (A) Hot.
   (B) Fine.
   (C) Tired.
   (D) Sorry.

56. What does the man tell the woman to do?

   (A) Hurry.
   (B) Get thinner.
   (C) Put on boots.
   (D) Change her dress.

57. How is the weather?

   (A) It's snowing.
   (B) It's raining.
   (C) It's fine.
   (D) It's hot.

58. Where are the speakers going?

   (A) To work.
   (B) To a show.
   (C) To a dinner.
   (D) To the shoe store.

59. Where are the speakers?

   (A) In an office.
   (B) In a clothes store.
   (C) In a health club.
   (D) In an exercise equipment store.

60. How long will the man stay?

   (A) One hour.
   (B) Four hours.
   (C) Until 4:00.
   (D) Until 8:00.

61. How can the man get more information?

   (A) Call.
   (B) Read a book.
   (C) Ask the woman.
   (D) Go online.

62. Where are the speakers?

   (A) At a concert.
   (B) At a lecture.
   (C) At a movie.
   (D) At a play.

63. How much did the tickets cost?

   (A) $50 each.
   (B) $100 each.
   (C) $115 each.
   (D) $150 each.

64. How does the man feel about the cost of the tickets?

   (A) Sad.
   (B) Glad.
   (C) Angry.
   (D) Comfortable.

65. What did the man order?

    (A) Pens.
    (B) Pencils.
    (C) Envelopes.
    (D) Notebooks.

66. How many did he order?

    (A) Four dozen.
    (B) Five dozen.
    (C) Four hundred.
    (D) Five hundred.

67. When will the order arrive?

    (A) Tuesday.
    (B) Wednesday.
    (C) On the weekend.
    (D) Next week.

68. Why does the man have to go to the office early?

    (A) To have breakfast there.
    (B) To attend a meeting.
    (C) To finish a report.
    (D) To get ready for a trip.

69. When will Mr. Park return to the office?

    (A) Tonight.
    (B) Tomorrow morning.
    (C) Tomorrow afternoon.
    (D) Tomorrow night.

70. When does the man plan to leave home?

    (A) 4:08.
    (B) 6:00.
    (C) 6:30.
    (D) 8:00.

GO ON TO THE NEXT PAGE

PART 4

Directions: You will hear some talks given by a single speaker. You will be asked to answer three questions about what the speaker says in each talk. Select the best response to each question and mark the letter (A), (B), (C), or (D) on your answer sheet. The talks will not be printed in your test book and will be spoken only one time.

71. Where would one hear this announcement?

    (A) At a movie theater.
    (B) In a cafe.
    (C) In a phone booth.
    (D) At an airport.

72. Why is this message being broadcast?

    (A) Someone has a message.
    (B) Security is at risk.
    (C) No one is paying attention.
    (D) The air is polluted.

73. What does Mr. Bajarin have to do?

    (A) Sit at his desk.
    (B) Show his ticket.
    (C) Go to the courtesy desk.
    (D) Get some fresh air.

---

74. Why is this building important?

    (A) It is very old.
    (B) Its architecture is unusual.
    (C) It contains statues of kings.
    (D) It has been excavated.

75. How is it known that the whole statue was 7 meters high?

    (A) The statue was measured.
    (B) An architect's records were discovered.
    (C) It was estimated from the size of the head.
    (D) Another statue of Damatian was 7 meters high also.

76. Where would this announcement most likely be heard?

    (A) In a museum.
    (B) In a classroom.
    (C) On a tour bus.
    (D) At church.

---

77. Why is this message being played?

    (A) The receptionist is not in.
    (B) Randall Svetlanovich is not in.
    (C) The voice mail is being tested.
    (D) The receptionist is busy.

78. How can the caller contact Randall Svetlanovich?

    (A) Send him a present.
    (B) Leave a voice mail message.
    (C) Mail him a letter.
    (D) Call later.

79. What will happen if the caller waits?

    (A) Randall Svetlanovich will pick up the phone.
    (B) The caller will be able to speak to the receptionist.
    (C) The caller will hear Randall Svetlanovich's e-mail address.
    (D) A voice mail will be sent to the caller.

---

80. How is the sky described?

    (A) High.
    (B) Blue.
    (C) Cloudy.
    (D) Sunny.

81. What is covering the region?

    (A) A high pressure system.
    (B) Light clouds.
    (C) Sun.
    (D) Picnics.

82. How high will the temperature be?

    (A) Around 17.
    (B) In the high teens.
    (C) Just below 70.
    (D) In the 70s.

---

310   PRACTICE TEST TWO

83. What crime was Mr. Robbins charged with?

(A) Embezzlement.
(B) Insider trading.
(C) Tax evasion.
(D) Gambling.

84. How did the Argentinean authorities find Ruiz?

(A) They had a tip from a local merchant.
(B) They obtained information from U.S. authorities.
(C) They carried out extensive investigations.
(D) They traced bogus tax statements.

85. What will happen to Mr. Robbins now?

(A) He will change his name to Ruiz.
(B) He will go to jail in Argentina.
(C) He will work as a florist.
(D) He will be returned to the United States.

---

86. What does this announcement concern?

(A) Rainy weather.
(B) Weekly duties.
(C) Late employees.
(D) Late buses.

87. How often are employees late?

(A) Three times a week.
(B) Five times a week.
(C) Ten times a week.
(D) Every day.

88. What problem do late employees cause?

(A) The bus driver has to stand in the rain.
(B) Employees at other stops wait longer for the bus.
(C) The late employees lose their pay.
(D) The punctual employees are on time.

---

89. What type of company is this?

(A) Clothing store.
(B) Restaurant.
(C) Camping equipment store.
(D) Baby furniture store.

90. How long is the sale?

(A) Half a day.
(B) Two days.
(C) All spring.
(D) All year.

91. How much are infants' clothes?

(A) Half price.
(B) $5.95.
(C) $7.98.
(D) $9.95.

---

92. What happened in downtown Riverdale?

(A) A water pipe broke.
(B) People were injured.
(C) There was an accident.
(D) People had to leave their homes.

93. How high did the water rise?

(A) Half a meter.
(B) A little less than one meter.
(C) Just over one meter.
(D) More than a meter and a half.

94. When did the rain stop?

(A) Saturday afternoon.
(B) Sunday evening.
(C) Monday evening.
(D) Wednesday morning.

GO ON TO THE NEXT PAGE

95. What type of company would leave this message?

   (A) An airline company.
   (B) A movie theater.
   (C) A travel company.
   (D) A phone company.

96. What happens if the caller presses 2?

   (A) The caller hears a movie schedule.
   (B) The caller can buy tickets.
   (C) The caller hears a flight schedule.
   (D) The caller can buy luggage.

97. How can the caller speak with a person?

   (A) Press 1.
   (B) Wait.
   (C) Call for a ticket agent.
   (D) Look for the number online.

98. Where will the concert be?

   (A) In a parking lot.
   (B) In City Hall.
   (C) In a library.
   (D) In a park.

99. When will the concert be held if the weather is bad?

   (A) Friday.
   (B) Saturday.
   (C) Sunday.
   (D) Monday.

100. How much are the tickets?

   (A) Free.
   (B) $3.00.
   (C) $7.00.
   (D) $30.00.

Stop! This is the end of the Listening test. Turn to Part 5 in your test book.

READING TEST

In the Reading test, you will read a variety of texts and answer several different types of reading comprehension questions. The entire Reading test will last 75 minutes. There are three parts, and directions are given for each part. You are encouraged to answer as many questions as possible within the time allowed.

You must mark your answers on the separate answer sheet. Do not write your answers in the test book.

PART 5

Directions: A word or phrase is missing in each of the sentences below. Four answer choices are given below each sentence. Select the best answer to complete the sentence. Then mark the letter (A), (B), (C), or (D) on your answer sheet.

---

101. Now that the company has changed ownership, we can expect to _____ a great many changes to our staff and structure.

    (A) undermine
    (B) underlie
    (C) undergo
    (D) underdo

102. _____ direct link exists between acidic soil and tooth decay, according to public health officials.

    (A) There is a
    (B) A
    (C) That there is a
    (D) Because

103. Passengers are hereby notified that all luggage _____ one hour before the scheduled departure time.

    (A) will check
    (B) will be checked
    (C) checks
    (D) has checked

104. People who do not _____ with the rules set forth in this notice will be asked to leave.

    (A) comply
    (B) agree
    (C) analyze
    (D) experiment

105. _____ in large quantities is not necessarily an indication of its quality.

    (A) A product is sold
    (B) It is a product sold
    (C) That a product is sold
    (D) A product sells

106. The new security guard on the first floor is _____ person that everyone likes him.

    (A) a such nice
    (B) a so nice
    (C) such nice
    (D) such a nice

GO ON TO THE NEXT PAGE

PRACTICE TEST TWO   **313**

107. No one is allowed on the _____ without a pass from the security desk.

(A) promises
(B) premises
(C) compromises
(D) comprises

108. The cost of the necklace depends _____ the quality of the gold.

(A) to
(B) on
(C) of
(D) about

109. We have _____ responsibility for the budget to Samantha, so Max is no longer in charge of it.

(A) accounted
(B) expected
(C) dismissed
(D) assigned

110. I wish I _____ the answer to your question so I could help you.

(A) would know
(B) knew
(C) know
(D) have known

111. We ask that all important correspondence be sent by registered _____ certified mail.

(A) or
(B) however
(C) but
(D) yet

112. The assistant jumped up on a chair and screamed when he saw a mouse _____ across the lounge.

(A) ran
(B) run
(C) runs
(D) had run

113. _____ the plumber could repair the toilet, he still would not do it.

(A) Therefore
(B) However
(C) So
(D) Even if

114. The laborers were _____ with mud after spending all day digging the ditch.

(A) covering
(B) cover
(C) covered
(D) coverage

115. _____ his joining the group late, his manager is confident that he will fit right in.

(A) Even though
(B) Despite
(C) If
(D) However

116. I filed my report last week, but now I wish I _____.

(A) have waited
(B) waited
(C) had waited
(D) wait

117. The doctors will be ready to go home as soon as they _____ their rounds.

(A) will finish
(B) will have finished
(C) are finishing
(D) finish

118. Vice President D'Agostino had her driver _____ her husband at the airport.

(A) picking up
(B) to pick up
(C) pick up
(D) picked up

314 PRACTICE TEST TWO

119. Mrs. Kurtoglu is a fast learner, and she has _____ mastered the drafting techniques.

    (A) already
    (B) ever
    (C) yet
    (D) still

120. We have to complete the project because we still have a _____ obligation.

    (A) contract
    (B) contractual
    (C) contracts
    (D) contracting

121. Who _____ how many of our clients can contact us at our new office?

    (A) knows
    (B) is knowing
    (C) has known
    (D) are knowing

122. The advertising staff has been working hard but has not finished the campaign _____.

    (A) still
    (B) yet
    (C) anymore
    (D) already

123. The high gross _____ product is an outcome of their work ethic.

    (A) nationally
    (B) nationwide
    (C) nation
    (D) national

124. Our company has chosen the Swedish vendor _____ they guarantee the best after-sales service.

    (A) and
    (B) because
    (C) but
    (D) so

125. The employee manual needs to be revised because much of the _____ is out of date.

    (A) contempt
    (B) contest
    (C) content
    (D) contend

126. Most small business owners are required to file their taxes _____.

    (A) quarterly
    (B) usually
    (C) anymore
    (D) still

127. We plan to hire a number of new staff members and will have to _____ our workspace in order to have room for them.

    (A) expend
    (B) enormous
    (C) extent
    (D) enlarge

128. Because of the strong economy, there has been an increase in exported _____ imported goods.

    (A) and
    (B) though
    (C) or
    (D) still

129. If Fujikin, Inc. _____ more available capital, they would have expanded their European operations.

    (A) has
    (B) had had
    (C) were having
    (D) has had

130. _____ the patient's condition get worse, the nurse will call in an internist.

    (A) Might
    (B) Unless
    (C) Should
    (D) If

PRACTICE TEST TWO 315

131. For reasons of public safety, the firefighters will not respond _____ the call is verified.

(A) and
(B) until
(C) even
(D) because

132. All shareholders must fill out a _____ slip in order to get money.

(A) withdraw
(B) withdrawing
(C) withdrawal
(D) withdrawn

133. The training staff does not have to attend the meeting, _____ they will anyway.

(A) but
(B) and
(C) or
(D) already

134. I will never forget _____ the beautiful country of Thailand during the summer after I graduated from college.

(A) to visit
(B) visited
(C) visiting
(D) visit

135. You can get _____ from the company for any money you spend on business travel.

(A) confidence
(B) expansion
(C) completion
(D) reimbursement

136. Our friends offered _____ us some of their camping equipment for our trip to the mountains.

(A) lending
(B) to lend
(C) to have lent
(D) on lending

137. All trainees _____ eighty hours of instruction by the end of March.

(A) complete
(B) will have completed
(C) will be completing
(D) have completed

138. After we announced the job opening, we received hundreds of _____ for the position.

(A) applications
(B) employments
(C) supervisors
(D) advertisements

139. I broke a tooth when I _____ into a piece of hard candy.

(A) bite
(B) had bitten
(C) have bitten
(D) bit

140. If Dr. Puri did not like jazz, he _____ to it so much.

(A) would listen
(B) would not listen
(C) would not have listened
(D) would be listening

316   PRACTICE TEST TWO

PART 6

Directions: Read the texts that follow. A word or phrase is missing in some of the sentences. Four answer choices are given below each of the sentences. Select the best answer to complete the text. Then mark the letter (A), (B), (C), or (D) on your answer sheet.

Questions 141–143 refer to the following letter.

HTCD Bank
20 State Street
Trenton, New Jersey 08625

June 17, 20___

Ms. Nukket Topal
451 West Huron Drive
Chicago, Illinois 60239

Dear Ms. Topal:

We received your e-mail requesting to close your savings account. Unfortunately, we are unable
to _____ with the request because it was sent by e-mail.

    141. (A) comply
        (B) compliant
        (C) compliance
        (D) complicate

To close your account, please mail us a letter stating that you wish to close your savings account.
Don't forget to include your sixteen-digit account number and the mailing address where you
would like to receive your remaining balance. You can also close your account by visiting our
nearest branch.

We always strive to give our customers the best possible service. We hope that you have been
happy with _____ and will consider using our bank again in the future. If you are

    142. (A) me
        (B) us
        (C) him
        (D) them

closing your account because you have had an _____ experience, please contact our

    143. (A) adequate
        (B) efficient
        (C) interesting
        (D) unsatisfactory

customer service representatives to discuss how we can serve you better.

If we may be of further assistance, please contact us any time. We look forward to working with
you.

Sincerely,

Erich Gleisner

Erich Gleisner
Account Manager

318 PRACTICE TEST TWO

Questions 144–146 refer to the following e-mail.

From: Marika Fiehne
To: Astrid Anderson
Subject: New office equipment request

Thank you for welcoming me to Ontel. My first week working here has been wonderful.

You asked me to e-mail you about the _____ of my office. Overall, it is very

144. (A) color
     (B) location
     (C) condition
     (D) dimension

nice and suits most of my needs. However, I would like a few small changes. Could I get a different chair? The current chair is really too small for me. I'd also like a conference table for _____ with clients.

145. (A) meet
     (B) to meet
     (C) meeting
     (D) will meet

My office also needs some technology upgrades. The computer's Internet connection is slow and frequently freezes in the afternoons. It is very frustrating. Also, I don't have the ability to participate in video teleconferencing. Would it be possible for me to get this? I am expected to participate in weekly conferences with our partners in other countries.

I will need a visit from the IT specialist. I should have antivirus software installed on my computer. Maybe my current computer has it, but I _____ find it.

146. (A) should not
     (B) could not
     (C) must not
     (D) may not

Thank you.

GO ON TO THE NEXT PAGE

PRACTICE TEST TWO   319

Questions 147–149 refer to the following memo.

From: Sarah Spencer
To: Eduardo Allende
Re: Vacancy on Information Technology Committee

Maria Robles has _____ from her position on the IT Committee.

147. (A) reacted
(B) resigned
(C) rejoined
(D) resisted

You have been recommended to fill the open spot. I hope that you want to participate on this important committee.

Your time commitment would be minimal; however, the _____ is an

148. (A) respond
(B) responsible
(C) responsibly
(D) responsibility

important one. As you know, criminals have broken into our competitors' computer systems. These hackers have cost our industry millions in lost and compromised data. To prevent this electronic theft, we have installed anti-hacking measures on our company's computers. This is one of the IT Committee's best achievements.

Our company's sales _____ because news spread about our

149. (A) have stagnated
(B) have increased
(C) have declined
(D) have stalled

anti-hacking devices. Customers trust us to protect their financial data.

The IT Committee agrees that you are our ideal new member. Please consider this invitation and get back to me within the next few days.

Thanks.

Questions 150–152 refer to the following e-mail.

From: Sigmund Ferdinand
To: Mendel Wagner
Subject: Itinerary

Dear Mendel,

I wanted to let you know that I booked our train tickets for the upcoming business trip. The price of the tickets was higher than I expected. I don't know if the train is always so expensive or if this is considered a peak time of year for _____ travel.

150. (A) air
     (B) road
     (C) rail
     (D) sea

In any case, Waterworks will cover the cost for us.

Since the conference is free _____ charge for all GBC members,

151. (A) at
     (B) in
     (C) by
     (D) of

Waterworks has offered to put us up in a 5-star hotel. I booked us two single rooms at Champlain Manor. It has a spa, a heated indoor pool, tennis courts, and three restaurants. We definitely won't be _____ there.

152. (A) bore
     (B) bored
     (C) boring
     (D) boredom

Let me know if you have any questions about these trip plans.

Yours,

Sigmund

PRACTICE TEST TWO **321**

PART 7

Directions: In this part you will read a selection of texts, such as magazine and newspaper articles, letters, and advertisements. Each text is followed by several questions. Select the best answer for each question and mark the letter (A), (B), (C), or (D) on your answer sheet.

Questions 153–154 refer to the following announcement.

Yamitomo International continues to be a pioneer in the digital revolution. As one of the first companies to manufacture compact discs, we continue to develop and implement the latest techniques.

At Yamitomo we manufacture compact discs, analog and digital cassettes, and records, as well as CD-ROM, Video CD, CD-1, and we are ready to deliver the next generation of sound carriers. We have carefully built a reputation of excellence in quality and customer service, providing not only manufacturing but also printing, packaging, drop-shipping, marketing, and distribution of music and media products.

We are ready to provide you with complete factory-to-store shelf service. Our complete wholesale catalog can be viewed online. To order, create your customer account by clicking on "new accounts." In addition, new accounts can be created and orders made by calling our wholesale customer line at 1-800-555-9098. Online or on the phone, you can always count on the high quality of our products.

153. What kind of company is Yamitomo International?

(A) An electronics manufacturer
(B) A computer distributor
(C) A music company
(D) A moving company

154. What is the focus of this passage?

(A) Musical artists are given much freedom with Yamitomo.
(B) Analog cassettes were developed by Yamitomo.
(C) Music and media products are sold by Yamitomo.
(D) Yamitomo has a reputation of excellence, diversity, and innovation.

322   PRACTICE TEST TWO

Questions 155–156 refer to the following advertisement.

Choose the magazine that meets your sourcing needs better...
And get a FREE sample copy!!!

As a regular or potential importer of Japanese-made electronics, computer products, and components, you know how important the latest marketing information is. You must also be alert to **what, where,** and **how** to get the most competitive offers to maintain your competitive edge.

Each of these magazines, *Purchasing Components, Purchasing Computer Equipment,* and *Purchasing Electronics,* is published monthly and reports on the Japanese exporting industries in each of these specialized fields. In addition to advertisements, they also contain surveys of new products, corporate and technological developments, details on market changes, and other valuable information to help you in your purchasing decisions.

Fill out the **Request a Free Sample Copy** form on the next page to receive a complimentary copy of the magazine that is right for your business. You will receive your copy in two to four weeks. In order to serve you better, we also ask you to take a few minutes to complete the survey at the bottom of the form. As a thank-you gift, we will send you, absolutely free, a copy of our *Guide to Japanese Electronics Companies.* This is an exclusive offer made available only to our customers. This book is not available in stores or online.

---

155. Who is the audience for this advertisement?

    (A) Japanese electronics manufacturers

    (B) Security system installation companies

    (C) Electronics wholesalers

    (D) Magazine publishers

156. What is offered in this advertisement?

    (A) Electronics components

    (B) Corporate changes

    (C) Magazines

    (D) Computer products

GO ON TO THE NEXT PAGE

PRACTICE TEST TWO

Questions 157–159 refer to the following letter.

Dear 25-Year Club Members,

The massive changes taking place within Anderson Industries may be somewhat unsettling for our longer-term employees. Yet, as we pause to recognize our 25-Year Club members, it is appropriate that we also acknowledge the need to adapt and grow. For this, we need the knowledge and experience of you and of all our employees to guide us successfully through this journey.

Most of you will realize that the manufacturing processes that we utilize and the methods that we use to guide our business have changed very little over the years. In today's constantly changing world, it is the innovative companies with continuous improvement of flexible manufacturing systems and modern business practices that capture the attention of their customers. This is the kind of company that we are striving to become.

You are aware that we have been working over the past several months with a team of experts to discuss innovations in our manufacturing processes and business practices. I want to ensure that you are also aware that we have built into this discussion process numerous opportunities to consult with our 25-Year Club members. No one knows better than we do that the perspective gained from experience is an essential part of any innovation process.

Anderson Industries has a solid reputation in the automotive industry, thanks to the efforts of you, the 25-Year Club members. Now it is time for all of us to create the necessary changes in our company to ensure that our 25-Year Club will grow in membership for years to come.

Thank you all for your loyalty and commitment to the success of Anderson Industries.

Sincerely,

Karl Anderson

Karl Anderson
CEO

---

157. Why was this letter written?

(A) To show appreciation to long-term employees

(B) To explain the changes that have taken place

(C) To explain that changes are necessary in the near future

(D) To recruit new members

158. What does the writer of this letter hope for?

(A) Innovation in the manufacturing process

(B) Customers

(C) A growth in club membership

(D) A reputation in the automotive industry

159. Where would this letter be most likely to appear?

(A) In a trade publication

(B) In a company newsletter

(C) In an executive memo

(D) In a community newspaper

324 PRACTICE TEST TWO

Questions 160–161 refer to the following passage.

Flying over Venezuela's Lake Maracaibo, one is struck by the deep orange color of the water spewing from a river into the lake. This is not a natural phenomenon but the result of aggressive mining practices carried out in western Venezuela, where tons of earth and rock are flushed away every day in the search for valuable diamonds. As the river carries the earth and rock away from the mining areas, it carries it into other areas, most particularly to Lake Maracaibo. Tons of silt flow into the lake every day, with dire consequences for the natural environment and the people who live there. On the one hand, the silting of Lake Maracaibo increases the risk of flooding, thus endangering the lives and livelihoods of people living in the area. In addition, the mining is also destroying fishing grounds that have been a major source of protein food for the country, as well as an important part of the economy.

160. What is the most noticeable characteristic of the river?

(A) Its location
(B) Its direction
(C) Its rate of flow
(D) Its color

161. What has been the outcome of the silting of Lake Maracaibo?

(A) Fishing grounds have been increased.
(B) The loss of protein has been offset by the economic development of the mining.
(C) There has been an increase in the risk of flooding.
(D) Mining and flooding have been kept in check.

GO ON TO THE NEXT PAGE

PRACTICE TEST TWO **325**

Questions 162–163 refer to the following notice.

The monthly luncheon meeting of the National Society of Fundraising Executives will be held at noon on Friday, May 5, in the Hall of World Cultures at the Knotty Pines Center, located at 4141 East State Street. The cost is $35 per person. Reservations are due by April 21 and should be sent directly to the Hall of World Cultures at the Knotty Pines Center. Following lunch, there will be a brief membership meeting with committee reports, then we will hear from our guest speaker. This month's speaker is Miranda Bottomley of Grantwriters, Inc., who will speak on the topic "Tapping into Old Money." Please note that this event is for members only. All those who are interested in joining the society in time to attend this month's meeting should contact our membership coordinator, Dr. Kamil Srivastava, at (312) 555-1298 before April 21.

---

162. Where should one send reservations?

(A) To Dr. Srivastava's office
(B) To the Hall of World Cultures of Knotty Pines
(C) To the luncheon hall
(D) To the National Society of Fundraising Executives' office

163. Who should contact Dr. Srivastava?

(A) Potential society members
(B) Current society members
(C) Any international representatives
(D) Fundraising experts

326   PRACTICE TEST TWO

Questions 164–166 refer to the following chart.

Manufacturer's Value of Shipments of Selected Types of Mining Equipment in the Industry*			
TYPE OF MACHINERY	$ AMOUNT IN MILLIONS	$ AMOUNT IN MILLIONS	% OF INCREASE OR DECREASE
Portable crushing, pulverizing, and screening machinery	63.7	85.1	+25
Stationary crushing, pulverizing, and screening machinery	160.3	132.1	–18
Underground mining machinery	381.8	318.8	–17
Mineral-processing equipment	90.2	86.6	–4
Portable drilling rigs	295.3	252.8	–14
Mine conveyors, hoists, and locomotives	56.6	82.8	+46

*Please note: For an analysis of the information on this chart, please see page 10 of this publication. The information on this chart presents shipment values from the past two years. For projected values for the next five years, please see the chart on page 15 of this publication.

164. What type of chart is this?

(A) An inventory list
(B) An industry report
(C) An advertisement
(D) A sales report

165. What was the decrease in mineral processing equipment?

(A) 3 percent
(B) 4 percent
(C) 14 percent
(D) 18 percent

166. Which product saw the largest increase in shipments?

(A) Portable crushing machinery
(B) Portable drilling rigs
(C) Mineral-processing equipment
(D) All mining machinery and related equipment

GO ON TO THE NEXT PAGE

PRACTICE TEST TWO 327

Questions 167–169 refer to the following advertisement.

NARTAGAZ

The 10th annual
International Trade Fair
for
Equipment for the Oil & Gas Industry
will take place at
Korbutt Andropov Park and Fairgrounds, Moscow, Russia
June 10–15, 20__

Sponsored by:
NGJ International GmbH
Stuttgart, Germany

Exhibitors and attendees should contact:
NGJ International
1151 Park Street
Baltimore, MD 22899
(410) 555-9292

Exhibitors:
Please ask for an application package.
Applications due: January 1, 20__

Attendees:
Visitors packages will be available February 1, including:
• A list of exhibit highlights
• Information on local accommodations
• Information on discounted travel and hotel packages

---

167. Who is sponsoring this event?

(A) U.S. Department of Commerce
(B) City of Moscow
(C) Oil & gas industry
(D) NGJ International

168. Where should one write for more information?

(A) Baltimore
(B) Moscow
(C) Stuttgart
(D) Washington, D.C.

169. Who will attend this trade fair?

(A) Politicians
(B) Oil and gas executives
(C) Environmentalists
(D) Trade negotiators

Questions 170–172 refer to the following advertisement.

DYNA BOLD

Most European financial institutions agree that an ATM is not just a purchase, it is an investment. That is why more than 50 percent of banks that have ATMs have invested in ours.

At DynaBold we have always built our ATMs to last. But since we are continually developing new technologies, we have made them adaptable, too. Years ago we created the industry's first modular ATM that could be upgraded without changing the housing. Today these ATMs are still yielding dividends for their original investors.

However, we do much more than protect your investment. With more than 100 years of security expertise, we make sure your ATM is secure, too. Our service organization responds 24 hours a day, 365 days a year. Also, all our service engineers are trained to maintain everything from electronic components to security features.

It is no wonder that the majority of European financial institutions use our ATMs. They know their money is securely invested.

Shouldn't you invest your money wisely, too? Call DynaBold today to find out how. We will arrange to send a DynaBold representative to visit you at your place of business to discuss our complete line of products and show you how a DynaBold ATM system can save you valuable time and money in ways that other ATM systems cannot. Various maintenance and upgrade packages are available. Our representative will help you select the best system and packages to serve your needs. Call today.

---

170. What kind of company is DynaBold?

(A) An ATM manufacturer
(B) An investment firm
(C) A bank
(D) A security service

171. What did DynaBold develop?

(A) Modular homes
(B) New investment methods
(C) A chain of banks
(D) Upgradable ATMs

172. How does the company maintain its ATMs?

(A) By upgrading them often
(B) Through a 24-hour service program
(C) By making them secure
(D) By developing new technologies

GO ON TO THE NEXT PAGE

Questions 173–176 refer to the following passage.

Drug advisory committees report to the Ministry of Health. It is the responsibility of these committees to protect consumers, most of whom have little chemical or biological knowledge with which to evaluate medications. Drug advisory committees provide the Ministry of Health with the necessary information for evaluating the proper degree of access to medications by the consumer. Drug advisory committees also oversee the preparation of materials that provide clearly explained information about commonly available drugs in a manner that is readily understandable to the layperson. Drug education may take the form of literature, advertisements, training of health care personnel, or other means as deemed appropriate by each committee. Drug advisory committees should be composed of physicians, registered nurses, epidemiologists, and pharmacologists. Members must posess specific scientific expertise and must have considerable experience working with consumers so that they can assess the impact of their decisions and projects on consumers. Each committee must have 10–15 members, who will be evaluated every two years by officials from the Ministry of Health.

173. Who is the audience for this passage?

(A) Nurses
(B) Medical doctors
(C) Lab workers
(D) Consumers

174. What is the purpose of these committees?

(A) To advise the Ministry of Health on the safety of drugs
(B) To sell drugs
(C) To serve as consumer advocates
(D) To evaluate the Ministry of Health

175. The word "advisory" in line 1 is closest in meaning to

(A) performance
(B) advocacy
(C) testing
(D) consulting

176. Which topic would a drug advisory committee discuss?

(A) Causes of cancer
(B) Availability of over-the-counter drugs
(C) Hospital drug-dispensing systems
(D) Ministry of Health budget cuts

Questions 177–180 refer to the following advisory.

> Having the proper documentation when you travel abroad is very important. Remember that immigration and customs officials are very document-minded, so failing to obtain the proper paperwork before entering a country or losing your passport in a foreign city can cause many complications. When traveling, you should always know where your passport is. Always carry it in a safe place on your person or, if not going far, leave it in the hotel safe. Do not leave it lying about in your hotel room or easily visible in a pocket. If staying in a country for several weeks, it is worthwhile to register at your embassy or consulate. Then, if your passport is stolen, the process of replacing it is simpler and faster. It is also recommended to keep photocopies of essential documents as well as some additional passport-sized photographs.
>
> Remember that it is your responsibility to ensure that your passport is stamped in and out when you cross borders. The absence of entry and exit stamps can cause serious difficulties and could invalidate your visa. Therefore, it is important to seek out the proper officials if the stamping process is not carried out as you cross the border. Also, do not lose your entry card. Replacing it can cause a lot of headaches and expense. Citizens of countries that require visas, such as France and Korea, can expect more delays and problems at border crossings.

177. Where would this advisory most likely appear?

    (A) In a newspaper
    (B) In an embassy pamphlet
    (C) In an airline in-flight magazine
    (D) In a travel guidebook

178. What should travelers do if staying in a country for a month?

    (A) Register with their embassy
    (B) Leave their passport in the hotel
    (C) Find a good hotel
    (D) Have extra passport photos taken

179. If border officials do not stamp the passport, what should a traveler do?

    (A) Request that it be stamped as soon as possible
    (B) Refrain from entering the country
    (C) Go to the embassy
    (D) Get help at the hotel

180. The word "ensure" in paragraph 2, line 1, is closest in meaning to

    (A) fasten
    (B) tighten
    (C) make certain
    (D) protect

PRACTICE TEST TWO 331

Questions 181–185 refer to the following letter and memo.

Lumpkin's Computer Center
88 Chestnut Street
Winterdale, MN 90480

July 26, 20___

Dear Neighborhood Business,

Lumpkin's Computer Center has just opened in your neighborhood. We offer all the computer supplies you need for your daily business. In addition, we do computer repair and sell refurbished computers. Best of all, we offer a convenient location close to your place of business. Please stop by and find out what we have to offer that will make your work easier. Our specials this week include brand-new printer ink cartridges @ $25 each and computer paper @ $7 for a package of 500 sheets. Show this letter for an additional 10% off your first purchase at Lumpkin's. See you soon!

Your neighbors,

Robert Oscar

Robert and Oscar Lumpkin

Holloway & Svenson
Attorneys-at-Law

Office Memorandum

From: Myra Holloway
To: Yoshi Phipps
Re: Computer Center

Please look at the attached letter. What a convenience to have a computer supply store on the same block as we are! Why don't you go today and pick up some things, let's say 5 ink cartridges and 10 packs of paper. Don't forget to take the letter with you for the discount. Then you can pop around the corner to Crawford's Stationery on Maple Avenue for some manila envelopes and anything else you think we need. Thanks.

---

332   PRACTICE TEST TWO

181. Who probably received this letter?

   (A) Local attorneys only
   (B) Holloway & Svenson only
   (C) All neighborhood businesses
   (D) Businesses throughout the city

182. Who are Robert and Oscar Lumpkin?

   (A) Attorneys
   (B) Software trainers
   (C) Computer manufacturers
   (D) Owners of the Computer Center

183. According to the letter, what can you do at the Computer Center?

   (A) Buy a used computer
   (B) Learn to use a computer
   (C) Have your printer repaired
   (D) Recycle your ink cartridges

184. Where is the office of Holloway & Svenson located?

   (A) On Maple Avenue
   (B) On Chestnut Street
   (C) On Crawford Street
   (D) On Lumpkin Avenue

185. If Yoshi follows Myra's instructions, how much will he spend at the Computer Center?

   (A) $112.50
   (B) $125.00
   (C) $175.50
   (D) $195.00

GO ON TO THE NEXT PAGE

PRACTICE TEST TWO **333**

Questions 186–190 refer to the following two letters.

September 9, 20___

Mr. T. Sachimoto
Human Resources Director
The Spindex Corporation
1809 35th Street
Mayfield, AL 20812

Dear Mr. Sachimoto:

I recently received my master's degree in Accounting from Pitt University and am currently seeking a position as an accountant. I graduated from Carson College with a bachelor's degree in Economics and worked for three years as a bookkeeper for Harrison Telemarketing, Inc. before I entered graduate school. I would be interested in applying for any opening you may have for an accountant. I am enclosing my résumé and two letters of reference. I also have copies of my college transcripts available if you are interested in seeing them.

Sincerely,

Gina Degenaro

Gina Degenaro

September 30, 20___

Ms. Gina Degenaro
71 Fern Lane
Mayfield, AL 20812

Dear Ms. Degenaro:

Thank you for your letter expressing interest in working for the Spindex Corporation. You have an impressive background. I was especially interested to see that you went to the same graduate school that I did.

We generally find that the best way to get a professional position in a large company like Spindex is to begin in one of the lower level jobs. Then you have the opportunity to show what you can do, and when an opening in your field comes up, you are well positioned to apply for it.

We currently have an opening in our Accounting Department, which you might be interested in applying for. It is for an administrative assistant. If you are interested in such a position, please call my assistant, Ms. Rogers, at 593-555-0954 to set up a time for an interview. When you come in, please bring the documents you mentioned in your letter. I look forward to meeting you.

Sincerely,

T. Sachimoto

T. Sachimoto

---

334   PRACTICE TEST TWO

186. Why did Ms. Degenaro write the letter?

(A) To ask for advice
(B) To answer an ad
(C) To apply for a job
(D) To ask for a reference

187. What job does Mr. Sachimoto offer to Ms. Degenaro?

(A) Accountant
(B) Bookkeeper
(C) Telemarketer
(D) Administrative assistant

188. Where did Mr. Sachimoto go to graduate school?

(A) Pitt University
(B) Carson College
(C) Harrison College
(D) University of Mayfield

189. Who is Ms. Rogers?

(A) Head of the Accounting Department
(B) Ms. Degenaro's former employer
(C) Mr. Sachimoto's assistant
(D) Director of Spindex

190. What should Ms. Degenaro take with her to the interview?

(A) Her résumé
(B) Her phone number
(C) Her college transcripts
(D) Her letters of reference

GO ON TO THE NEXT PAGE

PRACTICE TEST TWO **335**

Questions 191–195 refer to the following itinerary and e-mail.

Trip Itinerary for Akiko Ono

Monday, May 12th	Sydney	Meeting with Mr. Andrews of BelAir Corp.
Tuesday, May 13th– Wednesday, May 14th	Melbourne	Visit to the offices of Holiday, Inc.
Thursday, May 15th– Sunday, May 18th	Darwin	Global Marketing Assoc. Conference
Monday, May 19th	Singapore	Meeting with Ms. Chang of World Market
Tuesday, May 20th	Hong Kong	Visit to Technomarket branch office
Wednesday, May 21st	Home	

To: Tamako Sato
From: Akiko Ono
Subject: My Trip
Attach: Itinerary

Hello Tamako,

I am attaching the itinerary for my upcoming trip. Please take care of the following for me:

1. I'll need the photos for the new ad campaign to show at the Global Marketing Conference, but I don't think they'll be ready before I leave. I'll be staying at the Hotel Internationale during the conference. Please send the photos to me there.
2. I will discuss with Ms. Chang the visit she plans to make here. It will be very soon. I'll call you from her office to let you know the exact dates so you can start getting ready for her.
3. Please note that Mr. Andrews no longer works for Holiday, Inc. Correct his contact information in our files.

Thanks.

191. How many days will Akiko stay in Melbourne?

(A) One
(B) Two
(C) Three
(D) Four

192. When will she be in Hong Kong?

(A) May 12th
(B) May 13th–14th
(C) May 15th–18th
(D) May 20th

193. What company does Mr. Andrews work for?

(A) BelAir Corporation
(B) Holiday, Inc.
(C) World Market
(D) Technomarket

194. Where will Akiko be when she receives the photos?

(A) Sydney
(B) Melbourne
(C) Darwin
(D) Singapore

195. When will Akiko call Tamako?

(A) May 18th
(B) May 19th
(C) May 20th
(D) May 21st

GO ON TO THE NEXT PAGE

PRACTICE TEST TWO **337**

Questions 196–200 refer to the following two letters.

October 17, 20___

Dear Roberto,

I have some interesting news for you. My company is sending me to Greendale to work on a project in our branch office there. I will spend about three months at that branch office. I wondered if you could give me some advice about housing. The office can arrange a hotel for me, but I'd rather find something more comfortable. Since my family won't be with me, I'll only need a small apartment. Our office is downtown, right across from Greendale Park, so I'll need to be able to get there easily by public transportation. I won't have a car. I would like to pay no more than $1,500 a month. Is that possible in Greendale? I would appreciate any advice you could give me.

I'm also looking forward to seeing you. I plan to stay two weeks after my assignment is finished to travel around the area. I plan to spend most of that time at the beach. Maybe you would like to join me on this vacation. I'll see you soon.

Your friend,

Luis

Luis Silva

October 31, 20___

Dear Luis,

I was very happy to receive your news. I know you'll enjoy your time in our wonderful city. I have a good recommendation for you. There are several hotels that have special suites that are like small apartments. They all have kitchens and are very comfortable to live in for a few months. They are also inexpensive— about $300 less than the price you said you could pay. All of these hotels are located in the North End of the city. There are hotels in the business district, close to your office, but they don't have these comfortable suites. I am enclosing some brochures so you can pick the hotel you like the best.

I look forward to seeing you and joining you on the vacation you have planned.

Your friend,

Roberto

Roberto Mendez

196. Why is Luis going to Greendale?

(A) To take a vacation
(B) To buy house
(C) To visit Roberto
(D) To work

197. How long will Luis be in Greendale?

(A) Two weeks
(B) Three weeks
(C) Two months
(D) Three months

198. How much are the hotel suites that Roberto recommends?

(A) $300
(B) $1,200
(C) $1,500
(D) $1,800

199. Where are the hotel suites that Roberto recommends?

(A) Downtown
(B) Near a park
(C) In the North End
(D) In the business district

200. According to his letter, what will Roberto do during Luis's stay in Greendale?

(A) Work with him
(B) Take him to the park
(C) Invite him to his house
(D) Go to the beach with him

Stop! This is the end of the test. If you finish before time is called, you may go back to Parts 5, 6, and 7 and check your work.

PRACTICE TEST THREE

You will find the Answer Sheet for Practice Test Three on page 385.
Detach it from the book and use it to record your answers. Play the audio
program for Practice Test Three when you are ready to begin.

LISTENING TEST

 In the Listening test, you will be asked to demonstrate how well you understand spoken English. The entire Listening test will last approximately 45 minutes. There are four parts, and directions are given for each part. You must mark your answers on the separate sheet. Do not write your answers in the test book.

PART 1

Directions: For each question in this part, you will hear four statements about a picture in your test book. When you hear the statements, you must select the one statement that best describes what you see in the picture. Then find the number of the questions on your answer sheet and mark your answer. The statements will not be printed in your test book and will be spoken only one time.

Example

Sample Answer

Statement (C), "They're standing near the table," is the best description of the picture, so you should select answer (C) and mark it on your answer sheet.

342   PRACTICE TEST THREE

1.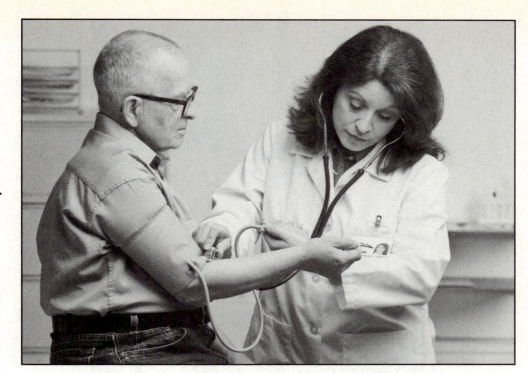

2.

GO ON TO THE NEXT PAGE

PRACTICE TEST THREE 343

3.

4.

5.

6.

7.

8.

9.

10.

GO ON TO THE NEXT PAGE

PRACTICE TEST THREE 347

PART 2

Directions: You will hear a question or statement and three responses spoken in English. They will not be printed in your test book and will be spoken only one time. Select the best response to the question or statement and mark the letter (A), (B), or (C) on your answer sheet.

Example

Sample Answer

You will hear: Where is the meeting room?

You will also hear: (A) To meet the new director.
(B) It's the first room on the right.
(C) Yes, at two o'clock.

Your best response to the question "Where is the meeting room?" is choice (B), "It's the first room on the right," so (B) is the correct answer. You should mark answer (B) on your answer sheet.

11. Mark your answer on your answer sheet.
12. Mark your answer on your answer sheet.
13. Mark your answer on your answer sheet.
14. Mark your answer on your answer sheet.
15. Mark your answer on your answer sheet.
16. Mark your answer on your answer sheet.
17. Mark your answer on your answer sheet.
18. Mark your answer on your answer sheet.
19. Mark your answer on your answer sheet.
20. Mark your answer on your answer sheet.
21. Mark your answer on your answer sheet.
22. Mark your answer on your answer sheet.
23. Mark your answer on your answer sheet.
24. Mark your answer on your answer sheet.
25. Mark your answer on your answer sheet.
26. Mark your answer on your answer sheet.
27. Mark your answer on your answer sheet.
28. Mark your answer on your answer sheet.
29. Mark your answer on your answer sheet.
30. Mark your answer on your answer sheet.
31. Mark your answer on your answer sheet.
32. Mark your answer on your answer sheet.
33. Mark your answer on your answer sheet.
34. Mark your answer on your answer sheet.
35. Mark your answer on your answer sheet.
36. Mark your answer on your answer sheet.
37. Mark your answer on your answer sheet.
38. Mark your answer on your answer sheet.
39. Mark your answer on your answer sheet.
40. Mark your answer on your answer sheet.

PART 3

 Directions: You will hear some conversations between two people. You will be asked to answer three questions about what the speakers say in each conversation. Select the best response to each question and mark the letter (A), (B), (C), or (D) on your answer sheet. The conversations will not be printed in your test book and will be spoken only one time.

41. Why will the woman be late for the meeting?
    (A) She has to buy something at the store.
    (B) She has to go to the dentist.
    (C) She has to prepare a report.
    (D) She has an appointment with a client.

42. What time will she arrive for the meeting?
    (A) 9:30.
    (B) 10:00.
    (C) 11:00.
    (D) 11:30.

43. What will be discussed at the meeting?
    (A) Marketing.
    (B) The budget.
    (C) Staff changes.
    (D) Plans for the future.

44. Where does this conversation take place?
    (A) On an airplane.
    (B) On a train.
    (C) At a travel agency.
    (D) At an airport.

45. Which row is the woman's seat in?
    (A) 1.
    (B) 2.
    (C) 3.
    (D) 4.

46. What will the woman probably do next?
    (A) Exchange her ticket.
    (B) Order a steak.
    (C) Go to another gate.
    (D) Ask for a refund.

47. How many copies does the woman need?
    (A) Two.
    (B) Eight.
    (C) Fifteen.
    (D) Fifty.

48. When does she need them?
    (A) This morning.
    (B) Right after lunch.
    (C) Tomorrow morning.
    (D) Tomorrow afternoon.

49. Where will the man put the copies?
    (A) In the conference room.
    (B) In the lunch room.
    (C) In the woman's office.
    (D) In the hallway.

50. What will the woman have for lunch?
    (A) Spaghetti.
    (B) Meat.
    (C) Rice.
    (D) Sandwich.

51. How much will she pay?
    (A) $8.00.
    (B) $8.15.
    (C) $8.50.
    (D) $15.00.

52. Where will she eat her lunch?
    (A) In the park.
    (B) In her car.
    (C) In her office.
    (D) In the restaurant.

GO ON TO THE NEXT PAGE

53. What time is it now?

    (A) Noon.
    (B) 7:00.
    (C) 9:00.
    (D) 11:00.

54. What does the woman want to do?

    (A) Go for a run.
    (B) Write a report.
    (C) Get a bus ticket.
    (D) Finish reading a book.

55. Who will help the woman?

    (A) The man.
    (B) The clients.
    (C) Her boss.
    (D) Her assistant.

56. How many tickets does the woman have?

    (A) Two.
    (B) Four.
    (C) Six.
    (D) Eight.

57. What are the tickets for?

    (A) A concert.
    (B) A movie.
    (C) A play.
    (D) A tennis match.

58. What will the man do tonight?

    (A) Mail a package.
    (B) Move to a new apartment.
    (C) Pack boxes.
    (D) Play tennis.

59. Where is the woman going tonight?

    (A) To work.
    (B) To class.
    (C) To the park.
    (D) To the garage.

60. How will she get there?

    (A) Bus.
    (B) Walking.
    (C) Car.
    (D) Train.

61. What's the weather like?

    (A) Snow.
    (B) Rain.
    (C) Cold.
    (D) Warm.

62. Why isn't Ms. Clark available?

    (A) She's making a phone call.
    (B) She's with her accountant.
    (C) She's at a meeting.
    (D) She has an appointment.

63. How does the man feel about the situation?

    (A) Mad.
    (B) Sorry.
    (C) Happy.
    (D) Disappointed.

64. When will Ms. Clark be available to see the man?

    (A) Monday.
    (B) Tuesday.
    (C) Thursday.
    (D) Friday.

65. Where does the woman ask the man to go?

    (A) The bank.
    (B) The banquet.
    (C) The printer's.
    (D) The cafeteria.

66. When will he go?

    (A) At noon.
    (B) After lunch.
    (C) On Tuesday.
    (D) Next week.

67. What will the man bring back with him?

    (A) Some ink.
    (B) A newspaper.
    (C) A briefcase.
    (D) Some paper.

68. What does the woman invite the man to do?

    (A) Play golf.
    (B) Have lunch.
    (C) Go to the beach.
    (D) Attend a conference.

69. When does she want him to do it?

    (A) Monday.
    (B) Saturday.
    (C) Next week.
    (D) Next month.

70. Why doesn't the man accept the invitation?

    (A) He has to work.
    (B) He will be away on vacation.
    (C) He isn't a member of the club.
    (D) He's been feeling weak.

GO ON TO THE NEXT PAGE

PART 4

 Directions: You will hear some talks given by a single speaker. You will be asked to answer three questions about what the speaker says in each talk. Select the best response to each question and mark the letter (A), (B), (C), or (D) on your answer sheet. The talks will not be printed in your test book and will be spoken only one time.

71. What kind of business is Chittendale?
    (A) Bank.
    (B) Accounting firm.
    (C) Real estate agency.
    (D) Small business consulting.

72. What time does Chittendale close on Saturdays?
    (A) Noon.
    (B) 3:00.
    (C) 8:00.
    (D) 9:00.

73. What happens when you press 4?
    (A) You speak with an office manager.
    (B) You get information about your account.
    (C) You get information about a new program.
    (D) You speak with a customer service representative.

74. What will be the topic of today's show?
    (A) Clothes.
    (B) Résumés.
    (C) Consultants.
    (D) Newsletters.

75. How long has Mr. McLean been in business?
    (A) Fifteen months.
    (B) Sixteen months.
    (C) Fifteen years.
    (D) Sixteen years.

76. What will be on the radio after The Business Hour?
    (A) An interview.
    (B) The news.
    (C) An author talk.
    (D) The weather.

77. What product is advertised?
    (A) Computer.
    (B) Printer.
    (C) Paper.
    (D) Ink.

78. How much does it cost?
    (A) $30.
    (B) $40.
    (C) $50.
    (D) $60.

79. Where is it sold?
    (A) In stores.
    (B) At a factory.
    (C) Online.
    (D) In a catalog.

80. How is the weather?
    (A) Warm.
    (B) Clear.
    (C) Rain.
    (D) Wind.

81. When will the weather change?
    (A) This afternoon.
    (B) At 10:00.
    (C) This evening.
    (D) Tomorrow morning.

82. What is the temperature now?
    (A) 40.
    (B) 45.
    (C) 58.
    (D) 68.

352   PRACTICE TEST THREE

83. What is this advice about?

    (A) How to pack suits.
    (B) How to choose suits.
    (C) How to keep suits neat.
    (D) How to remove spots from suits.

84. What is recommended?

    (A) Choose a dark suit.
    (B) Iron your suit yourself.
    (C) Wear a different suit everyday.
    (D) Never buy a checked suit.

85. How many pairs of shoes are needed?

    (A) One.
    (B) Three.
    (C) Four.
    (D) Ten.

86. What is Harvey Miller's job?

    (A) Résumé writer.
    (B) Office assistant.
    (C) Paralegal.
    (D) Lawyer.

87. What days is the office open?

    (A) Tuesday, Friday, and Saturday only.
    (B) Tuesday through Saturday.
    (C) Tuesday through Friday only.
    (D) Sunday and Monday.

88. How can you make an appointment?

    (A) Call back later.
    (B) Send an e-mail.
    (C) Leave a message.
    (D) Visit the office.

89. What kind of event is announced?

    (A) A sale.
    (B) A dinner.
    (C) A graduation.
    (D) A food exhibit.

90. Where will the event take place?

    (A) A mall.
    (B) A hotel.
    (C) A school.
    (D) A restaurant.

91. How many days will the event last?

    (A) One.
    (B) Two.
    (C) Three.
    (D) Seven.

92. When will passengers board the train?

    (A) In 5 minutes.
    (B) In 15 minutes.
    (C) Tonight.
    (D) Tomorrow afternoon.

93. What is the weather like?

    (A) Rain.
    (B) Snow.
    (C) Clear.
    (D) Hot.

94. What are passengers asked to do?

    (A) Get their tickets now.
    (B) Check all luggage.
    (C) Have a reservation.
    (D) Bring their own lunch.

GO ON TO THE NEXT PAGE

PRACTICE TEST THREE **353**

95. What problem caused traffic jams?

    (A) Too many cars were parked.
    (B) There was an accident.
    (C) A bus broke down.
    (D) Police were investigating a crime.

96. Where did the problem happen?

    (A) Near the police station.
    (B) In the park.
    (C) At the hospital.
    (D) Downtown.

97. When will the street be open again?

    (A) At noon.
    (B) In an hour.
    (C) This afternoon.
    (D) Tomorrow.

98. What is being advertised?

    (A) A resort.
    (B) A hotel.
    (C) A beach house.
    (D) A restaurant.

99. When is the special offer available?

    (A) September.
    (B) October.
    (C) November.
    (D) December.

100. What is included with the special offer?

    (A) Theater tickets.
    (B) Store coupons.
    (C) Continental breakfast.
    (D) A book about the city.

Stop! This is the end of the Listening test. Turn to Part 5 in your test book.

READING TEST

In the Reading test, you will read a variety of texts and answer several different types of reading comprehension questions. The entire Reading test will last 75 minutes. There are three parts, and directions are given for each part. You are encouraged to answer as many questions as possible within the time allowed.

You must mark your answers on the separate answer sheet. Do not write your answers in the test book.

PART 5

Directions: A word or phrase is missing in each of the sentences below. Four answer choices are given below each sentence. Select the best answer to complete the sentence. Then mark the letter (A), (B), (C), or (D) on your answer sheet.

101. We need a _____ person like Mr. Griegs working for our company.

(A) decide
(B) decision
(C) decisive
(D) decisively

102. If you pay the entire bill before the end of the month, they _____ you any interest.

(A) don't charge
(B) won't charge
(C) aren't charging
(D) wouldn't charge

103. You cannot put _____ that task any longer; it needs to be done before the end of this week.

(A) on
(B) up
(C) off
(D) out

104. Mr. Sterling was very unhappy to hear about Peter's absence from the meeting and made certain to _____ him for it.

(A) reprove
(B) improve
(C) approve
(D) disprove

105. We had to go into the office and finish up work on the report _____ it was a Saturday.

(A) therefore
(B) because
(C) since
(D) even though

106. You can just leave your hat and gloves _____ the closet shelf and proceed to the conference room.

(A) in
(B) between
(C) on
(D) through

GO ON TO THE NEXT PAGE

PRACTICE TEST THREE **355**

107. When I arrived at the Emergency Responders meeting, coffee _____.

(A) was serving
(B) was being served
(C) served
(D) had served

108. We overspent our budget last year, so we really need to _____ this year.

(A) economy
(B) economize
(C) economics
(D) economist

109. _____ she got this job, she worked for a large company on the West Coast.

(A) Before
(B) First
(C) Prior
(D) Earlier

110. Sam has contributed a lot to the company since he started working here, and I think we should consider _____ him a raise.

(A) give
(B) given
(C) giving
(D) to give

111. Because of the company's expansion, several new employees _____ over the next few months.

(A) hire
(B) will hire
(C) are hiring
(D) will be hired

112. I think you will find that your staff will do the extra work more _____ if you provide a bonus.

(A) read
(B) reading
(C) ready
(D) readily

113. We kept on interviewing candidates _____ we found the right person for the job.

(A) after
(B) because
(C) until
(D) although

114. _____ is very important in my office, so I try never to arrive late.

(A) Punctual
(B) Punctually
(C) Punctuate
(D) Punctuality

115. Everyone _____ extra hours at the moment until the project is completed.

(A) works
(B) is working
(C) had worked
(D) work

116. If you are unhappy with your work situation, you need to _____ your dissatisfaction to your boss.

(A) express
(B) repress
(C) impress
(D) oppress

117. We _____ all this office furniture from a discount vendor last year, and he gave us a very good price.

(A) purchased
(B) revived
(C) polished
(D) rejected

118. He usually ends up disappointed because his _____ are too high.

(A) expects
(B) expect
(C) expectant
(D) expectations

356   PRACTICE TEST THREE

119. The interns who worked with us last summer _____ very helpful.

(A) was
(B) were
(C) are
(D) is

120. His business wasn't at all _____ and he lost a great deal of money.

(A) comparable
(B) fallible
(C) agreeable
(D) profitable

121. Everyone was late for the meeting _____ the traffic was so terrible.

(A) although
(B) but
(C) because
(D) despite

122. You could _____ your boss to get someone to help you with this extra work.

(A) to ask
(B) asking
(C) ask
(D) will ask

123. They _____ to look for new clients after the first of the year.

(A) intern
(B) intact
(C) intend
(D) intake

124. He _____ drives his car to work because he doesn't like dealing with the traffic in the city.

(A) never
(B) always
(C) usually
(D) mostly

125. We will need to call your references in order to _____ the information you included in your job application.

(A) conform
(B) confirm
(C) conflict
(D) confine

126. If you had told me you were coming, I _____ the documents ready for you.

(A) would have had
(B) will have
(C) had had
(D) have had

127. They hope _____ the report well before next Friday's deadline.

(A) finish
(B) to finish
(C) finishing
(D) will finish

128. They took the bus _____ New York, and arrived there in about five hours.

(A) in
(B) at
(C) to
(D) by

129. If you are not happy with the agenda, we can _____ the order of the presentations.

(A) vary
(B) variable
(C) variety
(D) variation

130. _____ have to be signed by all parties involved or they are not valid.

(A) Contract
(B) The contract
(C) A contract
(D) Contracts

GO ON TO THE NEXT PAGE

PRACTICE TEST THREE **357**

131. You can contact me _____ by e-mail or by telephone.

(A) but
(B) both
(C) either
(D) neither

132. I think you will find that Ms. Lang is _____ on that subject than anyone else in this office.

(A) knowledgeably
(B) knowledgeable
(C) most knowledgeable
(D) more knowledgeable

133. Any _____ merchandise can be returned to the store for a complete refund.

(A) deflective
(B) detective
(C) deductive
(D) defective

134. They had _____ most of the brochures before anyone else even had a chance to look at them.

(A) take
(B) took
(C) taken
(D) taking

135. _____ your résumé and references to my assistant before the end of the week.

(A) To give
(B) Give
(C) Giving
(D) Given

136. Jim _____ in the same house since he was a child.

(A) lives
(B) lived
(C) is living
(D) has lived

137. The rent here is high, but it is _____ office in the building.

(A) the largest
(B) larger
(C) large
(D) enlarge

138. Your _____ will help us get the work done on time.

(A) cooperate
(B) cooperation
(C) cooperative
(D) cooperatively

139. We thought about _____ extra help but then decided that it wouldn't be necessary.

(A) hire
(B) hiring
(C) to hire
(D) hired

140. The suits in this store _____ much less than those other suits, and the quality is just the same.

(A) cost
(B) price
(C) money
(D) bill

PART 6

Directions: Read the texts that follow. A word or phrase is missing in some of the sentences. Four answer choices are given below each of the sentences. Select the best answer to complete the text. Then mark the letter (A), (B), (C), or (D) on your answer sheet.

GO ON TO THE NEXT PAGE

PRACTICE TEST THREE   359

Questions 141–143 refer to the following letter.

Dear Member,

It's time to renew your membership in the Professional Business Association (PBA). PBA has been providing its members with professional business support since 1965. As a member of PBA, you form part of the most well-regarded community of business professionals in the country. Your membership _____ you to numerous benefits, including: a subscription to our monthly

    141. (A) entices
          (B) entitles
          (C) entities
          (D) entireties

newsletter, *The Business Professional*; reduced rates at our annual conference; access to professional legal advice; discounts on health and life insurance; as well as many other benefits. Please complete the membership renewal form below and send _____ in with your

    142. (A) it
          (B) them
          (C) they
          (D) us

membership fee. If you renew your membership before May 15, you _____, as our thanks,

    143. (A) receive
          (B) receives
          (C) received
          (D) will receive

an autographed copy of *The Ladder to Professional Business Success*, written by PBA member Harlan McGee.

Sincerely,
Angelina Park
Angelina Park
BPA President

Questions 144–146 refer to the following article.

There are many steps involved in preparing to give a presentation. You need to plan exactly what you are going to say, and you need to organize your visuals. But in addition to the content of your presentation, you also need to consider your own appearance. The way you _____ is just as important as the information you impart. You need to pay

144. (A) speak
    (B) arrive
    (C) dress
    (D) enter

as much attention to your clothes as you do to your charts and graphs. If you look professional, your audience will take you seriously and pay attention to what you say. If, _____, you seem unconcerned with your appearance, your audience will probably

145. (A) therefore
    (B) on the other hand
    (C) as a result
    (D) moreover

be equally unconcerned with anything you have to say. _____ the clothes you will

          146. (A) Choose
              (B) Will choose
              (C) Choosing
              (D) Chosen

wear is an important part of preparing to give a presentation.

GO ON TO THE NEXT PAGE

PRACTICE TEST THREE **361**

Questions 147–149 refer to the following memo.

To: All Apex, Inc. Employees
From: Ken Ferguson
Re: Parking
Date: July 9, 20—

This is a reminder about the parking situation in our building. All employees of Apex, Inc. may park in the building garage free of charge. However, a parking sticker must _____ on the lower right-hand corner of your windshield. If you do not have a

147. (A) display
    (B) displays
    (C) will display
    (D) be displayed

sticker, please let me know. Your parking sticker allows you to park in spaces marked "Apex" only. If you park in any other space, your car will be subject to fines and towing, whether or not you have a sticker. Please be careful about this. The garage attendants are very _____ about the parking rules.

    148. (A) strict
        (B) stricken
        (C) strident
        (D) strike

Also, please _____ your clients that they may park in the spaces marked "visitor,"

    149. (A) advice
        (B) advise
        (C) advisor
        (D) advisory

but they must have a visitor parking pass. These are available from our receptionist. Thank you for your cooperation.

362   PRACTICE TEST THREE

Questions 150–152 refer to the following e-mail.

To: Andrew Jones
From: Eliza Higgins
Date: September 22
Subject: Office Space

Hi Andrew,

I wanted to let you know that I am looking for a new office space and to ask you to keep an eye
out for me. My business is _____ and I have hired several new employees

    150. (A) exciting
         (B) demanding
         (C) expanding
         (D) decreasing

over the past few months, so I really need a bigger office. My _____ is to be downtown

    151. (A) ideal
         (B) ideally
         (C) idealistic
         (D) idealize

although I know it might be difficult to find something there. At the very least, I would like to be
near the major bus and subway lines so that my business is accessible to my clients. Since my
business has been doing so well, I can afford to pay a higher rent than I am paying now. Please
let me know if you hear of any offices that might be _____ to my needs.

    152. (A) suit
         (B) suite
         (C) suiting
         (D) suitable

Thanks.
Eliza

PRACTICE TEST THREE **363**

PART 7

In this part, you will read a selection of texts, such as magazines and newspaper articles, letters, and advertisements. Each text is followed by several questions. Select the best answer for each question and mark the letter (A), (B), (C), or (D) on your answer sheet.

Questions 153–156 refer to the following news report.

World News
Local News
Weather
Sports
What To Do
Home

Downtown businesses were closed for several hours yesterday due to a power outage that affected several blocks in the heart of the shopping district. Stores lining Mayfield Avenue and Brownstone Street, the city's main shopping streets, were dark for several hours. "This couldn't have happened at a worse time," said Bob Withers, owner of Bob's Place. "We're right in the middle of the holiday shopping season. We had large crowds of people down here yesterday doing their holiday shopping, buying gifts for their friends and toys for their children. I get a lot of the holiday shoppers in here for lunch and afternoon coffee. It really hurt my business to have to close yesterday, and I know my colleagues in the neighborhood have also been really hurt by the incident."

Jane Wright, President of the Neighborhood Business Association and owner of The Corner Bookstore, agreed that yesterday's incident would have serious repercussions on area businesses. "We bring in the most profit during the holidays," she explained. "No one can afford to be closed for even one hour at this time of year." The power outage occurred just after noon and continued until around 5:00, the start of the evening rush hour. Most stores, however, remained closed overnight but were ready for business at the usual hour this morning.

---

153. Why were businesses closed yesterday?

(A) It was a holiday.
(B) The electricity went out.
(C) Crowds got out of control.
(D) Streets were being repaired.

154. What kind of business is Bob's Place?

(A) Restaurant
(B) Gift shop
(C) Toy store
(D) Bookstore

155. The word "repercussions" in paragraph 2, line 2 is closest in meaning to

(A) occasions
(B) losses
(C) results
(D) recoveries

156. When did businesses reopen?

(A) In the morning
(B) After one hour
(C) At 5:00
(D) In the evening

364 PRACTICE TEST THREE

Questions 157–160 refer to the following instructions.

> Remove item from box and examine carefully. If there are any signs of damage visible, replace the item in the box and return to the store, accompanied by a receipt, for a full refund, or contact manufacturer. See page 54 for contact information.
>
> Place the item on a flat location away from areas where it might be exposed to water or steam, as dampness could affect efficient operation. Also locate it where it will not interfere with radio and television reception and away from cordless phones.
>
> To set the timer, press the "timer" button. The display will show 00:00. Press the number keys to enter the correct time, and then press "start." When the set time is reached, the beeper will beep five times. See page 13 for recommended cooking times for a variety of common foods.
>
> To clean, use a soft damp cloth. Use warm, not hot, water and wipe the inside walls gently. Do not scrub. Avoid the use of detergents and abrasives, however, you may add a small amount of mild dish soap to the dampened cloth. To clean the glass plate turntable, remove it and wash it in the sink. It can also be washed in the dishwasher. The glass plate turntable is made of durable, tempered glass. If it should break, do not attempt to repair it yourself. Contact the manufacturer for a replacement. See page 54 for contact information.

157. What item are these instructions for?

    (A) Phone
    (B) Clock
    (C) Oven
    (D) Television

158. Where should the item be put?

    (A) On a flat surface
    (B) In a damp location
    (C) Next to a radio
    (D) Near a receiver

159. How should the item be cleaned?

    (A) By scrubbing hard
    (B) By wiping with a cloth
    (C) By washing with abrasives
    (D) By adding detergents

160. What should be done if the glass plate turntable breaks?

    (A) Return it to the store.
    (B) Follow the instructions on page 13.
    (C) Repair it carefully.
    (D) Ask the manufacturer to send a new one.

Questions 161–163 refer to the following brochure.

Do you enjoy traveling to other countries?
Why not make it into a career?

Graduates of the Hotchkiss Institute are offered jobs in all parts of the world, from Iceland to Argentina to Bali. At Hotchkiss, you will learn all aspects of operating a hotel, from customer service to employee management to budgeting and bookkeeping, and everything in between. Our two-year program also includes coursework in foreign languages and cross-cultural communication. When you graduate from Hotchkiss, you will be qualified to work in five-star hotels anywhere in the world. Our placement office will help you find the job you dream of. There's no need to spend three or four years preparing for your career, as some other programs require. There's no need for previous experience or a college degree. Hotchkiss accepts applicants from high school graduates. Don't wait! Contact us today and start on the road to the career of your dreams.

161. What kind of career does Hotchkiss train for?

    (A) Hotel manager
    (B) Language teacher
    (C) Tour guide
    (D) Bookkeeper

162. How long does the training program last?

    (A) One year
    (B) Two years
    (C) Three years
    (D) Four years

163. What is required of applicants to the program?

    (A) Previous travel abroad
    (B) Prior experience
    (C) College degree
    (D) High school diploma

Questions 164–165 refer to the following notice.

Skyland Office Building
Notice to all tenants

The building fire alarm system will undergo routine maintenance tomorrow, October 17. The alarm will sound more than once over the course of the day. This is a normal part of the maintenance work. In the case of a real emergency, each office will be notified by a member of the building maintenance staff. Work should be completed by the end of the day. We regret any inconvenience this may cause. Any questions should be addressed to the Chief of Maintenance in Room 7.

---

164. Why will the alarm sound?

   (A) There will be a fire.
   (B) There will be an emergency.
   (C) A new alarm system will be installed.
   (D) The alarm system will be repaired.

165. When will the alarm sound?

   (A) Once during the day
   (B) Several times during the day
   (C) At the end of the day
   (D) After tomorrow

GO ON TO THE NEXT PAGE

PRACTICE TEST THREE   **367**

Questions 166–168 refer to the following invoice.

Gypsy Insurance Company
45 Compton Boulevard
Grenville, IN

Policy type: Renter's   Policy No. 4028577583020

Customer:
Harlan and Myers Engineering
PO Box 56
Grenville, IN

Total Amount Due: $450   Minimum Payment: $40

Please pay by September 30.

If you choose to pay with the installment plan, please pay the designated minimum amount
due plus the $5 service charge. You must pay at least this amount by the due date or you
will be charged a $12 late fee. Checks returned by your bank are charged $30.

Questions? Call:	
555-0988	For billing and payment information
555-0987	To make a claim
555-0986	To report a change of address
555-0985	For policy changes

---

166. What is the least amount the customer owes now?

(A) $5
(B) $40
(C) $45
(D) $450

167. What happens if the customer pays after September 30?

(A) The policy will be dropped.
(B) The total amount due will have to be paid.
(C) Two installments will be due.
(D) Twelve more dollars will be charged.

168. Why would a customer call 555-0988?

(A) To get a new policy
(B) To ask a question about the invoice
(C) To give a new address
(D) To find out how to report an accident

368 PRACTICE TEST THREE

Questions 169–172 refer to the following memo.

> To: All office staff
> From: Myra Jansen, Office Manager
> Re: Photocopier
> Date: February 15, 20__
>
> This is to notify office staff that the large photocopy machine at the end of the hall is out of service as of late this morning. Constant paper jams have made it impossible to use. These recurring breakdowns of the photocopier are due, at least in part, to misuse of the machine. For example, it has come to my attention that some users are placing pages that are stapled or paper-clipped together into the document feeder. This jams up the delicate internal machinery. The instruction manual for the photocopier is kept on the shelf with the extra paper. Please consult it if you are unsure about any steps involved in operating the machine. It thoroughly describes all the machine's features as well as giving step-by-step instructions for such routine procedures as changing the toner and adding more paper. If the machine becomes jammed or otherwise stops working while you are using it, please don't attempt to fix it yourself. Please inform me or my assistant, as we are trained in troubleshooting the machine.
>
> I put a call into the photocopier company this afternoon, and they will send someone out to work on the machine tomorrow. In the meantime, if you have any critical photocopying needs, you can use the small machine in my office. Otherwise, I would request that you save all your photocopying jobs until after the large machine is repaired.

169. What is the problem with the photocopier?

   (A) The toner needs changing.
   (B) It has a paper jam.
   (C) The stapler doesn't work.
   (D) It needs paper added.

170. What should you do if you don't know how to operate the photocopier?

   (A) Read the instruction manual.
   (B) Ask Myra Jansen for help.
   (C) Call the photocopier company.
   (D) Speak with the assistant office manager.

171. When will the repairperson arrive?

   (A) This morning
   (B) This afternoon
   (C) Tomorrow
   (D) Next week

172. The word "critical" in paragraph 2, line 2 is closest in meaning to

   (A) dangerous
   (B) current
   (C) judging
   (D) important

PRACTICE TEST THREE **369**

Questions 173–174 refer to the following advertisement.

Urban Car Rental and Leasing Company

We offer the best rates and largest selection of cars in the city.
Rates start at just $23 per day!*
All cars come equipped with a cutting-edge GPS navigational system and a
top-quality radio and CD player, as well as a full tank of gas.
See chart below for sample rates.

Car Type	Daily	Weekly
Compact	$28	$185
Mid-size	$35	$225
Luxury	$42	$280

(Insurance is extra. See agent for details on available plans.)

Call Urban today! 555-7749
We accept all major credit cards.

* On 30-day paid-in-advance contracts for compact cars only.

173. How can a customer get the $23 a day rate?

(A) Lease a mid-size car.
(B) Pay for 30 days at once.
(C) Rent by the week.
(D) Use a credit card.

174. What is not included in the price of each car?

(A) Gasoline
(B) Radio
(C) GPS
(D) Insurance

370   PRACTICE TEST THREE

Questions 175–178 refer to the following information sheet.

Visitor's Guide
Central Regional Airport

Welcome to the Central Regional Airport. We strive hard to make your travels pleasant and comfortable.

Airline Information
All airline check-in counters are located on the main level. Ticket offices are also located there. Baggage pick-up is located on the ground level near the south exits. Baggage carts are available for your convenience. Flight arrival and departure times are posted near the escalators on each level.

Local Travel
The Visitor Information Desk is located on the second level and has information on local hotels and restaurants, maps, guided tours, and other tourist information. The agents there are also available to help you with hotel and rental car reservations. The taxi stand is located just outside the main entrance on the ground level. City buses and the subway also serve the airport. Maps and schedules are posted near the taxi stand.

Airport Services
A food court is located on the third level, serving a variety of foods available for eating there or to go. For more formal dining, the Sky View Restaurant is also located on that level and offers a full bar as well as lunch and dinner. Rest rooms are located on each level and are clearly marked. The Airport Gift and Bookshop is located on the second level near the Visitor Information Desk. It sells tea, coffee, and soft drinks as well as gifts and books. Also for your pre-boarding convenience, a newsstand is located by the gates just past the security area.

175. Where can you eat a meal?

    (A) Ground level
    (B) Main level
    (C) Second level
    (D) Third level

176. What can you buy near the gates?

    (A) Drinks
    (B) Books
    (C) Newspapers
    (D) Gifts

177. How can you find information about local transportation?

    (A) Look near the main entrance.
    (B) Ask at the Information Desk.
    (C) Go to the second level.
    (D) Inquire at the check-in counter.

178. What is near the escalators?

    (A) Baggage carts
    (B) Flight information
    (C) Rest rooms
    (D) Taxis

GO ON TO THE NEXT PAGE

Questions 179–180 refer to the following advertisement.

> **For Rent**
> 1,000 square feet in small professional building. Located close to downtown. On second floor, above stores, tenant and customer parking available in rear. Suitable for lawyer, dentist, other professional. Available for April 1 move in. Open house Saturday, 2-4.
> Offered by: Franklin Realty, 123 Main St., Norwich
> 555-6775, Monday-Friday, 9-5

179. What is for rent?

(A) Office
(B) Store
(C) Parking space
(D) Apartment

180. What will happen on Saturday?

(A) The new tenant will move in.
(B) The space will be shown.
(C) The realty office will be open.
(D) The stores will close.

Questions 181–185 refer to the following schedule and e-mail.

Doing Business in the New Millennium
Conference Schedule
Wickford Hotel

Time	Event	Location
9:00	Opening Remarks	Main Hall
9:30-10:30	Workshops A, B, and C*	Rooms 101, 102, 103
10:45-11:45	Workshops D, E, and F*	Rooms 101, 102, 103
12:00-1:00	Lunch	Main Hall
1:15-2:15	Workshops G, H, and I*	Rooms 101, 102, 103

* See page 2 for workshop descriptions

372 PRACTICE TEST THREE

To: Meredith Bergman
From: Josue Silva
Date: April 8
Subject: Conference

Meredith,

The conference is coming up next Tuesday. That's just a week from today, so we need to finalize some things. I've attached a draft of the schedule. Thank you for getting us the space at the hotel, since the City Conference Center just wouldn't have worked for a small conference like ours. But, would you find out if we can get one more room for the workshops? I'm adding two more workshops to the schedule because I talked to Bill Smith this morning and he agreed to do one on marketing in the morning and one on customer relations in the afternoon. Please call the hotel manager about that before 12:00 today, and then I'll make the changes to the schedule and get it printed up.

Janet Newman, the guest speaker, will be flying in the night before the conference. Her plane arrives at 7:00. Please pick her up at the airport and drive her to her hotel. It's the Runway View Suites, right near the airport. Before you do that, you should call the hotel restaurant and make sure the plans for the conference lunch are all set. Then on the morning of the conference, I'd like you to arrive an hour before everything begins and make sure everything is in order.

Thanks for all your hard work.
Josue

---

181. When will the conference take place?

(A) April 8
(B) April 9
(C) April 15
(D) April 18

182. Where will the conference take place?

(A) At a hotel
(B) Near the airport
(C) At a restaurant
(D) At a conference center

183. How many workshop rooms will be needed?

(A) One
(B) Two
(C) Three
(D) Four

184. What will Meredith do on Monday?

(A) Call the hotel manager.
(B) Get the schedule printed.
(C) Pick up someone at the airport.
(D) Talk to Bill Smith about workshops.

185. What time will Meredith have to arrive for the conference?

(A) 7:00
(B) 8:00
(C) 9:00
(D) 12:00

GO ON TO THE NEXT PAGE

PRACTICE TEST THREE   **373**

Questions 186–190 refer to the following advertisement and e-mail.

Are you looking to enter the exciting world of business?
Do you want to improve your business skills?
The Business Training Institute
can help you achieve your goals.

We offer classes in:

*Computer Software Training
  • Word Processing
  • Spreadsheets
  • HTML
  and more!
  (20-hour courses offered evenings and
  weekends/$500 per course)

*Accounting
*Advertising
*Product Development
(35-hour courses offered evenings only/$800 per course)

Courses start the first Monday or Saturday of the month.
For more information or to register, visit us at:
www.bti.com
info@bti.com

374   PRACTICE TEST THREE

To: info@bti.com
From: Mark Fortescue
Date: Thursday, August 21
Subject: Courses

Hi,
I saw your ad in yesterday's newspaper, and I'm interested in registering for a course. I took some software courses from your program a couple of years ago, and I thought they were excellent. Now I am interested in taking your advertising course. I currently work as an assistant in the accounting department of a mid-size firm, but I am interested in moving into market research. The company completely supports me in this goal and our personnel office will cover 25 percent of the cost of any courses I take towards this, and I would be responsible for paying the other 75 percent. Unfortunately, I have to be out of town during the first week of next month, so I won't be able to start until the following month. Because of that, I'd like to know how many weeks your courses last. I'd like to be finished with the course by the end of December because I have some other obligations coming up in January. If the course will end before January, then please put my name on the list and let me know, and I will get the payment to you right away. Thank you very much for your help.

Mark Fortescue

186. When did Mr. Fortescue see the ad in the newspaper?

(A) Monday
(B) Wednesday
(C) Thursday
(D) Saturday

187. What is Mr. Fortescue's current job?

(A) Accounting assistant
(B) Market researcher
(C) Software trainer
(D) Personnel officer

188. What course does Mr. Fortescue want to take?

(A) Word Processing
(B) Accounting
(C) Advertising
(D) Product Development

189. How much will Mr. Fortescue pay for the course he wants to take?

(A) $75
(B) $500
(C) $600
(D) $800

190. When does he want to start his course?

(A) August
(B) October
(C) December
(D) January

Questions 191–195 refer to the following employee's manual chapter and request form.

Widget, Inc.   Employee Manual

Chapter 8: Community Volunteer Program

As part of our Give Back to the Community Initiative, we encourage all Widget employees to work as volunteers in a community organization. To facilitate this goal, any employee can request up to five hours per month Volunteer Leave to volunteer in a local organization. In order to be approved for this leave, the employee must do the following:

1. Choose an approved community organization from the list below. Contact the volunteer coordinator at the organization and make an arrangement for your volunteer assignment and schedule. To be eligible for leave hours, volunteer work must take place during our normal business hours: 9-5, Monday-Friday, excluding holidays.
2. Get permission from your supervisor to be absent from your duties for volunteer work.
3. Fill out a Volunteer Leave Request Form.
4. Submit the form to the personnel director at least one month in advance of the volunteer work start date.

Approved Community Organizations:
Teen Drop-In Center
Community Gardens Group
Wynsdale Public Library
Wynsdale Nursing Home
Eastland Park Beautification Committee
Wynsdale Renewable Energy Commission

Please direct any questions about this program to the community outreach coordinator.

**Volunteer Leave Request Form
Widget, Inc.**

Date: June 5
Name: Maria Streltsov
Position: Design Assistant
Supervisor: Paolo Galasso

Community organization where you will volunteer:
Eastland Park Beautification Committee
Volunteer Coordinator contacted:
Will Shuman   date contacted: May 28
Volunteer duties:
help with planting and maintaining gardens
Schedule:
every Tuesday, 3-5

I give this employee permission to be absent from his/her duties during the hours described above for the purposes of community volunteer work.
Signed: Paolo Galasso
Date: June 6

Approved: Yes ____ No ____

191. What days does Maria want to volunteer?

    (A) Mondays
    (B) Tuesdays
    (C) Fridays
    (D) Mondays and Fridays

192. What is the earliest date Maria can begin volunteer work?

    (A) May 28
    (B) June 3
    (C) June 5
    (D) July 5

193. What kind of volunteer work does Maria want to do?

    (A) Help with a garden
    (B) Clean up a park
    (C) Work at the library
    (D) Make some designs

194. Who should Maria submit this form to?

    (A) Paolo Galasso
    (B) Will Shuman
    (C) The personnel director
    (D) The community outreach coordinator

195. Why won't Maria's request be approved?

    (A) She asked for too many hours of leave per month.
    (B) She forgot to contact the volunteer coordinator.
    (C) She didn't choose an approved organization.
    (D) She didn't get her supervisor's permission.

PRACTICE TEST THREE 377

Questions 196–200 refer to the following e-mail and brochure.

To: shenderson@execcater.com
From: lhong@nonesuch.com
Date: Thursday, February 1
Subject: Catering job

Dear Ms. Henderson,
I was referred to your company by my former classmate, Emily Pearson, who used your catering services for the training workshop her office put on last November. We are planning an all day meeting for our entire staff for Friday of next week, and I was wondering whether you would be available to cater it. We would like lunch and also would like to have snacks served in the middle of the afternoon. We expect around 25 people to attend. Also, do you provide linens and silverware? We would need you to bring those and are willing to pay extra if necessary. We already have plenty of tables and chairs here so we won't need to rent any furniture from you. I was also wondering whether you include vegetarian options in your menus. Some of our staff members don't eat meat. Please let me know if you are available for this job. If you have a brochure, please send me a copy.
Thank you.
Lulu Hong
Office Manager
Nonesuch, Inc.

378   PRACTICE TEST THREE

Executive Caterers
Specializing in Business Events

We are available to cater all your business events: workshops, conferences, retirement parties, and more!

Lunch Includes sandwich trays, salad trays, dessert trays, tea, coffee, juice
Snack Includes fruit trays, cake and cookie trays, tea, coffee, juice
Dinner A variety of menus is available. Call us for more information and prices.

Prices:
Lunch   10 people $50
        25 people $125
        50 people $225
        100 people $450
(Vegetarian options are available. Add $1 per person)

Snacks 10 people $30
        25 people $75
        50 people $130
        100 people $250

Extras:
Linens and silverware are included in the prices of all lunches, dinners, and snacks. Chairs and tables are available for rental. Call us for more information.

To see a complete description of our menus, visit us at www.execcater.com.
To place an order* or for more information, e-mail us at info@execcater.com or call 555-9522.

*Please place your order at least two weeks in advance of your event. Orders made with less notice are sometimes possible. Please call our office to discuss.

196. How did Ms. Hong find out about the Executive Caterers company?

- (A) She found the company's website on the Internet.
- (B) She attended an event catered by this company.
- (C) A friend of hers told her about it.
- (D) Someone sent her a brochure.

197. What kind of event does Ms. Hong need catering for?

- (A) Party
- (B) Meeting
- (C) Workshop
- (D) Conference

198. What extras does she want the catering company to supply?

- (A) Linens only
- (B) Chairs only
- (C) Linens and silverware
- (D) Tables and chairs

199. How much will the catering for her event cost?

- (A) $75
- (B) $125
- (C) $200
- (D) $225

200. How should she place her order with the catering company?

- (A) Make a phone call
- (B) Send an e-mail
- (C) Visit the website
- (D) Fill out a form

Stop! This is the end of the test. If you finish before time is called, you may go back to Parts 5, 6, and 7 and check your work.

ANSWER SHEETS

ANSWER SHEET: Listening Comprehension Review

Name

Listening Comprehension

Part 1 Part 2 Part 3 Part 4

ANSWER SHEET: Reading Review

Reading

Part 5 Part 6 Part 7

382   ANSWER SHEET: LISTENING COMPREHENSION REVIEW/READING REVIEW

ANSWER SHEET: Practice Test One

Name _____

Listening Comprehension

Part 1 **Part 2** **Part 3** **Part 4**

The answer grids are arranged in columns labelled "Answer."

Part 1 (1–10): options A B C D
Part 2 (11–40): options A B C
Part 3 (41–70): options A B C D
Part 4 (71–100): options A B C D

#	Answer	#	Answer	#	Answer	#	Answer	#	Answer	#	Answer	#	Answer	#	Answer	#	Answer	#	Answer
1	A B C D	11	A B C	21	A B C	31	A B C	41	A B C D	51	A B C D	61	A B C D	71	A B C D	81	A B C D	91	A B C D
2	A B C D	12	A B C	22	A B C	32	A B C	42	A B C D	52	A B C D	62	A B C D	72	A B C D	82	A B C D	92	A B C D
3	A B C D	13	A B C	23	A B C	33	A B C	43	A B C D	53	A B C D	63	A B C D	73	A B C D	83	A B C D	93	A B C D
4	A B C D	14	A B C	24	A B C	34	A B C	44	A B C D	54	A B C D	64	A B C D	74	A B C D	84	A B C D	94	A B C D
5	A B C D	15	A B C	25	A B C	35	A B C	45	A B C D	55	A B C D	65	A B C D	75	A B C D	85	A B C D	95	A B C D
6	A B C D	16	A B C	26	A B C	36	A B C	46	A B C D	56	A B C D	66	A B C D	76	A B C D	86	A B C D	96	A B C D
7	A B C D	17	A B C	27	A B C	37	A B C	47	A B C D	57	A B C D	67	A B C D	77	A B C D	87	A B C D	97	A B C D
8	A B C D	18	A B C	28	A B C	38	A B C	48	A B C D	58	A B C D	68	A B C D	78	A B C D	88	A B C D	98	A B C D
9	A B C D	19	A B C	29	A B C	39	A B C	49	A B C D	59	A B C D	69	A B C D	79	A B C D	89	A B C D	99	A B C D
10	A B C D	20	A B C	30	A B C	40	A B C	50	A B C D	60	A B C D	70	A B C D	80	A B C D	90	A B C D	100	A B C D

Reading

Part 5 **Part 6** **Part 7**

#	Answer	#	Answer	#	Answer	#	Answer	#	Answer	#	Answer	#	Answer	#	Answer	#	Answer	#	Answer
101	A B C D	111	A B C D	121	A B C D	131	A B C D	141	A B C D	151	A B C D	161	A B C D	171	A B C D	181	A B C D	191	A B C D
102	A B C D	112	A B C D	122	A B C D	132	A B C D	142	A B C D	152	A B C D	162	A B C D	172	A B C D	182	A B C D	192	A B C D
103	A B C D	113	A B C D	123	A B C D	133	A B C D	143	A B C D	153	A B C D	163	A B C D	173	A B C D	183	A B C D	193	A B C D
104	A B C D	114	A B C D	124	A B C D	134	A B C D	144	A B C D	154	A B C D	164	A B C D	174	A B C D	184	A B C D	194	A B C D
105	A B C D	115	A B C D	125	A B C D	135	A B C D	145	A B C D	155	A B C D	165	A B C D	175	A B C D	185	A B C D	195	A B C D
106	A B C D	116	A B C D	126	A B C D	136	A B C D	146	A B C D	156	A B C D	166	A B C D	176	A B C D	186	A B C D	196	A B C D
107	A B C D	117	A B C D	127	A B C D	137	A B C D	147	A B C D	157	A B C D	167	A B C D	177	A B C D	187	A B C D	197	A B C D
108	A B C D	118	A B C D	128	A B C D	138	A B C D	148	A B C D	158	A B C D	168	A B C D	178	A B C D	188	A B C D	198	A B C D
109	A B C D	119	A B C D	129	A B C D	139	A B C D	149	A B C D	159	A B C D	169	A B C D	179	A B C D	189	A B C D	199	A B C D
110	A B C D	120	A B C D	130	A B C D	140	A B C D	150	A B C D	160	A B C D	170	A B C D	180	A B C D	190	A B C D	200	A B C D

ANSWER SHEET: Practice Test Two

Name _____

Listening Comprehension

Part 1

	A B C D
1	Ⓐ Ⓑ Ⓒ Ⓓ
2	Ⓐ Ⓑ Ⓒ Ⓓ
3	Ⓐ Ⓑ Ⓒ Ⓓ
4	Ⓐ Ⓑ Ⓒ Ⓓ
5	Ⓐ Ⓑ Ⓒ Ⓓ
6	Ⓐ Ⓑ Ⓒ Ⓓ
7	Ⓐ Ⓑ Ⓒ Ⓓ
8	Ⓐ Ⓑ Ⓒ Ⓓ
9	Ⓐ Ⓑ Ⓒ Ⓓ
10	Ⓐ Ⓑ Ⓒ Ⓓ

Part 2

	A B C
11	Ⓐ Ⓑ Ⓒ
12	Ⓐ Ⓑ Ⓒ
13	Ⓐ Ⓑ Ⓒ
14	Ⓐ Ⓑ Ⓒ
15	Ⓐ Ⓑ Ⓒ
16	Ⓐ Ⓑ Ⓒ
17	Ⓐ Ⓑ Ⓒ
18	Ⓐ Ⓑ Ⓒ
19	Ⓐ Ⓑ Ⓒ
20	Ⓐ Ⓑ Ⓒ
21	Ⓐ Ⓑ Ⓒ
22	Ⓐ Ⓑ Ⓒ
23	Ⓐ Ⓑ Ⓒ
24	Ⓐ Ⓑ Ⓒ
25	Ⓐ Ⓑ Ⓒ
26	Ⓐ Ⓑ Ⓒ
27	Ⓐ Ⓑ Ⓒ
28	Ⓐ Ⓑ Ⓒ
29	Ⓐ Ⓑ Ⓒ
30	Ⓐ Ⓑ Ⓒ
31	Ⓐ Ⓑ Ⓒ
32	Ⓐ Ⓑ Ⓒ
33	Ⓐ Ⓑ Ⓒ
34	Ⓐ Ⓑ Ⓒ
35	Ⓐ Ⓑ Ⓒ
36	Ⓐ Ⓑ Ⓒ
37	Ⓐ Ⓑ Ⓒ
38	Ⓐ Ⓑ Ⓒ
39	Ⓐ Ⓑ Ⓒ
40	Ⓐ Ⓑ Ⓒ

Part 3

	A B C D
41	Ⓐ Ⓑ Ⓒ Ⓓ
42	Ⓐ Ⓑ Ⓒ Ⓓ
43	Ⓐ Ⓑ Ⓒ Ⓓ
44	Ⓐ Ⓑ Ⓒ Ⓓ
45	Ⓐ Ⓑ Ⓒ Ⓓ
46	Ⓐ Ⓑ Ⓒ Ⓓ
47	Ⓐ Ⓑ Ⓒ Ⓓ
48	Ⓐ Ⓑ Ⓒ Ⓓ
49	Ⓐ Ⓑ Ⓒ Ⓓ
50	Ⓐ Ⓑ Ⓒ Ⓓ
51	Ⓐ Ⓑ Ⓒ Ⓓ
52	Ⓐ Ⓑ Ⓒ Ⓓ
53	Ⓐ Ⓑ Ⓒ Ⓓ
54	Ⓐ Ⓑ Ⓒ Ⓓ
55	Ⓐ Ⓑ Ⓒ Ⓓ
56	Ⓐ Ⓑ Ⓒ Ⓓ
57	Ⓐ Ⓑ Ⓒ Ⓓ
58	Ⓐ Ⓑ Ⓒ Ⓓ
59	Ⓐ Ⓑ Ⓒ Ⓓ
60	Ⓐ Ⓑ Ⓒ Ⓓ
61	Ⓐ Ⓑ Ⓒ Ⓓ
62	Ⓐ Ⓑ Ⓒ Ⓓ
63	Ⓐ Ⓑ Ⓒ Ⓓ
64	Ⓐ Ⓑ Ⓒ Ⓓ
65	Ⓐ Ⓑ Ⓒ Ⓓ
66	Ⓐ Ⓑ Ⓒ Ⓓ
67	Ⓐ Ⓑ Ⓒ Ⓓ
68	Ⓐ Ⓑ Ⓒ Ⓓ
69	Ⓐ Ⓑ Ⓒ Ⓓ
70	Ⓐ Ⓑ Ⓒ Ⓓ

Part 4

	A B C D
71	Ⓐ Ⓑ Ⓒ Ⓓ
72	Ⓐ Ⓑ Ⓒ Ⓓ
73	Ⓐ Ⓑ Ⓒ Ⓓ
74	Ⓐ Ⓑ Ⓒ Ⓓ
75	Ⓐ Ⓑ Ⓒ Ⓓ
76	Ⓐ Ⓑ Ⓒ Ⓓ
77	Ⓐ Ⓑ Ⓒ Ⓓ
78	Ⓐ Ⓑ Ⓒ Ⓓ
79	Ⓐ Ⓑ Ⓒ Ⓓ
80	Ⓐ Ⓑ Ⓒ Ⓓ
81	Ⓐ Ⓑ Ⓒ Ⓓ
82	Ⓐ Ⓑ Ⓒ Ⓓ
83	Ⓐ Ⓑ Ⓒ Ⓓ
84	Ⓐ Ⓑ Ⓒ Ⓓ
85	Ⓐ Ⓑ Ⓒ Ⓓ
86	Ⓐ Ⓑ Ⓒ Ⓓ
87	Ⓐ Ⓑ Ⓒ Ⓓ
88	Ⓐ Ⓑ Ⓒ Ⓓ
89	Ⓐ Ⓑ Ⓒ Ⓓ
90	Ⓐ Ⓑ Ⓒ Ⓓ
91	Ⓐ Ⓑ Ⓒ Ⓓ
92	Ⓐ Ⓑ Ⓒ Ⓓ
93	Ⓐ Ⓑ Ⓒ Ⓓ
94	Ⓐ Ⓑ Ⓒ Ⓓ
95	Ⓐ Ⓑ Ⓒ Ⓓ
96	Ⓐ Ⓑ Ⓒ Ⓓ
97	Ⓐ Ⓑ Ⓒ Ⓓ
98	Ⓐ Ⓑ Ⓒ Ⓓ
99	Ⓐ Ⓑ Ⓒ Ⓓ
100	Ⓐ Ⓑ Ⓒ Ⓓ

Reading

Part 5

	A B C D
101	Ⓐ Ⓑ Ⓒ Ⓓ
102	Ⓐ Ⓑ Ⓒ Ⓓ
103	Ⓐ Ⓑ Ⓒ Ⓓ
104	Ⓐ Ⓑ Ⓒ Ⓓ
105	Ⓐ Ⓑ Ⓒ Ⓓ
106	Ⓐ Ⓑ Ⓒ Ⓓ
107	Ⓐ Ⓑ Ⓒ Ⓓ
108	Ⓐ Ⓑ Ⓒ Ⓓ
109	Ⓐ Ⓑ Ⓒ Ⓓ
110	Ⓐ Ⓑ Ⓒ Ⓓ
111	Ⓐ Ⓑ Ⓒ Ⓓ
112	Ⓐ Ⓑ Ⓒ Ⓓ
113	Ⓐ Ⓑ Ⓒ Ⓓ
114	Ⓐ Ⓑ Ⓒ Ⓓ
115	Ⓐ Ⓑ Ⓒ Ⓓ
116	Ⓐ Ⓑ Ⓒ Ⓓ
117	Ⓐ Ⓑ Ⓒ Ⓓ
118	Ⓐ Ⓑ Ⓒ Ⓓ
119	Ⓐ Ⓑ Ⓒ Ⓓ
120	Ⓐ Ⓑ Ⓒ Ⓓ

Part 6

	A B C D
121	Ⓐ Ⓑ Ⓒ Ⓓ
122	Ⓐ Ⓑ Ⓒ Ⓓ
123	Ⓐ Ⓑ Ⓒ Ⓓ
124	Ⓐ Ⓑ Ⓒ Ⓓ
125	Ⓐ Ⓑ Ⓒ Ⓓ
126	Ⓐ Ⓑ Ⓒ Ⓓ
127	Ⓐ Ⓑ Ⓒ Ⓓ
128	Ⓐ Ⓑ Ⓒ Ⓓ
129	Ⓐ Ⓑ Ⓒ Ⓓ
130	Ⓐ Ⓑ Ⓒ Ⓓ
131	Ⓐ Ⓑ Ⓒ Ⓓ
132	Ⓐ Ⓑ Ⓒ Ⓓ
133	Ⓐ Ⓑ Ⓒ Ⓓ
134	Ⓐ Ⓑ Ⓒ Ⓓ
135	Ⓐ Ⓑ Ⓒ Ⓓ
136	Ⓐ Ⓑ Ⓒ Ⓓ
137	Ⓐ Ⓑ Ⓒ Ⓓ
138	Ⓐ Ⓑ Ⓒ Ⓓ
139	Ⓐ Ⓑ Ⓒ Ⓓ
140	Ⓐ Ⓑ Ⓒ Ⓓ
141	Ⓐ Ⓑ Ⓒ Ⓓ
142	Ⓐ Ⓑ Ⓒ Ⓓ
143	Ⓐ Ⓑ Ⓒ Ⓓ
144	Ⓐ Ⓑ Ⓒ Ⓓ
145	Ⓐ Ⓑ Ⓒ Ⓓ
146	Ⓐ Ⓑ Ⓒ Ⓓ
147	Ⓐ Ⓑ Ⓒ Ⓓ
148	Ⓐ Ⓑ Ⓒ Ⓓ
149	Ⓐ Ⓑ Ⓒ Ⓓ
150	Ⓐ Ⓑ Ⓒ Ⓓ

Part 7

	A B C D
151	Ⓐ Ⓑ Ⓒ Ⓓ
152	Ⓐ Ⓑ Ⓒ Ⓓ
153	Ⓐ Ⓑ Ⓒ Ⓓ
154	Ⓐ Ⓑ Ⓒ Ⓓ
155	Ⓐ Ⓑ Ⓒ Ⓓ
156	Ⓐ Ⓑ Ⓒ Ⓓ
157	Ⓐ Ⓑ Ⓒ Ⓓ
158	Ⓐ Ⓑ Ⓒ Ⓓ
159	Ⓐ Ⓑ Ⓒ Ⓓ
160	Ⓐ Ⓑ Ⓒ Ⓓ
161	Ⓐ Ⓑ Ⓒ Ⓓ
162	Ⓐ Ⓑ Ⓒ Ⓓ
163	Ⓐ Ⓑ Ⓒ Ⓓ
164	Ⓐ Ⓑ Ⓒ Ⓓ
165	Ⓐ Ⓑ Ⓒ Ⓓ
166	Ⓐ Ⓑ Ⓒ Ⓓ
167	Ⓐ Ⓑ Ⓒ Ⓓ
168	Ⓐ Ⓑ Ⓒ Ⓓ
169	Ⓐ Ⓑ Ⓒ Ⓓ
170	Ⓐ Ⓑ Ⓒ Ⓓ
171	Ⓐ Ⓑ Ⓒ Ⓓ
172	Ⓐ Ⓑ Ⓒ Ⓓ
173	Ⓐ Ⓑ Ⓒ Ⓓ
174	Ⓐ Ⓑ Ⓒ Ⓓ
175	Ⓐ Ⓑ Ⓒ Ⓓ
176	Ⓐ Ⓑ Ⓒ Ⓓ
177	Ⓐ Ⓑ Ⓒ Ⓓ
178	Ⓐ Ⓑ Ⓒ Ⓓ
179	Ⓐ Ⓑ Ⓒ Ⓓ
180	Ⓐ Ⓑ Ⓒ Ⓓ
181	Ⓐ Ⓑ Ⓒ Ⓓ
182	Ⓐ Ⓑ Ⓒ Ⓓ
183	Ⓐ Ⓑ Ⓒ Ⓓ
184	Ⓐ Ⓑ Ⓒ Ⓓ
185	Ⓐ Ⓑ Ⓒ Ⓓ
186	Ⓐ Ⓑ Ⓒ Ⓓ
187	Ⓐ Ⓑ Ⓒ Ⓓ
188	Ⓐ Ⓑ Ⓒ Ⓓ
189	Ⓐ Ⓑ Ⓒ Ⓓ
190	Ⓐ Ⓑ Ⓒ Ⓓ
191	Ⓐ Ⓑ Ⓒ Ⓓ
192	Ⓐ Ⓑ Ⓒ Ⓓ
193	Ⓐ Ⓑ Ⓒ Ⓓ
194	Ⓐ Ⓑ Ⓒ Ⓓ
195	Ⓐ Ⓑ Ⓒ Ⓓ
196	Ⓐ Ⓑ Ⓒ Ⓓ
197	Ⓐ Ⓑ Ⓒ Ⓓ
198	Ⓐ Ⓑ Ⓒ Ⓓ
199	Ⓐ Ⓑ Ⓒ Ⓓ
200	Ⓐ Ⓑ Ⓒ Ⓓ

ANSWER SHEET: Practice Test Three

Name _____

Listening Comprehension

Part 1 **Part 2** **Part 3** **Part 4**

Reading

Part 5 **Part 6** **Part 7**

ANSWER SHEET: PRACTICE TEST THREE **385**

PRACTICE TEST SCORE CONVERSION

HOW TO CONVERT YOUR PRACTICE TEST SCORES

To convert your practice test scores, use the table on page 387.
Follow these simple steps.

1. Take a practice test.
2. Total the number of correct answers in the listening section.
3. Match the total number of correct listening answers with the corresponding practice score.
4. Total the number of correct answers in the reading section.
5. Match the total number of correct reading answers with the corresponding practice score.
6. Add the two scores together. This is your estimated total practice score.

Sample

Number of correct listening answers 56 = Practice listening score   290
Number of correct reading answers   82 = Practice reading score   + 405
    Estimated total practice score   695

Your score on Practice Test 1

Number of correct listening answers ____ = Practice listening score   _____
Number of correct reading answers ____ = Practice reading score   +_____
    Estimated total practice score   _____

Your score on Practice Test 2

Number of correct listening answers ____ = Practice listening score   _____
Number of correct reading answers ____ = Practice reading score   +_____
    Estimated total practice score   _____

Your score on Practice Test 3

Number of correct listening answers ____ = Practice listening score   _____
Number of correct reading answers ____ = Practice reading score   +_____
    Estimated total practice score   _____

PRACTICE TEST ESTIMATED SCORE CONVERSION TABLE

# CORRECT	PRACTICE SCORE	
	LISTENING	READING
0	5	5
1	5	5
2	5	5
3	5	5
4	5	5
5	5	5
6	5	5
7	10	5
8	15	5
9	20	5
10	25	5
11	30	5
12	35	5
13	40	5
14	45	5
15	50	5
16	55	10
17	60	15
18	65	20
19	70	25
20	75	30
21	80	35
22	85	40
23	90	45
24	95	50
25	100	60
26	110	65
27	115	70
28	120	80
29	125	85
30	130	90
31	135	95
32	140	100
33	145	110
34	150	115
35	160	120
36	165	125
37	170	130
38	175	140
39	180	145
40	185	150
41	190	160
42	195	165
43	200	170
44	210	175
45	215	180
46	220	190
47	230	195
48	240	200
49	245	210
50	250	215

# CORRECT	PRACTICE SCORE	
	LISTENING	READING
51	255	220
52	260	225
53	270	230
54	275	235
55	280	240
56	290	250
57	295	255
58	300	260
59	310	265
60	315	270
61	320	280
62	325	285
63	330	290
64	340	300
65	345	305
66	350	310
67	360	320
68	365	325
69	370	330
70	380	335
71	385	340
72	390	350
73	395	355
74	400	360
75	405	365
76	410	370
77	420	380
78	425	385
79	430	390
80	440	395
81	445	400
82	450	405
83	460	410
84	465	415
85	470	420
86	475	425
87	480	430
88	485	435
89	490	445
90	495	450
91	495	455
92	495	465
93	495	470
94	495	480
95	495	485
96	495	490
97	495	495
98	495	495
99	495	495
100	495	495

CD-ROM CONTENTS

MP3 AUDIO FILES FOR THE COMPLETE AUDIO PROGRAM:
Listening Comprehension Practice (CD 1, track 2–CD 3, track 9)
Listening Comprehension Review (CD 4, tracks 2–28)
Practice Test 1, Listening Parts 1–4 (CD 5, tracks 2–28)
Practice Test 2, Listening Parts 1–4 (CD 6, tracks 2–28)
Practice Test 3, Listening Parts 1–4 (CD 7, tracks 2–28)

PDF FILES FOR:
Complete Audioscript
Complete Answer Key (in specified editions only)